ALSO BY EDWARD M. HALLOWELL

CrazyBusy
Delivered from Distraction
Worry

the childhood roots of adult happiness

FIVE STEPS TO HELP KIDS
CREATE AND SUSTAIN
LIFELONG JOY

EDWARD M. HALLOWELL, M.D.

BALLANTINE BOOKS • NEW YORK

In memory of Josselyn Hallowell Bliss

School is out. It's June, and the backyard beckons.

I always have high hopes for the summer.

Summer is like childhood. It passes too fast. But if you're lucky, it gives you warm memories from which you take strength in the cold days ahead.

Summer is also like childhood, in that you may not think what you are doing matters very much while you are doing it, but later on you realize it mattered far more than you knew.

Summer is hot days, picnics, roads under repair, and the chance to swim. Summer is slower than the rest of the year, and its days are longer than any others. Summer embraces children. But like childhood, summer also warns: Love me now; I will not last.

Like a child, summer teaches us about the best in life. Summer asks us to do what we should help our children do: play, relax, explore, and grow.

I dedicate this book to summer and to all the children who play beneath its sun.

CONTENTS

ACKNOWLEDGMENTS

I turned to many people for help with this book. I interviewed parents, teachers, school principals, college professors, pediatricians, psychologists, social workers, psychiatrists, specialists in learning, and a host of others from disparate fields such as business, religion, martial arts, and sports. Without their help, I never could have written this book.

I also interviewed many children of all ages, and, of course, they were particularly helpful. They know so much about joy.

Many experts from the fields of psychology, learning, and medicine were especially helpful. Janine Bempechat, Robert Brooks, Mihaly Csikszentmihalyi, William Doherty, Anna Fels, Howard Gardner, Peter Jensen, Jerome Kagan, Mindy Kornhaber, Peter Metz, Michael Thompson, Priscilla Vail, and George Vaillant all generously gave me their assistance. Anna Fels was particularly helpful in explaining to me her ideas about the formative nature of recognition.

Dozens of school principals and teachers guided me as well. I especially want to thank Peter Barrett, Kathy Brownback, Paula Carreiro, Barbara Chase, Martha Cutts, Dary Dunham, Dick Hall, Gwen Hooper, Frank Perrine, Randy Plummer, Bruce Shaw, Sally Smith, Bruce Stewart, Marjo Talbot, Ty Tingley, and Aggie Underwood.

I informally interviewed so many other people that I think my friends grew weary of hearing me ask each new person I met, "Do you mind if I ask, what do you consider to be the childhood roots of adult happiness?" Once a person understood the question, he or she almost invariably got interested, gave careful thought, and offered a reply. The most common reply? Well, I can't give it away right here, but you will know by the time you finish reading this book.

However, the book is entirely my responsibility. Whatever flaws it has are my doing.

My oh-so-wise editor at Ballantine, Nancy Miller, and her marvelous assistant, Megan Casey, helped me with superb editorial suggestions. They improved this book immensely.

And my trusty agent for so many years, Jill Kneerim, blessings upon you. You are always there, and you have given me the agent's equivalent of unconditional love. I can never thank you enough.

Finally, I thank my children, Lucy, Jack, and Tucker, and their mother, my wife, Sue. The day I married Sue my life forever changed for the better. I know she would agree with me when I say that our three children have surprised us with more joy than we ever imagined we would find. I wrote this book because of Sue and because of Lucy and Jack and Tucker. My children created such an intense feeling in me of *I must find out what is best for them while there is still time to try to provide it* that I researched and wrote this book. I see their faces now in my imagination as I write these words, and I hope that someday, when they are grown-ups, they will read what I am writing now and smile, saying to themselves, *Yes, Dad, it worked. We're happy.*

WHAT'S IN THIS BOOK?

"What does *this* have to say?" I always ask when I pick up a book as I browse through a bookstore (one of my favorite pastimes—I always come out with more books than I will actually read). Like most people these days, I'm too busy to read many books all the way through. So I'll ask a friend, "What does that new book by So-and-so have to say?" and he or she will reply with a few pithy sentences that will allow me to file that book under "Done." Or I'll read a portion of a review, or I'll catch part of an interview with the author on *Charlie Rose* or *Oprah*, or I'll read an excerpt in some magazine, or I'll even buy the book and look at its cover now and then. Maybe one day I'll actually read ten pages of it. After a while I will have "absorbed" the book and believe I know what is in it. Unfortunately this is how many of us adults try to keep up in this era of information overload.

So what's in *this* book?

As the author, I would be most pleased if you'd actually read it to find out. I did my best not to waste pages. This book could easily have been ten times longer than it is.

But I sympathize with your desire to hear the short version first, or what businesspeople call the "the elevator pitch," in which you have only as much time as an average elevator ride to make your case.

OK, here's mine:

This book is about the roots of joy. I present specific steps you can take to increase the chances of a child's finding happiness and fulfillment in childhood that will deepen and grow in adulthood.

Based on current research, as well as my own experiences as a parent, teacher, and child psychiatrist, these pages usher you into the often-thought-about but rarely mapped world of happiness-in-the-making.

It's best not to leave happiness to chance alone. Parents, teachers, and all others who care about children should have a plan for creating a childhood that leads to lifelong joy.

Childhood lasts only about fifteen short, spellbound years. But what a lifelong spell those years do cast. How to cast it well?

I have evolved a five-step plan that parents and others can use to raise children who will stand the best chance of becoming happy, responsible adults. This book describes the plan in detail, cites the research on which it is based, and provides suggestions for how to implement it in daily life.

My plan is based on values that most people share. It is neither liberal nor conservative. It is based on the love of children and the power of childhood. We know what needs to be done. Now let's do it.

If we do it—if we restore childhood to the way it ought to be—we will not only serve our children, we will strengthen ourselves.

This book also celebrates what children give to us grown-ups, if we let them, and all that we can learn from children about how to be happier in our adult lives. Children really are our best experts on happiness.

the childhood roots of adult happiness

WHAT DO I *REALLY* WANT
FOR MY CHILDREN?

Think of your children. Bring their faces to your mind. Then ask yourself, "What do I really want for them in their lives?"

Don't assume you know. Before you spend another day as a parent (or as a teacher or a coach or anyone else involved with children), try to answer this deceptively simple question: What do I really want for my children?

Is it trophies and prizes and stardom? Do you want them all to grow up and become president of the United States? Is it riches and financial security? Is it true love? Or is it just a better life than the one you have now?

On some days you might quickly reply, "I just want them to clean up their rooms, do their homework, and obey me when I speak." On other days, when you are caught up in the pressures your children are feeling at school, you might desperately reply, "I just want my children to get high SAT scores and be admitted to Prestige College."

But if you linger over the question, your reply will almost certainly include one particular word: the simple, even silly-seeming word *happy*. Most of us parents just want our children to be *happy*, now and forever. Oh, sure, we also want them to be good people; we want them to contribute to the world; we want them to care for others and lead responsible lives. But deep down, most of us, more than anything else, want our children to be happy.

If we take certain steps, we can actually make it happen. Recent research has proved that parents and teachers can greatly increase the chances that their children and students will grow up to be happy, responsible adults by instilling certain qualities that might not seem of paramount importance but in fact are—inner qualities such as optimism, playfulness, a can-do attitude, and connectedness (the feeling of being a part of something larger than yourself). While traditional advice urges parents to instill discipline and a strong work ethic in their children, that advice can backfire when put into practice. The child may resist or do precisely the opposite of what is asked or even comply, but joylessly. That joylessness can last a whole life long.

We need a more reliable route to lifelong joy than can be provided by lectures on discipline or rewards for high grades and hard work. Of course, discipline and hard work matter, as do grades and civil behavior. But how you reach those goals is key. The engine of a happy life runs better on the power of connection and play than on the power of fear and guilt.

A happy life. Such a simple term for such a universal, heartfelt goal. You may not be able to define happiness, but you know it when you see it. Can you bring to mind a happy day from your own childhood? Let me tell you about one from mine.

I remember a day when I was eight years old, living in Chatham, Massachusetts. The night before, we'd had a big snowstorm, what they call in New England a nor'easter, and the storm had covered my little town on the elbow of Cape Cod with snowdrifts so high we could barely open our doors. Naturally school was closed that day.

I lived next door to my cousin Jamie, and I had spent the night at his house. When we woke up and found ourselves buried under snow, we let out a hoot. A snow day!

After shoveling out, we took the new toboggan Jamie had received for Christmas to the nearby golf course, which was full of hills. We trudged our way up the highest hill, each step spilling the powdery snow over the tops of our buckled galoshes and down into them, soaking our socks and feet. We were little mountaineers, scaling the summit of Mount Toboggan.

At last we made it to the top of what seemed like a sledders' heaven. We angled the toboggan this way and that, trying to figure out which route would give us the longest ride. I got in front, Jamie gave us a push and jumped on behind me, and our first ride began. We nearly tipped over right at the start, but we held steady, gathered speed, and zoomed down the hill, through the reeds surrounding the pond below, and out over the snow that covered the frozen water. When we came to a stop in the middle of what was called the lily pond, we both cried out, "Let's do that again!" and started the long trek back up the hill.

We tobogganed down that hill maybe fifty times that day. We added thrills to the rides by building moguls and banked curves on our course. As the snow packed down, icy spots propelled us to breakneck speeds. We never went home for lunch—we didn't even think about lunch—and no one came looking for us. They knew we were safe.

That was as happy a day as I have ever had. Even though the conditions of my life were far from perfect at the time—my parents had divorced because of my father's mental illness, and my mother was now seeing the man who would become the stepfather I grew to hate—that didn't matter. I felt loved and secure in the world, even though my world was insecure.

Jamie was my best friend. Although he was two years older than I, he treated me like a pal, not an annoying younger cousin. When we tobogganed down that hill, free from school, free from schedules, free to do exactly what we wanted to do, I felt as good as a person can feel. I was with my great friend Jamie, doing something that was exciting and fun.

I didn't know it at the time, but I was also doing what I recommend in this book. I was learning how to create and sustain joy, a tremendously important skill. I was also acquiring the all-important qualities of playfulness, optimism, a can-do attitude, and connectedness—qualities that have deepened in me since then, qualities that make me, for the most part, a happy man.

On that day, and on others just as special, I learned about the ingredients of happiness. I imagine you've had days like that, too. I want to remind you of those days in this book and give you some ideas about how to create them in children's lives today.

One way to define happiness is as a feeling that your life is going well. That feeling doesn't *have* to start in childhood, but that's a good place for it to start if you want it to become a habit that endures. The problem is that there is no foolproof plan for exactly *how* to start it there (or anywhere else). We are left to wonder why some children are happy while others are not, even though the circumstances of their lives may be similar; we also wonder why some happy children grow up to be unhappy adults while some unhappy children turn into happy adults. At first glance happiness can seem as if it depends on the luck of the draw.

I know. I am a parent myself. I am the father, and my wife, Sue, is the mother, of three young children, aged twelve, nine, and six as I write these words. I am also a child and adult psychiatrist still active in my practice, and I am the author of several books about children, families, and schools. I am immersed, both personally and professionally, in childhood. I researched and wrote this book because I wanted a reliable guide for myself and others about what can—and should—go right for children.

There is a psychologist with a name that seems impossible to pronounce, Mihaly Csikszentmihalyi, who is revolutionizing psychology, turning it from a field that studies mainly misery into a field that studies joy. (By the way, his name is pronounced ME-high Chick-sent-ME-high.) His detailed, empirical studies of the roots of happiness have led him to conclude, "Happiness is not something that happens to people but something that they make happen." His research shows that people are happiest in a state he has named "flow." In a state of flow, you are one with what you are doing.

Children know flow well. They call it play. Play is one of the childhood roots of adult happiness. But there are others—four others, to be exact—in the schema I outline in this book.

Parents can make sure their children learn the basics of the skill of happiness. You don't have to leave your child's happiness—now, later, or ever—merely to chance. We can't control everything, of course, but we can control a lot.

When I say "we," I mean both we as a society and we as individuals interested in the welfare of children. The societal "we" must address such questions as health insurance, poverty, and public education. But we as individuals do the raising of our children. If both "we's" work at it, we can plant the roots of adult happiness solidly in childhood, where they can grow sturdy and strong and last a whole life long.

As parents, we don't get unlimited time with our children to set down these roots. We get about fifteen years with our children of real, at-home, muddy-river, big-dream, go-out-and-play, kiss-me-goodnight, time-is-forever, I'll-never-die childhood. Then it's over. Recently, when my youngest child, Tucker, turned six, I saw how fast he was growing up. Grasping at straws, I desperately asked him, "Please, Tucker, could you try to find a way to grow up more slowly?"

Earnestly disappointed that he could not do what I asked, as Tucker is our one child who always tries to cooperate, he replied, "Dad, I just can't control my heightness!" He paused, to make sure I wasn't too sad, then added exuberantly, "I have to go up, up, and away!"

Yes, he does. So did we when we were children, so must Tucker, and so must all children. They leave. "Do you promise that they leave?" I can hear you parents of difficult teens and young adults asking. Yes, I promise. The years of childhood end. We all go up, up, and away to somewhere or other, sooner or later. No one can control anybody's heightness.

But we can do the next best thing. We adults can make every second count. We can protect children long enough for a good spell to be cast, letting the magic of childhood turn them into resilient and joyful adults.

Good News

Most parents these days are doing a great job. Don't let all the negative press get you down; the current generation of children is by and large quite wonderful. *Idealistic, ambitious, sane, hopeful, but a bit worried*—these are words I'd pick to describe today's children. Contrary to what you read in the press and various books, hear on talk radio, or watch on TV (after all, what makes for a catchy story? Certainly not good or balanced news!), most children in this country today are healthier, happier, and more productive than ever. It is the standard role of older generations to bemoan the state of the coming generation, and many adults have highlighted the downside of today's youth, but I can't join them. To the contrary, it is my observation that today's children comprise an excellent group. Parents, be glad and be proud.

These kids are not mere achievers. They are also more socially concerned than you might think. They are not as radical as we baby boomers were, but the times don't really call for that. Today's kids have their own style. While my generation grew up protesting a war, I think the idealism of today's generation finds expression less in fighting battles than in seeking balance and creating environmental and political safety (especially since September 11, 2001). Today's kids are less strident than we were, but they are just as strong, if not stronger. Caricaturists would have you believe that today's young people are spoiled, selfish, and want nothing more than ten million dollars (who doesn't want that?), but their life choices do not jibe with that cynical caricature. For example, one of the most popular majors at Harvard College is environmental studies. And volunteerism among teens around the country is on the rise, not on the decline. While most kids say they want jobs that pay well—again, who doesn't?—surveys show that they rank meaningfulness of their work higher than salary.

If you want vivid evidence of heart and grit in today's youth, consider these words, taken from an essay written by fourteen-year-old Latoya Hankey upon her graduation from the eighth grade at Boston's Mother Caroline Academy, an inner-city school for girls who come from underprivileged homes, mostly with single moms. Latoya grew up very poor; you can't get into Mother Caroline Academy unless you are poor. (The school does charge a nominal tuition of one hundred dollars per year, as a show of commitment on the parent's part.) I think as you read Latoya's words here, you will see the roots of adult happiness taking shape.

For the past four years I have trudged into school most mornings very tired and worn out from the day before. It was in these moments that I questioned whether the experience of Mother Caroline Academy was worth it. Although my mind did not always draw the same conclusion, most often I thought to myself that yes, this will pay off in the end. I truly believe that it was my classmates that motivated me during the most stressful of times, because they understood, but on the days when no one could have or should have given me that extra push, I was responsible for performing that task on my own. I am now extremely grateful for those tired mornings, because it is through them that I learned initiative. . . .

Success. Webster defines it as the achievement of something. . . . Although Webster was a very intelligent man, can't success also be described as assisting others in their achievements? Can't it be defined as a selfless act of giving? All of the volunteers who have given their time and support [most of the teachers at the school are volunteers] have shown me that success has several definitions. They have shown me that success is not solely defined by what you have, but most importantly by who you are and by what you do with your internal gifts. So because of this I have devised my own definition of success. Success is what you make of yourself and how you use yourself to contribute to the lives of others.

This girl, who had every reason to dream of material success above all else growing up with so little, did so well at Mother Caroline that she received a full scholarship to attend St. Paul's School, a prestigious boarding school in New Hampshire. Latoya will enter that high school with the dream not of material success but of contributing to the lives of others.

Or what about these words? They are taken from a twelfth grader's speech upon graduating from Phillips Academy in Andover, Massachusetts.

> Teamwork is a good thing. It does not allow for personal glory but offers its own important rewards. Many of us have given endless hours toward endeavors for which we received few individual dividends but learned, nonetheless, the thrill of pulling together to produce an outcome. Hang on to friends. A friend is someone who knows all about you and for some reason still likes you. We have not been perfect students, or roommates, or sons or daughters, but the people who can understand and forgive are the good guys. Life is not a résumé-building exercise. Despite what your parents may have told you, there are more important things than how you look on paper. Do what you love best. Maybe it will pay off in ways that matter . . . or maybe not, but you'll be a better person for having followed your passion.

This young man, graduating from one of the most prestigious secondary schools in the country, doesn't sound very interested in prestige. Instead, he is excited about "the thrill of pulling together."

In addition to reports of rampant selfishness of American children, we also read sententious accounts of the academic demise of our youth—the "dumbing down" of America. As with the reports of selfishness, there is some truth to them, but also as with the reports of selfishness, they exaggerate the bad news and omit the good news in order more dramatically to accentuate the bad, which grips our attention.

In fact, young people are working harder than ever to get into college. As high school students and their parents can ruefully attest, competition to get into elite colleges has never been stiffer. Why might this be? How can all these dumbed-down students be posting such excellent grades and high SAT scores? The answer is that most of them have not been dumbed down at all. If anything, they are too smartened up; in my view many schools press students too hard academically and leave them too little time to hang out and play. But our worried culture has children feeling the pinch of insecurity, and high school students are scrambling to compete for admission to the "best" colleges (I put "best" in quotes because many parents and students make the mistake of equating only high-prestige colleges with the best college *for that person*). In any case, there have never been as many highly qualified candidates for admission to college as there are today; for example, if it chose to, Harvard could fill its entire freshman class exclusively with high school valedictorians. That was not the case a generation ago.

So while many critics have pronounced this new generation shallow, spoiled, and careerist, those critics may merely be jealous of youth. In fact, today's children are full of ideas and energy and goodness, while tinged with the worry they feel in our insecure world. By and large, today's children are great.

However, "by and large" does leave out a hefty percentage of our children—children who desperately need help. About 25 percent of America's children have no medical insurance. About one-sixth are undernourished. Of the twenty million children under the age of five in this country, five million live in poverty. Illiteracy is common. Guns find their way into the hands of children every day. Violent behavior is epidemic, even though it may be on the decline. The prisons are full of adults who as children did not receive the diagnosis and treatment that they needed for their medical problems, learning disabilities, or mental illnesses. In the United States, unlike other countries, we actually have the money to provide adequately for these children. That we do not do it harms us all in many ways.

Without ever entering politics, we can all do a lot in our own lives to help children here and around the world. We can begin by raising our own children in the best way possible by giving them a connected, love-filled childhood. We can begin by turning on the magic.

Magic? What Magic?

Beyond food, clothing, and shelter, the single greatest need in a child's life is for emotional security, or what I call connectedness. Connectedness creates the magic.

I borrow the word *magic* from Selma Fraiberg, whose classic book *The Magic Years*, published originally in 1959, remains one of the best books on early childhood ever written.

I resist defining what I mean by *magic*, because it varies so widely from person to person. The magic of your childhood was not the same as the magic of mine, nor is it the same as the magic of your children's. Even among your children, the magic varies from child to child. But it almost always finds its origin, its genie's bottle, in some kind of connection, some kind of loving bond.

Childhood can be—and should be—a time of magic for all children, everywhere. Think for a moment. Close your adult, seen-it-all eyes and think back, seeing the world through the eyes of a child, when everything was new.

Remember when. Before you grew up. Before you learned what adults think about giants and gnomes and grinches and fairies. There was a time—you had it once, so did I—when days were much longer than they are for us now, and tomorrow never seemed to come, especially if you wanted it to, but that didn't matter because there was always something somewhere to look forward to or someone to get into mischief with or some cookie jar somewhere that had at least a few crumbs left in it for you to make off with.

Do you remember when your toys were all you ever needed? Or when one doll could occupy you for hours? Or when nail polish was about as exciting a substance as was ever invented? Or when a stuffed animal, or better yet an array of stuffed animals, gave you the warmth you needed when you were angry at the rest of the world? Or when your brother could turn a two-inch plastic figure he found in a drain on the street into a hero with superpowers? And when a frail, old grandma could make you feel safer and better than ten million dollars could do today?

There was a time when everything we needed could be found in a tattered, chewed-up, stained blanket or in a friend nobody liked but us or in a cozy corner with an old comic book or a Hollywood magazine. We didn't think about meeting our needs; we just tried to meet them.

But what actually *were* our needs? What *does* a child need most?

What children need is not all that complicated. What it takes to activate the magic of childhood is not all that complicated. Love activates the magic of childhood.

The magic itself is complicated—that's why I call it magic, having no idea how precisely it works—but setting it in motion is simple enough. The magic is mysterious, but getting it started is not. We know what to do. All we have to do is love. And no one is easier to love than a newborn baby. Just let the love flow. Trust in its power. That is what we parents need to do.

It is easy to forget how important emotional security and connectedness are and focus on prodding our children to achieve or simply to behave themselves. That's because, minute to minute, a parent's job is to maintain order and do what has to be done. But as much as we have to do, and as busy as we are, let us parents never, ever forget how deeply children need to feel that they are safe and that they are loved.

We grown-ups, with our education, sophistication, and distance from our own days as a child, can forget the pure joy of feeling safe and loved. If you are lucky enough to have had that when you were a child, simple moments of curl-up-in-bed-and-give-me-a-hug love, then you are blessed. If you didn't have it, then you know the ache of having missed it. One of the best ways I know to make up for having missed it is to give it to a child yourself. Suddenly that hole inside you gets filled.

Struggles and the hard knocks can be part of the magic. As long as there is unconditional love somewhere, the magic permeates and swells the seeds of adult happiness, and the seeds soon start to germinate. Love is not *all* that is needed, but there is little good without it. In a context of love, the struggles and hard knocks lead to growth. If trees could talk, they'd tell you about their struggles to grow tall; but since they can't talk, just ask any adult!

While in this book I describe a method for growing the childhood roots of adult happiness, I want to stress that there is no one path that the roots of happiness always follow. Indeed, there are as many root systems as there are happy adults.

One of the major mistakes good parents make is to assume that one certain root system is best. To continue my (I hope not over-extended) metaphor, these parents dig up the sapling of childhood over and over again trying to rearrange the roots just so, to comply with what they've been told is the best root system for that tree. But as any farmer can tell you, such work is best left to nature.

This is a lesson we parents learn slowly. How can we let nature take its course when it comes to our children? I am not recommend-ing that you be passive. Not at all. The whole point of this book is to show you what you can *do* and to offer a program of action that works. But just as the farmer picks where to plant and adds the right fertilizer and supplies water as needed and prays for good weather and pulls out the weeds but stops short of fiddling with the roots, allowing them to grow on their own, so should we parents stop short of trying to control every last detail to fit some preconceived blueprint of a happy life, right down to insisting that only one school is best, or one peanut butter, or one sport, or one friend. Children need to make some decisions for themselves.

Being a parent is like that old game of falling backward. Once you have done all you can to make sure someone will catch you, you just have to fall back and hope for the best. You can't run around yourself to catch yourself, and you can't run around to catch your child.

This is where we rely on the magic.

To illustrate what I mean, let me tell you about a little boy I once knew. This boy had a father who was put in a state mental hospital when the boy was four years old. The psychiatrists said his father was a lost cause, so two years later his mother divorced his father. After two more years, she got married again, to a man who turned out to be an abusive alcoholic. The little boy battled with his stepfather every day. His mother was unable to stop the fights or the drinking that caused them. At a loss for what to do, she sent the boy away to a boarding school when he was ten years old. Fortunately the boy found substi-tute parents at the boarding school, as well as friends and activities he enjoyed. Despite having learning disabilities, the boy became a good student, went on to college and medical school, became a child psychiatrist, and is now the lucky husband of a woman named Sue and the proud father of three children, Lucy, Jack, and Tucker. Yes, the same Tucker who can't control his heightness. I was that little boy. That boy has grown up to be the man who is writing this book, thanks to the magic of his—my—childhood.

If you look at what I had to contend with—a father with a chronic mental illness; parents divorcing when I was six; an alcoholic mother; an alcoholic, abusive stepfather; and two learning disabilities—you would say the outlook for me was bleak. You would say that the seeds of adult happiness were not planted well in my childhood. If anything, you would say the seeds of adult disaster were sown.

But you would be wrong.

Despite all the difficulty I had to contend with, I still found in my childhood the very ingredients that I describe in this book that lead to happiness in adult life. I learned how to deal with adversity. I learned how to create and sustain joy. I always knew my mother and father loved me, even though my dad had to leave me due to his mental illness and my mother was very often tipsy, to use the family word. While I felt that my stepfather hated me, as I hated him, I also felt, amazingly enough, that he would have loved me and I would have loved him had we had a second chance. In retrospect, I think that feeling stemmed from the fact that I knew my mother and real father loved me unconditionally, so much so that I felt deep down inside that I was good, acceptable, and OK; if someone was treating me as if I weren't, as my stepfather often did, well, there had to be some misunderstanding. I always felt love in my life, in spite of what any given day might bring. Like drunken fights. Like watching my mother get hit. Like lewd remarks I didn't understand but knew were slimy.

Still the roots of adult happiness were growing, even though my childhood was what we call a "troubled" one. I had love from both parents, however distant those parents had to be. I had friends. I was allowed to play. I found teachers who cared. I worked hard to please them. I found things I liked to do, so I did them often. I practiced. I achieved mastery. I gained recognition from my peers and teachers.

This, in turn, connected me back to the healthy part of the world, away from my troubled home.

I found a way into that healthy world and a happy life, a way that, when I was ten years old, no one would have predicted I'd find. Children will do this if given half a chance.

And if all you need is half a chance, imagine how well you can do with a full chance!

There is always, always hope.

What Do We Parents Need?

There is another side to the question of what children need that we usually do not think about: What do we parents need from our children? And more broadly, what does society at large need from its children? The answers to those questions run like a subplot throughout this book. Briefly put, we need the love that children bring out in us. To get it, all we have to do is let them bring it out. Just as to activate the magic of childhood, all we have to do is love the child, so for us to be given new life by our children, all we have to do is feel the love they feel. And let it flow. And trust in its power.

Loving a child proves the truth of the old saying, "It is in giving that we receive." The more we love our children, the more we receive the gifts our children have to give.

Whether we have children of our own or not, children give us all new life. Children disturb and distract us in ways we need to be disturbed and distracted. They get us to come out and play. They puncture our pomposity. They make us laugh, even when we try not to. They show us that there is more to life than getting ahead or getting sleep. They require our help, even when we don't know how to do whatever it is. They make us improvise. They show us how to take delight in the mundane in ways we had long ago forgotten (for children very little is mundane). They make us exercise. They teach us new words. They prevent us from getting set in our ways. They tease us. Finally they give us adults that elusive gift called meaning.

We also need children to ask the many questions that we can't answer.

Oh, those questions. There is an old anecdote about a conversation between a father and his daughter:

"Daddy, why is the sky blue?" the little girl asks.

"Sweetheart, I don't know," her daddy replies.

"Daddy, how does lightning get made?" the girl asks.

"Sweetie, I'm not sure of that, either," her daddy replies.

"Daddy, why can't I remember everything I learn in school?" the girl then asks.

"I don't know," her daddy answers.

"Daddy," the girl then asks, "do you mind that I ask you all these questions?"

"Of course not, honey," her daddy replies. "I am very glad you ask me questions. How else are you supposed to learn anything?"

We need children to look up to us and depend on us and give us a good reason to try as hard as we can.

The Advantages of Being a Parent Today

I can say without a second's hesitation that I am a much better parent than my parents were, not because I am a better person—I am not—but because, like most in my generation, I know more about what children need than my parents knew, and like most in my generation, I have made being a parent much more of a priority than it was for my parents.

The old ways have not disappeared: harsh, physical punishments; teaching by humiliation; telling children they should be seen and not heard; exploiting children. But these ways are fading, as more and more parents think that being a parent is the most important activity in their lives. We also know more now than ever before. We have learned a tremendous amount in the past fifty years about brain science, learning disabilities, depression and anxiety in children, pediatric medicine, and new methods of education. As we make use of what we've learned about children's needs, we become better parents, and our children become healthier children.

Most of us try to do our best for our children. But it helps if we define what "our best" actually means. What are we supposed to do? It helps, if you are a parent, to have a kind of "game plan," a basic strategy for raising your children.

You will see that I believe—and research shows—that a happy life rests mostly on having what I call a "connected childhood." This is good news, because it is within the power of all parents, not just the wealthy ones, as well as all schools, coaches, doctors, community leaders, politicians, clergy, neighbors, and everyone else who cares about children to create a connected childhood for our children.

But a connected childhood is only the starting point. I will describe a process that you can set in motion in childhood that will last a lifetime—a lifetime of what most people would call happiness.

For years experts have both underemphasized and overemphasized the possibilities of childhood: they have overemphasized how much parents can control, but they have underemphasized how much can go right. What goes right when you are a child can translate into years of satisfaction, productivity, and joy. That is why in this book I focus on what can go right.

We parents see, hear, and read about what can go wrong every day: the increase in stress and worry among children; the results of the latest study (and there always seems to be a "latest study" coming out, bound to upset or confuse us); the disappearance of childhood as the overscheduled child rushes from one activity to the next; the alarming number of children who can't read; the many children who receive inadequate medical care; the pressure on high school students to get into a good college; the perils of too much TV or too much computer time or what we call in my family "electronic time"; the decline in politeness; the ongoing problem of drug abuse; and on and on and on.

But what about the good news?

Children are the good news. Children are the best news life has got.

Not long ago I visited the Princeton Montessori School in Princeton, New Jersey, where I had the treat of spending a half hour on a carpeted floor with seventeen babies, ranging in age from twelve weeks to fifteen months. This was as close as I had come to finding heaven on earth in quite some time.

As I lay there on my stomach, my head propped up on my folded arms, I marveled at these busy bundles called babies. I marveled at all their activity, their lookings here and there, their lip-smackings, their elastic-faced yawns, their reachings for this and that, their tadpole kicks, and their rapt engagement with every specific object or person to which they turned.

The babies soon were looking at me, gurgling to me, some even waving at me (sort of). Several crawled over to me for an up-close visit. Others, who couldn't crawl, inchwormed their way to me. Once close, we made all sorts of faces at each other and talked that wonderful singsong language called baby talk, a language that makes both speaker and hearer feel good. The babies would say, "Oh, how interesting!" in their own particular ways, or, "I am so glad you came to visit me this morning," or, "Have you pooped yet today? I just did."

Gradually, as I fell into the rhythm of the room, and my brain took in the smells of powder and porridge and the sounds of infant communication and the sights of little humans at play, I felt an endorphin rush the likes of which I cannot remember ever having felt before. These babies were taking me into their group like a pod of dolphins swimming along connected in a surging but secure sea. A concentrated, positive energy filled the room, especially the floor area where the babies held sway.

Enjoy Your Children

In my work I have met thousands of children of all ages, not just babies, and not just my own children. I like to talk to children. I like to be with them. When I was in medical school, one of my favorite activities was to go into the newborn nursery and bask in the energy in the room, much as I did when I lay on the floor with the babies at the

Montessori school. And I always loved the pediatric wards, although they could be heartbreaking. Since finishing my training and becoming a child psychiatrist, I have always loved visiting schools. When you go into a school—any school: pre-, lower, middle, upper, high—you feel the power of childhood enveloping the school like a force field. It picks you up and takes you back, back to when you were young and free. When I walk by a row of lockers in a school, I often find myself absentmindedly looking for mine!

There is a point that many parenting books miss: children do more for us than we do for them. The most important advice in any parenting book ought to be this: *Enjoy your children.* Learn from your children, listen to what they say, play with them while you can, let them activate those parts of you that had already started to go dead before they were born, and let those parts of you energize your work, your friendships, your spiritual life, every part of your life that there is.

"What?!" you might scream. "You say my children do more for me than I do for them? My children do nothing! I do everything! They eat and make clothes dirty and watch TV. I cook and wash dirty clothes and pay for the electricity that powers their TV. How can you possibly say that they do more for me than I do for them?!" And you might want to add a few choice expletives to vent your contempt for my foolish words.

But after you've finished blowing off steam, and after your children have gone to bed or grown up and moved away, you know I am right. Yes, we parents do the providing—of food, clothing, shelter, organization, time management, opportunities, discipline, parties, presents, Red Sox (you can substitute your team's name here) tickets, visits to the doctor, TLC, and so forth. Even the providing is not so bad. If we weren't providing for them, for whom or for what would we be providing? Our personal fortunes? I know that since I've had children, I've gained purpose and direction, worked harder than ever, and gotten more done than I ever have before. This is because I have a reason greater than myself to go out and provide.

But for all we provide for them, look at what our children give us: Hope. Love. Energy. Purpose. Laughter. Sweet sorrow. Meaning. A chance to be a hero. A chance to love as we never knew we could love. A chance to worry more about someone else than about ourselves. A chance to make a life.

One of the best ways to be a great parent (and a happy adult) is to let yourself delve deeply into what it means to be a child and relish it, the way, for example, you once relished mud. Now you avoid mud, but once you probably jumped plop right into it and loved the sound it made and the mess it sent up. You may even have rolled in it or made pies out of it. If you want to be happy (and be a great parent), celebrate childhood in its specific details, not just in the abstract. Celebrate mud. And messes. And noise. And spooky things. And chocolate anything and ketchup on pizza. Celebrate what it feels like to go to bed really, really, really looking forward to tomorrow.

Children point a way to joy. If we watch and learn, we can follow.

If you spend time around children, they make you want to do everything you can to give them the right kind of start in life. You don't even ask yourself why. You simply find that you want to. Now. But *how*?

It isn't always obvious how to translate the powerful love you feel as a parent into the most helpful kinds of action.

Some Basic Questions (and Answers)

Here are some of the basic questions parents ask, along with some answers based on the specific steps offered throughout this book, steps that you can take to help your child.

Q: What do children need most?

A: Love. But then you have to wonder, How much love? Love from whom? What kind of love? How much love is too much? Is there hope for the child who does not get any love? For those answers see Chapter 7.

Q: Tell me, in terms that, as a parent, I can use and put into practice, what should I do when I am worried about one of my children?

A: There is one rule I put above all others when it comes to dealing with worry about a child (or worry about anything, for that matter). It is the best antiworry advice ever invented, and it has been proved effective by research many times over. It is simply this: Never worry alone. For more on how to control worry, see Chapter 2.

Q: What should my top priorities be in terms of spending money on my children?

A: Food, clothing, shelter, medical and dental care, education-related items.

Q: What expenses can I forget about?

A: Everything else if you must, although sports-related expenses rank right after education-related expenses in my estimation. Sports, when approached in the right way, can be as valuable as academics in the development of a happy child. Music lessons are great for the interested child if you can swing them. Birthday presents and other gifts need not be costly; we parents usually overspend. In particular, forget about spending lots of money on the snazziest computer (unless your child has a special need, the basic computer will usually do just fine), designer clothes, expensive toys, over-the-top vacations, or anything deemed necessary "because everyone else has one" or "everyone else does it."

Q: What about what the latest study said?

A: As I mentioned, there always is a "latest study." It is inescapable. You'll find it reported in *Newsweek* or *Time*, or you'll hear about it on the news as you drive your children to school, or you'll see it on *60 Minutes* or the *Today* show. It will be about the negative effect of day care on children, and you will cringe because as a working mom you have to use day care; or it will be about how divorce damages children, and you will cringe because this is your second marriage and two of your children came from your first marriage; or it will be about the harm done to children by Nintendo or TV or sugar or trampolines or immunizations or sunlight or toy guns or scooters. You will cringe because those "dangerous" items are part of your children's lives. Guess what? You need not cringe. If you stay in touch with your pediatrician, your children's teachers, and a few friends, you will combine enough common sense with all the latest studies to act sensibly.

Q: Are we doing the right thing putting such an emphasis on test scores and other kinds of achievement in school?

A: Absolutely, definitively no. Our emphasis has become dangerously unbalanced. We are overemphasizing the importance of grades and other measurable achievements, while we are underemphasizing the importance of resourcefulness, optimism, "people skills," a can-do attitude, creativity, and the many forms of connectedness, such as friendship, family, community, spirituality, love of nature, team play, and so forth. An abundance of research has shown that it is inner qualities—optimism, extroversion, a feeling of control over one's life, and self-esteem—that lead to happiness in adult life. It is fine to emphasize getting good grades, as long as you balance this by equally emphasizing and teaching the tools of emotional health. Empirical studies have shown that feeling connected at home and feeling connected at school are the two most powerful determinants of which adolescents will stay out of such troubles as severe emotional distress, depression, drug or alcohol abuse, violent behavior, dropping out of school, or unwanted pregnancy. In addition, the student who feels connected also tends to get the best grades. If we emphasized our students' "connectedness scores" as much as we do their SAT scores, students would be emotionally healthier *and* they would achieve at a higher level academically. They would be more apt to lead happy, productive lives. For further discussion of this, see Chapter 12.

Q: If it is true that childhood is disappearing, what can each of us do, in concrete, practical ways, to bring it back?

A: A lot. See Chapters 3, 15, and the rest of the book. Start by remembering your own childhood, which Chapter 3 will guide you in doing.

Q: Sometimes my children drive me crazy, and sometimes I feel as if I am a bad parent because I can't control them or get them to cooperate with me or even be nice to each other. What should I do?

A: Say hello to the real world. With rare exceptions, there is fighting in every family. Indeed, conflict is a sign of connectedness. How you work out conflict at home is part of what builds problem-solving abilities, resiliency, and the ability to share. The opposite of connectedness is not conflict but indifference. If you visited my house on any morning of your choosing, you could expect to hear bursts of yelling and shouting and sometimes tears and a slamming door. My children are what we euphemistically call "spirited," and Sue and I are not strong disciplinarians. I, in particular, need to work on that, as sometimes Sue gets stuck with the job of setting the limits while I come off as the "nice guy." Like every family, we are a work in progress, trying to get better at certain tasks while enjoying the whole process as much as we can. If you want help, you might consult with a professional, such as a child psychiatrist or a child psychologist or a social worker who specializes in family therapy. These people can help enormously. Just make sure you pick someone with whom you feel comfortable. Your pediatrician, another parent, or your school can give you a referral if you do not know of anyone yourself.

Q: How did the adults who came from troubled childhoods still manage to beat the odds?

A: They found one positive relationship with an adult. See Chapters 6, 7, and many other portions of the book for more detail.

My own children show me the answers to these questions every day. For example, one evening my wife, Sue, my three kids, and I were having dinner at a restaurant when I started to worry out loud about something or other—I can't even remember now what it was. After a minute or so of listening to me worry, Tucker, aged five at the time, piped up, "Dad! You could always look on the bright side."

The chances are good that Tucker will grow up to be a happy man.

Research shows that optimism in childhood correlates with happiness in adulthood.

A few days later I was out in the backyard, again with Tucker. He was jumping on our trampoline, showing me some games and routines he had invented before and others he was inventing on the spot. They were very elaborate, involving specific steps, jumps, and hops as well as certain precautions necessary to avoid the trampoline monster, not to mention how many leaps the rules allowed you to do on one foot. He also included the leaves and sticks that had blown onto the trampoline as part of the games and rules. It was all extremely complex.

Delighting in watching Tucker play, and feeling a tug on my heart for that time of life when trampolines are kingdoms and you are king, I asked my son, "Tucker, are you happy?"

Tucker, accustomed to the dumb questions his psychiatrist father tends to ask, just kept jumping. So I asked again, "Tucker, are you happy?"

Being the youngest and still the most cooperative of my three children, Tucker relented and replied. "Yes," he said, "except when I am sad or angry."

"And what makes you happy?" I asked, as he continued to jump.

This time he responded right away. "Mommy and Daddy," he said, still jumping, "and toys and trampolines and friends," and he kept jumping, then added, "and ice cream and candy and hugs, and more Mommy and Daddy," and then he paused before concluding, "and that's about it." Tucker's off-the-cuff compendium closely resembled my carefully thought out compendium, which I present in Chapter 5 as the childhood roots of adult happiness. But Tucker already knew. Most children do.

After a certain age they may not want to tell us any longer. For example, when I asked my then-eight-year-old son, Jack, what made him happy in his life, he responded tersely, "Stuff."

Since we parents often forget, and after a while our children do not always want to tell, I present in this book my program to help parents provide their children with the best chance of finding happiness in their lives.

However, I don't want you to think I am claiming to have solved the riddle of human happiness. I merely offer here the best program I have been able to devise.

You should also know that, to some extent, it doesn't matter what you do as a parent. A portion of the story of your child's life is fixed at birth, even at conception; some of the seeds of happiness are planted in the genes. But just as the growth of a crop depends on the gardener's care, so, too, does a child's happiness depend on the parents' care and the experiences of childhood.

More than most gardeners, we parents strive to do right. We want to do all we can to give our kids the best possible shot at living the full lives that we hope and dream for them as we rock them in our arms in the light of the moon or in the warmth of the sun when they are babies.

Oh, those hopes and dreams. I remember rocking Lucy, our first child, as I sat by a lake the summer she was born, a lake appropriately named for summer vacation, Lake Doolittle. The lake may have been Doolittle, but Sue and I sure had a lot to do, with this new baby. One of the most important but least strenuous things we did was hope and dream. As I held Lucy, I imagined her little face becoming the face of a young woman, and I saw her smiling an adult's smile. I imagined her running across the grass to greet someone I couldn't quite see, and I saw her standing proudly as she received her college degree on a gold and green morning in June.

I envisioned her reaching adulthood with the confidence I never quite found for myself. How often we do this: wish our children will gain skills we didn't and avoid pain we couldn't. I so hoped for Lucy that she would be confident and not fear the opinions and judgments of others, as I did and still do. I so hoped for Lucy that she would feel comfortable with herself in the world and be able to play without self-consciousness or fear. I hoped for her what I never had as a child and, despite the good things I have found in life, still do not have: a strong sense of security.

So far, twelve years since I held her as a baby that summer, she has found this, as have our other two children. It is incorrect (thank goodness!) that you can't raise emotionally healthy children if you have hang-ups yourself. Sue and I both had insecure childhoods that left us with permanent scars. But so far, we have not passed that pain along to our children, and I very much doubt that we will.

Sue and I started having hopes and dreams for our children before we even met each other. We both wanted to do it right. Once we got married, we started right in. I was thirty-nine and Sue was thirty-three, so there was no time to waste.

When Lucy was born, eleven months after our wedding, our lives changed forever. Once you become a parent, you become involved in the welfare of another person as you never have been before, and you will be until you die. Oddly enough, for most of us parents, this heavy obligation is also the greatest gift we've ever received. When Lucy was born, she unlocked the door to happiness for me. Sure, she unlocked the door to worry, fatigue, exasperation, frustration, and feeling inept as well. What parent doesn't feel inept now and then, every stage of the way? But the rewards of having a child? There's nothing better.

Sue and I filled our minds with dreams for Lucy, just as she filled our lives with dreams-come-true the minute she was born. She had to fight for her life in the beginning, so we knew worry and heartache right away as well. She was born with her heart on the wrong side (the right side) of her chest. Sometimes this condition, which is called situs inversus, is associated with life-threatening heart problems. But in Lucy's case, everything turned out to be fine. She came through it all in excellent shape.

But we shuddered at the warning fate had issued us. Things can go wrong. Now we knew this all too well. As we took the next step with Lucy in the long journey from infant to adult, the step from hospital to home, we felt—as opposed to merely "knowing"—how precious and fragile a baby truly is.

When we got home, Sue placed Lucy on our bed and took off her diaper. Just as soon as her diaper was off, Lucy started to pee, like a little water bubbler. Presented with this wee geyser, Sue started to cry. "I don't know how to be a mother," she sobbed, and I took her in my arms, fully aware that I had no idea of how to be a father. I was a doctor, Sue was a social worker, we both had taken care of patients in many different settings, but we both felt utterly unprepared for what we now had to do. As the little geyser of pee subsided and slowly spread out in a circular blotch, I held Sue and spoke the words we both needed to hear: "It will be OK. Lots of people have done this before. We'll learn." I hoped I was right.

Sue is in fact an extraordinarily competent woman, far more adept in daily life than I am, but that afternoon and evening we both felt humbled. What in the world were we supposed to do? How could we raise this little pee-and-poop machine to be a happy, secure, confident adult? It seemed all but impossible. Still, we were happy, so happy, even in the midst of our feelings of ineptitude. Just to look at Lucy was to feel happy. It was as if God knew we would feel scared and overwhelmed, so God gave Lucy—and gives all babies—a special power to captivate and enthrall adults, especially parents.

By evening, when it was time for dinner, I had prepared a meal for Sue and me. Sue was nursing Lucy; she had learned how to do this in the hospital. But what she had not learned how to do was eat her own food and nurse Lucy at the same time. She needed both her hands to hold Lucy and steady the nipple Lucy was sucking. She had no free hand with which to hold a fork and feed herself. When I put our plates down on the table, and Sue reflexively moved to get a bite of food for herself, she realized she couldn't do it without dropping Lucy, so she started to cry once again. "I can't even eat. And I'm really, really hungry," Sue moaned, tears streaming down her cheeks. She looked up at me desperately, still sobbing. "Does this mean I'll be a terrible mother? Oh, I want to be a good mother so much. But I am soooo hungry. Lucy wants to nurse, and I want to eat. Oh, oh, what am I going to do?" To hear Sue's lament, you would have thought she was being judged unfit right there on the spot unless she were willing to starve.

"But, honey," I said, as confidently as I could, "that's why you have me around. I can feed you, while you feed Lucy." And I picked up her fork, stuck a piece of chicken onto it, and placed it in her mouth. You should have seen the satisfied smile that filled her face. Ah, contentment at last. She could eat, Lucy could eat, and I could do something useful.

This is how it went at first. Each day, each moment presented new conundrums, new twists on what it means to be a parent. We didn't know what to do at first, and we felt scared. It is like this for most parents. One reason for my writing this book is to give some suggestions, some pointers I have learned, especially for when your children get a bit older than infancy and the problems become more complex than what to do with poop and pee.

Gradually we developed a routine. Our confidence grew. Lucy slept in an antique cradle we'd been given as a wedding present, which we placed right next to our bed. After a while we moved her into a crib in her own room and took another step in the journey.

After she moved into her own room, we would start our day by bringing Lucy into our bed. As she lay there, we would sing a little ditty to the tune of the Folger's coffee commercial (how pleased the advertisers would be!). The actual ditty went "The best part of waking up is Folger's in your cup," but we changed it to "The best part of waking up is Lucy in your bed." As we would lie there and watch her gurgle and pucker and look up and, yes, poop and cry, Sue and I were in heaven. It was indeed the best part of waking up to have Lucy in our bed. So good that we went on and had two more children.

When Jack was born and, three years later, Tucker, we hoped and dreamed for them, as we had for Lucy. I would stand over each of them when they were in the crib or rock them or just watch them from afar and imagine not too many specific scenes, just general states, happy states, states of joy and play and confidence, all of which we wanted so much for our children to find.

But, there is no guarantee. What can we do?

I am lucky enough to know many happy people. I am sure you do, too. Do you ever wonder where their happiness came from? Or if you are a more or less happy person yourself, do you ever wonder how you got this way? How much did your childhood have to do with it?

In short, what can be done in childhood to increase the chances of happiness in adulthood?

The answer to that question is the subject of the rest of this book.

2

A CRAZY LOVE THAT NEVER QUITS: THE PARENT'S MAGICAL TOOL

Being a parent is difficult. So is being a teacher or a coach or anyone responsible for guiding children. The unexpected abounds in childhood, and no one has all the answers. But let me give you some good news. You are almost certainly doing much better than you think!

When he was president, John F. Kennedy had a plaque on his desk that read, "O God the sea is so great and my boat is so small."

What parent hasn't felt that? I know Sue and I have. Often. Parents may not deal with issues as weighty as those facing the president of the United States, but sometimes it surely feels as if we do. The dangers from which we want to protect our children are so great. All the decisions we need to make—all the crucial moments when we want to say the right words, all the many, many times when we hope and pray that all goes well, realizing we do not have control over what school will bring or friends will do or fate will send—can serve to remind us, over and over again, how small our boat truly is.

We all need help in bolstering our little boats. And we need help in gaining perspective on the largeness of the sea. We need to be reassured that what we are doing has been done before. We need to be reminded that we have more knowledge than parents have ever had and much more help than we ever take advantage of.

Good parents—and the vast majority of parents are good parents—worry because they care so much. They also worry because most of the time it is not clear and obvious what the right course of action is.

When you care a lot and you are not sure what you should do, worry flares up like a brush fire.

You need tools to fight those fires. You need an assortment of tools, from knowledge to the support of others to money to physical strength to patience to a sense of humor (that's one of a parent's most important tools, for sure!). But one tool stands above the others as the most powerful of all. It is a tool you know about but whose power you probably underestimate. It is more powerful than money, brainpower, or even knowledge. It is love. I call it the crazy love that never quits. It is a magic wand, a wand that appears as if sent by God the moment your child is conceived. It is what keeps us going when the going gets tough. It is what makes being a parent such a deepening experience, a voyage right into the core of life.

Most of us parents are crazy in love with our children from the moment they are born. And while they do upset us and even torment us as they grow older, most parents never stop loving them. No matter what. I urge you to honor that feeling. Don't trivialize it by saying, "Oh, well, all parents feel this," or, "My love is not enough to deal with my child's problem," or, "My child doesn't care about love, she just wants a ride to the mall." Instead, trust the feeling. The more you trust in it and honor it, the more powerful it becomes. It brings out the best in you, and over the long haul it brings out the best in your child. Feel proud of that love, turn to it in times of trouble, reinforce it in others, and celebrate it as perhaps the most valuable and noble emotion we humans ever feel.

A parent's love is like the favorite stuffed animal our children carry around while they are young. Over the years it loses an ear or perhaps an eye, gains a few gashes that get repaired with Band-Aids or tape, becomes faded and floppy, develops amazing flexibility, and all the while becomes stronger and stronger in the hold it exerts upon our hearts.

But love is not all we need. In addition to the crazy love that never quits, we need knowledge as well. We also need the support of others. And we need to know how to handle worry. I have a very effective, practical, three-step process I use myself and recommend to others for controlling excess worry (and no one worries more than us parents).

The process, which incorporates both emotion and intellect, is as follows:

1. *Never worry alone.* Simply talking to another person helps, even if you do not solve the problem. Get together for a cup of coffee or talk on the telephone. Suddenly what seemed like a huge problem feels smaller. The ocean becomes a little less vast, and your boat feels a little less small.

2. *Get the facts.* As we all know, knowledge helps. Sometimes we feel afraid to ask, we're embarrassed, or we do not want to be a burden. I encourage parents to do what I do and let the crazy love that never quits push me past whatever timidity I might feel. One reason I call this love "crazy" is that it emboldens us to do deeds we otherwise wouldn't dare to do. Once I think of how much I love my children, I pick up the phone and call whomever I need to speak to, no matter who the person is, whether I am a burden or not! And most of the time, your fears are unfounded and the people are pleased to help and give you the facts you need. So speak to the teacher, call the doctor, ask the expert on whatever the problem is. Many times excessive worry is based on wrong information or lack of information.

3. *Make a plan.* Take action. Even if the only action you take is to go back to step 1 and simply speak to someone else, that's fine. Just don't be passive and bury yourself under the bedclothes. Worry feasts on passive people. If you are active in trying to solve the problem, whatever it is, you will feel more in control and less vulnerable. This, in turn, will lead you to worry less and solve more.

Never worry alone. Get the facts. Make a plan. You can rely on these three steps to help you almost any time you feel worried, which means just about every day if you're a parent. I have spent many years helping people who worry a lot (including my wife and me), so what I recommend has been tested in real and messy life.

By the way, that goes for all the advice you will find in this book. Although this is not an academic book, the answers I offer are based on a wide range of research, conducted by many different people.

One of the most exciting areas of research in the past twenty years has been research on learning. When I was a child, *smart* and *stupid* were the two "diagnostic" words used to describe a child's learning style. Now, thanks to the pioneering work of Howard Gardner, Mel Levine, Robert Sternberg, Priscilla Vail, and many others, we have a whole new way of looking at learning.

This seemingly rarefied research is, in fact, quite practical. For example, thanks to concepts introduced by Howard Gardner, we can say that a child is strong in musical intelligence and intrapersonal intelligence, but less strong in linguistic intelligence and logical mathematical intelligence; that is much more accurate, and helpful, than to say she is bad at school but good at piano and daydreaming. The difference is more than semantic. The old vocabulary carries with it what can feel like condemnation, which in turn translates into lower self-esteem and reduced effort, which translate into lowered achievement, which further reduces self-esteem, which in turn translates into (as the research of David Myers has shown) lower happiness in adulthood.

In addition to the groundbreaking work on how children learn, a whole new field of research into the ingredients of happiness has sprouted in the past few decades. This research was tremendously helpful to me in writing this book, allowing me to cite data rather than merely speculate. Pioneers like Martin Seligman (*Learned Optimism* and *The Optimistic Child*), Mihaly Csikszentmihalyi (*Flow*), George Vaillant (*Adaptation to Life* and *The Wisdom of the Ego*), and David Myers (*The Pursuit of Happiness*) have scientifically investigated the question What makes for joy in life? Their research has given us specific and reliable answers, answers upon which I have drawn heavily in writing this book. We now have a solid idea of what can go right, not just wrong, what can be changed and what can't, and what children need in order to stand the best chance of finding happiness later on.

For example, Martin Seligman's research has shown how powerful childhood optimism is as a protector against depression and anxiety later on, as well as how strongly it correlates with a happy adulthood. He has also shown that while genetics influence the development of optimism, it can also be learned, and learned at any age.

Csikszentmihalyi's research into happiness brought us the marvelous concept of *flow*, that state of mind in which you become one with what you are doing, be it skiing or writing an essay or playing tennis or setting up an experiment in a chemistry lab. Csikszentmihalyi's carefully conducted research shows that we are happiest in states of flow. You usually reach a state of flow when both the challenge the activity poses and your skill at that activity are high. In other words, an expert skier finds flow when he or she is skiing the toughest slope. When high skill meets high challenge, flow is apt to occur. Teachers, coaches, and parents should know this.

Vaillant has been looking into the ingredients of a happy life for decades now, since he became involved with the Grant Study of Adult Development in 1967. The study itself has been going on since 1937 and has provided us with empirical data, as opposed to theoretical speculation, as to what leads to joy in life. Among Vaillant's many findings is the central one that how a person deals with stress is pivotal. And how you deal with stress is something that you can learn, as opposed to simply being born with. For a parent this finding translates into knowing that the goal should not be to prevent stress in a child's life but rather to help the child learn healthy ways of accommodating it. For example, teach your child to ask for help rather than pretend there is no problem with the math homework. In this way you can steer your child away from denial as a means of dealing with stress and toward reaching out, which is one of the best ways of all to manage stress. Or teach your child to put herself in the shoes of the child who is being teased and speak up in her defense instead of joining the teasing crowd. In this way you can steer your child away from submission as a way of dealing with stress and toward empathy and altruism, both highly adaptive life skills. Or require your child to perform chores around the house and get a paying job as a teenager rather than allow all the work to be done by parents or hired others. In this way you can introduce your child to work as an integral part of life— indeed, as a chance to contribute to the family and achieve mastery— rather than allowing avoidance to become your child's main means of dealing with the stress of work. Or upon the death of a loved pet, show the child how to grieve rather than just going out and buying a new pet or telling the child to buck up, life is hard. In this way you can teach your child how to manage sadness in a healthy way rather than relying on denial or "toughness."

Myers, a psychologist at, appropriately enough, Hope College in Michigan, has been studying and writing about happiness for years. All of his findings are based not on speculation but on an immense amount of research, conducted both by him and by many others. The four factors his research has shown to correlate most closely with happiness in adulthood—optimism, extroversion, a feeling that you have control over your life, and self-esteem—certainly take root in childhood. If parents and schools would promote these qualities with the verve and ingenuity they promote getting good grades, the emotional health of children (and the adults they become) would skyrocket.

In addition to the research into learning and into happiness, the past decade or so has seen the publication of a number of very helpful books that challenge, if not overturn, old assumptions or dispel recent fads. *The Nurture Assumption,* by Judith Rich Harris, put a dent in the idea that parents alone determine the fate of their children and showed what a great influence the peer group exerts. *Reviving Ophelia,* by Mary Pipher, and the more recent *Raising Cain,* by Dan Kindlon and Michael Thompson, and *Real Boys,* by William Pollack, gave fresh, new advice on raising girls and boys and challenged the old stereotypes in the process. *Raising Resilient Children,* by Robert Brooks and Sam Goldstein, gave practical, research-based advice on how to instill the qualities—like hope, optimism, and confidence—that translate into resilience. *The Hurried Child,* by David Elkind, and the more recent *Hyper-parenting,* by Alvin Rosenfeld and Nicole Wise, as well as *Ready or Not,* by Kay Hymowitz, called to task our whole society's emphasis on speed, achievement, and "enrichment" at the expense of having a playful, adventurous childhood. And *The Myth of the First Three Years,* by John T. Bruer, debunked the fad, based on a misreading of new brain science, that children's brains are permanently set by three years old and that they should be force-fed all kinds of mind-enhancing activities during these years, from Mozart to mobiles. Finally, the Dr. Spock for my generation of parents, T. Berry Brazelton, teamed up with one of the great child psychiatrists in this country,

Stanley Greenspan, to delineate as specifically as possible what children need to grow, learn, and flourish in a marvelous book called *The Irreducible Needs of Children.*

But on the day Sue and I brought Lucy home from the hospital and helplessly watched as Lucy peed on our bed, we were at a loss for what to do next. I hadn't read all the research; indeed, most of it had not yet been published. Even if it had, research wasn't what I needed just then.

What I really needed was someone to tell me what most of the books don't tell you, because they are busy making arguments, elucidating complex problems, or explaining the latest piece of research.

Sue and I needed something much more basic and practical. We needed someone to say, "Just lift up Lucy's ankles and raise her bottom so you can slip this diaper underneath. Then fold . . ." And we desperately needed some reassurance and encouragement. We needed someone to say, "Don't worry. It will be OK. Raising children is not as hard as you think it is. Lots of people have done it well, and you will do it well yourself." We needed someone to tell us that our worst fears would not come true. We needed someone to tell us that our worries were normal and that most people respond with fear when asked to do something they fervently want to do well but for which they feel completely unprepared. Imagine if you were asked to jump out of an airplane and all you were given was a parachute, with no instructions. That's how a new parent feels. Only maybe without the parachute.

We needed someone to tell us that love was our parachute. Love would let us land safely. Love would motivate Sue and me to do whatever else we needed to do, whether it was change a diaper, find and read an instruction book, call a doctor, find the right school, or stay up late into the night hassling with a teenager over a curfew time.

We needed someone with experience, someone we could trust and believe, to tell us that the odds were heavily on our side, that as long as we showed up for the tasks of being a mom and a dad and didn't disappear, as long as we didn't really *try* to botch it up, we would be good parents.

Often new parents' own parents do this for them: after the baby is born, they reassure their grown children that everything will be OK, and they often teach them the basic skills they need to learn to take care of a newborn. Grandparents can appear as if sent from heaven.

Since both of my parents were deceased when Lucy was born, and since Sue's parents lived far away, my cousin Josselyn jumped into the role of adviser. Having five children of her own, she was certainly an expert. I loved Josselyn like a sister, and so did Sue, so when she came to stay with us for a few days right after Lucy was born, we hung on her every word as if she were a revered sage. She gave us advice, she taught us little tricks she had learned, she made us laugh, and she gave us confidence. Tragically, a few months before the publication of this book, Josselyn died of myeloma at the age of fity-six; but the love she gave lives on through her five children, her husband, Tom, and the hundreds of others, like us, whom she so deeply touched.

I have also learned a sad irony since then. The people who *should* worry about whether or not they are good parents don't; and the people who don't need to worry about it *do.* The ones who do not have the crazy love that never quits, the ones who ignore or mistreat their children, are usually troubled in ways that prevent them from reflecting upon what they are doing and then changing their ways.

The mistakes I have seen people make in parenting are so obvious that they are hard to miss; all you have to do is be willing to see them when some brave soul tells you about them. You don't need a complex psychological dissection of the dynamics of the family to do right by your children. Such analysis can be interesting, but it is rarely necessary.

What *is* necessary is what you already know is necessary: it is necessary to *be there.* Be there to clean up the poop, be there to provide the food, be there to fix the leak in the roof or to find somebody who can, be there to sing "Happy Birthday," be there to read aloud at night or make breakfast in the morning or help steady the bike your child is learning to ride. The key to being a good parent is wanting to be a good parent strongly enough to make the time to do it. And the crazy love that never quits makes most of us want to do it, even when we thought we didn't want to!

So let me say to you what Sue and I needed to hear when we got started being parents. Being a parent really is not as hard as you think.

It is not easy, but there is a lot of help out there for you when you hit problems. All you have to do is let the love catch you up and carry you on. All you have to do is give in to it and let it take you where you've never been before.

The mere fact that you are reading this book identifies you as a good parent because you care enough to read it. I'd like to say, "Close up the book and go play; you already know all you need," but before you do, I do have a few points to make that I think will be useful to you in doing what is, after all, the most important work in the world: raising a child.

My first point is simply this: you already have the tools that you really need. That crazy love, for starters. Time. Friends and/or relatives. Some money. Access to help, like your own parents or your equivalent of Josselyn, plus a pediatrician and a school. That's pretty much all you need.

Let me dispel a few myths that I would have liked to have had dispelled for Sue and me when baby Lucy lay there peeing on the bed:

• You do not have as much control or influence as you think. This is good news. It means our children can survive our mistakes.

• There is no one right way to raise children. If you hear conflicting pieces of advice, like cotton diapers versus Pampers, or some TV versus no TV, or "clean your plate" versus "just eat until you're full," take heart. *There is no one right way.* So talk it over with your friends, your pediatrician, your spouse, your mother or mother-in-law, and whomever else you turn to, maybe your sister or a teacher or your clergy. And then decide for yourself. Concerning the decisions that really matter, you'll find that almost everyone agrees. Concerning the rest, it won't matter what you do.

• You do not need to be the picture of emotional health in order to be an excellent parent. You can even be like me and come from a crazy family background, have many insecurities and hang-ups, and still be a darn good parent (if I do say so myself).

• You do not have to bone up on all the latest research. If you read the parenting magazines, you'll find so much information that it will make you dizzy. And after you've read for a while, you'll find that some of it is helpful and some of it is not, and some of it is even contradictory. (Don't be upset by contradictory advice from experts. Instead, be glad. It proves that there is no one right way.) Some of it you will remember, and some you will not. That is just fine. You don't have to take a test on what you've read. The magazine articles are simply meant to offer support, not make you feel like an unprepared student.

• Your child's eventual fate is not all in the genes. Nor is it all in your hands, either. Nature and nurture combine. Studies of identical twins who were given up for adoption and raised apart from each other prove that genes don't tell the whole story, as those individuals do not end up exactly alike. But they do end up similar. So genes matter. But so does life experience.

Take heart. You can do it. In fact, you will do it. Your child is as lucky to have you as you are to have your child.

I so easily remember Sue and me huddled together that first day home with Lucy, wondering what would happen to her and to us. Now that I have three young children, my panic has subsided and been replaced by a constant question. Now I wonder if Sue and I are doing all that we can do to maximize the chances that our kids will grow up to become those blessed, happy adults we all know.

My wondering has prompted me to ask many experts what are the childhood roots of adult happiness, including Jerome Kagan, professor of psychology at Harvard and one of the world's leading authorities on child development. He said that my question was difficult to answer but then went on to say that if you had a happy childhood, that probably meant you would not report you were as happy as an adult, adult life being as difficult as it is; and that if you had a moderately unhappy childhood, the odds were in favor of your reporting being happier later on, because you'd suffered the worst already. Kagan was being his typical, thought-provoking self. He then told me that the happiest person he knew was a man in Boston who had a very difficult childhood, having grown up as an orphan. This did not surprise me, as I knew from my own childhood experience that even in the direst of circumstances, a child can often find what he needs.

Kagan then added that although he couldn't tell me exactly what the childhood roots of adult happiness are, he could tell me what the childhood roots of adult *unhappiness* are.

"What might they be?" I eagerly asked.

"Parents who expect more from a child than the child can possibly deliver," Kagan replied. "Parents who set up goals and standards the child can never meet. I know people who are at the very top of their fields, people who have even won the Nobel Prize, who still are not happy and never will be happy because they are trying to please a parent, now long dead, whom they never will be able to please. It is a curse parents place upon a child, to expect too much."

If the parents about whom Kagan was talking had not pushed so hard, perhaps their child would not have won the Nobel Prize. But then one might ask, "So what?" As a parent, would you prefer to raise a child who becomes a happy adult or raise a Nobel Prize winner?

Stop. Don't answer that question, because the question is booby-trapped. It implies that you have to make a choice, when, in fact, you do not. You can both be happy and win the Nobel Prize. It is not an either/or proposition.

I emphasize this point, because many parents, schools, teachers, and coaches teach the opposite. They say that the child must choose between happiness and high achievement. They imply that the only way to reach the top is to sacrifice all your free time and work, work, work.

But, as I will point out in later chapters, research has shown that if you are doing the right kind of work for you, work and happiness can go hand in hand. When you are doing what you love, you want to work at it as hard as you can. You want to stay up late and get up early. You want to work out in the weight room or put in extra hours practicing a difficult sonata or get the key to the lab so you can run experiments on weekends.

My work with the Harvard Chemistry Department, where there are five Nobel Prize winners, has taught me how the joy of discovery fuels the urge to work. These great scientists are not trying to please an unpleasable parent; they are trying to satisfy a curiosity that burns inside of them. To be sure, they work extremely hard and often contend with disappointment. The ability to deal with adversity is an absolute prerequisite for being a great scientist.

But what drives the best of them, the ones who are happy in what they do, is not fear but rather an unstoppable curiosity and enthusiasm. This may include a desire to win, to get to the goal first, to beat the competition, but it is a healthy competitive spirit, not a fear-driven, to-lose-means-to-die attitude. They work hard because they want to, not because they fear not to.

As a parent it is good to encourage hard work. But you need to adapt your approach to the temperament of your child. As all coaches can tell you, some athletes do best with a demanding coach, while other athletes need a gentler touch to bring out their best.

As I will explain in future chapters, the goal for a parent should be to help the child find his or her domains of curiosity and desire and then let curiosity and desire provide the pressure and the motivation. You may have to push your child to take the first lesson or try out for the first play, but sooner or later your child should find a strong enough interest to begin to push herself from within. Finding something you love to do when you are a child is one of the keys to happiness in adult life. If, when you grow up, people are willing to pay you to do the thing you love to do, then you've got it made!

Kagan's warning not to expect too much from your child does not warn against pressure *per se* as much as it warns parents to make sure the pressure is of the right kind. "Do your best" is advice that instills a good kind of pressure. "Please me," on the other hand, is a request that can haunt a child forever, instilling toxic pressure.

You want to make sure that your child knows you love her, no matter what. Conditional love from a parent does great harm. Children should know that their parents love them no matter what, now, always, and forever. The value of such constant love is summed up beautifully in the reply of a famous man who was asked how he had achieved so much in his life. He said, "In my mother's eyes I only saw smiles."

We parents have such a short time to smile those smiles, to instill whatever it is that we are going to instill. We have to do our best to get it right because we can't go back and do it over again. However we intend to point our children toward a happy life, we have to do it now.

I recognize the limitations on the concept of a happy life. I know that happiness comes and goes and is usually appreciated only in recollection, not as it is happening. I know that happiness is a by-product that comes as the result of doing other things and so should not be a goal in itself. I know that many wise people dismiss the word *happy* as a fleeting state at best, no more worthy of pursuit than the pot of gold at the end of the rainbow and at worst as the goal of selfish pleasure seekers.

Still, I want my children to grow up to be . . . happy. More than anything, that's what I want for them. To be happy. As for a definition of happiness, my favorite was told me by Sissela Bok. "Happiness," she said, "is the feeling that your life is going well."

I want to do everything I can to set my children up to lead a life they will feel is going well.

There is a truckload of books about what can go wrong. I know, because I have written one myself, entitled *When You Worry about the Child You Love*. These are useful books (you knew I'd say that, right?). But we need a book that can serve as a guide to what can and should go *right* in childhood. It is time to examine the childhood roots, not of adult unhappiness but of adult happiness.

It is time now because now we have a great deal of new evidence about what children need in order to do well later on in life.

But before plunging into that, I want to invite you to pause and reflect for a moment on your own life and your own childhood.

3

THINK BACK . . . :
LET YOUR OWN CHILDHOOD
TEACH YOU NOW

Research has shown that one of the crucial determinants in being a good parent is the ability to reflect upon your own childhood and learn from it. Parents who can learn from what went right or wrong back then are far less likely to repeat mistakes, while those who are unable to recall and reflect are likely to repeat the same mistakes their parents made.

For example, parents who abuse their children were often abused themselves. However, they are less likely to be abusive as adults if they are able to reflect upon and learn from their own experiences of abuse, to acknowledge what happened, recall the pain of it, and find other means of dealing with stress in their own lives than taking it out on their children.

While your concerns may be far more subtle than worrying about abusing your child, the same finding applies: the ability to reflect on and learn from your own childhood improves your ability to be a good parent.

We try to preserve and pass along to our children what was good from our own childhoods. And we try not to make the mistakes that were made with us.

But wait a minute; do you actually remember, and can you put into words, exactly what was good and what was not from way back then? It is worth the effort to try.

A noted British psychologist, Peter Fonagy, found in his recent studies that mothers in a relatively high-stress (deprived) group characterized by single-parent families, parental criminality, unemployment, overcrowding, and psychiatric illness would be far more likely to have securely attached infants if their reflective function was high. This is preliminary support for the Freudian notion (1920) that those who do not remember and come to terms with the past are destined (and more likely) to repeat it, at least with their children.[1]

Certainly one of the major childhood roots of adult happiness is the feeling of safety that comes from having a secure attachment to one or two parents. Even if you did not get this yourself in your childhood, Fonagy's research shows that if you reflect on why you didn't, you are far less likely to repeat the mistakes that were made with you. In other words, it is worthwhile to remember your childhood and learn from what you remember. That is why I am devoting an entire chapter of this book to the simple act of helping you organize those memories.

Do you remember saying to yourself when you were a child or a teenager, *I will never forget how I feel right now, and I will never, ever do to my children what is being done to me now*? Do you remember how angry you would get at statements like, "You are just going through a phase," or, "You'll get over it"? Do you remember when people my age would tell you how great it is to be young and to enjoy it while you can, you would think to yourself, *Yeah, right; well, it stinks being my age, and I will never, ever become a sentimental old fool like that guy and forget how hard it is to be a kid?*

As much as we might have told ourselves we would never forget, we forget. But with a bit of effort, we can remember.

Let a poet, William Wordsworth, set the stage. In 1802, when he was thirty-two years old, he wrote the following words:

My heart leaps up when I behold
    A rainbow in the sky:

So was it when my life began;
So is it now I am a man;
So be it when I shall grow old,
    Or let me die!
The Child is father of the Man. . . .

Wordsworth vows to hold on to the wonder that comes so naturally to a child. But it can be like holding on to ice; in time it melts away.

In a poem completed five years later Wordsworth, now only thirty-seven, already feels the sense of wonder slipping away:

—But there's a Tree, of many, one,
A single Field which I have looked upon,
Both of them speak of something that is gone:
    The Pansy at my feet
    Doth the same tale repeat:
Whither is fled the visionary gleam?
Where is it now, the glory and the dream?

If you can get past the dated, poetic language, words like *doth* and *whither*, and forgive Wordsworth his trees and pansies, you will find in his words a feeling with which you and I and everybody else must contend: the feeling that we had something extraspecial back then, when we were children, and we do not have it anymore.

Whither is fled the visionary gleam? Where is it now, the glory and the dream?

The closest we can get to it now may be to remember it.

You and I stopped for rainbows once, when we were young. And our hearts leaped up. Maybe it wasn't a rainbow that did it. Maybe it was that cute boy or girl you were secretly hoping to catch a glimpse of. Or maybe it was a good-night kiss from your mother or father. Or maybe it was victory in kickball. I don't know what it was for you. But I know it happened. Many times.

The Best Expert You'll Ever Find

You are your own best, most trusted expert. Not only are you your best expert, you are also the person who makes your decisions. It is you who finally decides what you want to do with and for your children. It is you who decides what makes for the best kind of childhood, and it is you who tries to provide it. That's why it is important that you recall the "data"—your own childhood—upon which you base your conclusions.

So close your eyes now, please, and think back. I don't mean that you review your whole childhood, just bring to mind a scene or two. When you return, I will have a few things to ask. Take your time. There's no hurry. Take as long as you like. I'll wait.

Welcome back. Now that you have brought childhood up into your consciousness, I invite you to ask yourself a very interesting, complex question—one that most adults rarely, if ever, ask. The question is this: What went right in your childhood? What (if anything!) from back then has led to whatever happiness you have found today?

Most of us adults can state immediately what our childhood roots of unhappiness are. A bad teacher. Not enough money. A cruel or distant parent. Few opportunities. Illness. Moving too often. A lousy school. A troubled fifth-grade year. Bad genes.

But set those aside for a moment and think, as specifically as you can, about what went right. What are you grateful for from back then? What are you glad about?

This is such an important question that I want to help you organize your thinking on it by offering the following fourteen groups of questions as a guide. I hope you will take time with each one and let the memories rush in. The answers to the questions will bring back your childhood and set up a data bank to which you will consciously and unconsciously be referring as you read the rest of this book.

I would suggest you take a notebook or piece of paper and jot down your answers to these questions so you can refer to them now and then, even after this book is long forgotten. Your notes will make for very interesting reading.

1. Try to think of some happy moments with your mother and/or with your father (if you are adopted, think of your adoptive mother and father). Can you remember a few now in some detail? They need not be "important" or "significant." All that matters is that they make you smile as you recall them. Sometimes the most trivial moments—like licking the knife that spread the frosting—can warm your heart the most.

2. Try to think of some happy moments with your siblings and/or friends. Try to recall a few now in some detail. Again, it does not matter how deep or meaningful they might or might not have been, just that you remember them and they make you smile.

3. Now that you've recalled some happy moments, think about what went wrong. This will help you decide what *not* to do with your children. What went wrong in your childhood? Try to think of a few specific moments.

4. Try now to get back into the world of your youth. Try to remember how the world looked and felt when you were around age eleven or twelve. What did your yard look like? What did your bedroom look like? What kind of refrigerator did you have? Did you take showers or baths? What was your favorite dessert? Can you remember a movie you liked back then? What did you think of adults? What did your classroom look like? What did cars look like? How about the main street of your town or the street where you lived? Can you remember a pet you really loved? What were your favorite holidays or special occasions (like birthday parties or sleepovers)? Can you think back on a couple of good ones and recall what went on?

5. Who were your best friends from childhood? Can you name a few who still stand out in your mind?

6. Can you remember happy times with grandparents? Spend a few moments in your mind with your grandparents now, remembering.

7. What person outside your family influenced you most significantly in a positive way during your childhood? How did this person

change you? Spend a moment or two remembering him or her in your mind now. What was it that he or she did? Was there a specific moment that stands out as significant? Or was it a series of moments? Or just the relationship as a whole?

8. What are your most positive memories from school? What teaching style worked best for you? What did you get from school that you use in your life today? What in your schooling went wrong? What do you want to make sure your children never experience in school that you experienced?

9. What form of discipline or behavioral regulation, if any, would you say helped you the most? What did *not* help? What kind of discipline that was applied to you do you want to make sure you never apply to your children? And what discipline or motivational strategy worked well enough for you to want to use it with your children?

10. What are a few of your happiest, random childhood memories? What did you do that you hope you can encourage your own children to do? Reading by yourself? Making time for friends? Looking on the bright side?

11. What do you wish now had happened during your childhood that didn't?

12. What traits did you have as a child that you value the most today (regardless of whether you think you still have them)?

13. What are the childhood roots of whatever happiness you feel you have found today?

In answering these questions, you have called to mind some of the most important years of your life. The beginning years.

Let me ask you one more question:

14. What can you learn from your answers to the preceding questions about how you are or should be raising your children today?

4

CONFIDENT, CAN-DO KIDS: WHERE DO THEY COME FROM?

Most people who reflect on what went right in their own childhoods, as I invited you to do in the previous chapter, bring up two kinds of memories. First, they think of joyful moments, bringing to mind people who loved them and guided them or special moments of victory and mastery. Second, they think of problems that they dealt with, moments of defeat or injustice, difficult times that they managed to survive that shaped them. The research done by Csikszentmihalyi, Seligman, Vaillant, and many others supports the idea that the two preeminent skills on which happy adults rely are the ability to deal with adversity and the ability to create and sustain joy.

It is especially heartening to know that these skills can be learned. You do not have to be born with the right genes to become able to deal with adversity or create and sustain joy.

How a child (or you or I) can learn those two all-important skills is the subject of the next few chapters.

How to Deal with Adversity

At first glance you might think that the childhood roots of adult happiness are obvious. If you have good genes and you have a happy childhood, then you will grow up to be a happy person. If you don't, you won't.

But it doesn't work out that way. Far from it. From the genetic standpoint, there are millions of adults who have overcome "bad" genes; they overcame inherited problems like a learning disability or a congenital heart disorder or depression. And from the standpoint of life experience, there are millions of unhappy adults who had pleasant childhoods, while there are many happy adults who had harrowing childhoods.

Let me tell you about the early years of Shantwania Buchanan and then invite you to guess what she is doing today.

Shantwania was born in Mississippi to a crack-cocaine–addicted mother who had no money. Four years later her sister was born, and three years after that her little brother. They had no money and essentially no mother. Drugs came in and out of the house, their mother came in and out of the house, and their only caretaker was an aging, ill grandmother. Shantwania learned how to cook and clean under her grandma's direction, and she was taking care of her siblings by the time she was seven. By the time Shantwania was eleven, her grandma had died and her mother had up and left. Shantwania and her siblings were out on the street.

But her grandmother, while not able to leave her money, had managed to instill in Shantwania something more valuable: certain feelings. One was a feeling that she had power and could solve whatever life sent her way. Another was a fierce feeling of loyalty to and connectedness with her siblings. Rather than separate and go into different foster homes, which would have happened had they appealed for the services of the state, Shantwania elected to live on the streets of Jackson, Mississippi, with her little brother and sister. She made money shooting dice in street craps games. She and her siblings slept under stairwells and sometimes in people's backyard doghouses. They would use the public rest rooms in gas stations or McDonald's, and they would scrounge for clothes in other people's discarded trash. Shantwania did whatever she had to do to survive and protect her siblings. She made up her mind that the three of them would make it as a family, together, no matter what.

Where do you suppose she is today? Statistics would predict that she and her siblings would be on drugs or in jail or living a marginal life, barely eking out an existence.

But Shantwania and her brother and sister didn't believe in statistics. In June of 2001 Shantwania graduated from Brown University Medical School and in July started a residency in obstetrics and gynecology. Her sister recently graduated from junior college, and her brother is in the marines.

You could say that Shantwania's story is miraculous—and it is. But it is not incomprehensible. You could say that God did it; but then why did God do it for Shantwania and not for so many others? You could say it's a mystery, and so it is. But here's a clue to the mystery: God works through other people. Various human beings helped Shantwania and her siblings, some profoundly, others just in passing. To be sure, Shantwania relied on her personal strength; her motto is "Suck it up." But that strength did not come out of the vapors. It came from her grandmother and other people with whom she connected along the way. This led her to a feeling of wanting to give back, a feeling we call altruism. According to Vaillant's data, the development of altruism as a means of dealing with stress is one of the healthiest of all strategies, one that correlates strongly with satisfaction in life. As Shantwania puts it, in describing how she envisions her career now as a doctor, "For some reason, God has always put people in my life to get me through. Now, I want to look after them."

Even though we probably do not identify with or share Shantwania's experience in its details (who does?), I think we can look at her and learn something that we can apply in our own lives instead of simply feeling awestruck by her—and distant from her life.

Shantwania can teach us all about the extraordinary power of love when it becomes a reverberating circuit within a group of people, like a family. The love she felt for and from her grandmother and the love she felt for and from her siblings gave her superhuman strength. Each day, in order to survive, she did what she had to do, not only for herself but for two other children who depended on her totally. She had a mission, fueled by love, tested in the extreme by the grimmest realities.

Shantwania's grandmother was the charismatic adult whom Dr. Robert Brooks's research shows almost always can be found in the childhood of an adult who has beaten the odds, as Shantwania did. Shantwania's grandmother was charismatic in that she inspired Shantwania to find more within herself than she knew she had, to try hard no matter what, and to feel connected to a grand mission in life. Brooks, who along with Sam Goldstein has meticulously reviewed the considerable research that has been done into what makes for resilient children, states that the most important factor is this one, charismatic adult. One adult—often a parent or a teacher but sometimes another relative or a coach or some other adult who luckily appears in a child's life—can transform a broken child into a heroic survivor. One adult who cares, and who is able to inspire the child, can set into motion what amounts to a miracle.

Although most children do not need to work the miracle Shantwania worked, all children contend with hard times once in a while. Disappointments and setbacks of many kinds befall all children, from minor ones, like not getting invited to a certain party, to larger ones, like not getting into a certain school, to major ones, like the death of a relative or a friend or even a parent. The same kind of reverberating circuit of love that saved Shantwania and her siblings can save all families, like yours and mine, from being destroyed by whatever grim realities, minor or major, we have to face.

Most of all, what I learn from Shantwania's story is not a precept (something that you learn like a lesson) but rather a feeling (something that you come to know without having to take lessons). When I think of Shantwania, I feel hopeful. If she could do what she did, then there's hope for just about anyone. You don't have to win the lottery or find a benefactor. All you have to do is find that reverberating circuit of love, somewhere.

From the basic loving connection, emotional strength will grow. Recent findings from Peter Fonagy, whom I mentioned in the previous chapter, as well as other specialists in attachment research underscore the power of the loving connection in creating emotional strength, even under adverse circumstances.

That research, which is some of the most exciting work being done in child development today, enlarges upon the classic work of John Bowlby, whose research half a century ago showed that children who did not develop a secure attachment to their mothers were more likely to show signs of "*partial deprivation*—an excessive need for love or for revenge, gross guilt, and depression—or *complete deprivation*—listlessness, quiet unresponsiveness, and retardation of development, and later in development signs of superficiality, want of real feeling."[1]

One of the best ways to do well in life is to have a secure, lasting attachment to one person, usually your mother, when you are very young.

I know many people who have beaten the odds, and I imagine you do, too. You may be one of them yourself. They—you—handle adversity well. That is something that distinguishes happy people in general. They are not knocked off their pins by hard times. And since life is sure to offer up to every one of us a hefty helping of adversity, dealing with it well must be one key to what we call happiness.

One way to gain such an ability is by having a strong and secure attachment early on. But if you didn't get that, can such an ability be taught and learned? Well, some very good research suggests that it can.

Some of this ability is in the genes. We can't do anything about that. But a great deal of it can be learned. Martin Seligman's research has proved that optimism—a can-do, want-to-do attitude—can be taught. And optimism in childhood is one of the chief variables that correlates with happiness in adulthood. I daresay that Shantwania's grandmother was a master teacher of optimism and Shantwania a master student. Leaders in business will tell you that what they look for in a potential employee is not so much a stellar academic record as a can-do, want-to-do attitude, an ability to tackle a problem and stick with it until it is solved, using Scotch tape and spit and whatever brainpower he or she has got. So it is in the lives of people who report that they are happy. When a problem arises, they swing into action. They gather their resources, limited though they may be. They find help, limited though it may be. They don't give up.

I got one clue to how such resourceful people get to be that way when I interviewed Ty Tingley, the principal at Phillips Exeter Academy, a boarding school in New Hampshire that accepts students from all over the world, grades nine through twelve. I asked him the question I have been asking experts of all kinds for years now, as I prepared to write this book: "What do you think are the childhood roots of adult happiness?"

This question usually makes the person pause, as it did Ty. It is also a question that usually brings a smile to the person's face, as it did to Ty's. Then, the person usually says something like what Ty said to me, "Gee, that is a very good question." For such an obviously important question, it is not one that most of us have ever been asked or thought about in much detail. But almost everyone has a reply, after giving it a little thought, as did Ty. His reply was one of the most unusual, but I think on-the-mark, of any of the hundreds of replies I have collected.

"I can tell you one very important way we prepare kids here, while they are at Exeter, to be happy in their adult lives," Ty said with a little mischief in his eye, as he knew I was not expecting the answer he was about to give. "We teach them how to fail. We give them many, many chances to fail. We see to it that they fail. And then we help them get back up again." Exeter is a school with high academic standards. It is hard to get admitted to Exeter, and it is hard to get good grades once you are there. Students who do get in expect to excel. Then they don't do as well as they expected. I know. It happened to me.

I arrived at Exeter as a ninth grader in 1964. I had been the number one student in my class at my previous school. I expected to be the same at Exeter. But I wasn't. I thought I would get straight A's. I didn't. In fact, in that ninth-grade year, I didn't even get one A.

At first I went into a tizzy. How could this be! But then, with the help of my adviser and the other kids, all of whom, like me, were discovering that they were not nearly the smartest people in the world, I gradually learned how to handle this bit of adversity. I learned how, in Ty Tingley's intentionally ironic words, to fail. That was one of the most important lessons of my childhood. I didn't have to be number one to be happy. I didn't have to be perfect in order to be OK.

That is not to say I became complacent. To the contrary, I worked harder at Exeter than I ever had before. But I realized that even when I worked as hard as I possibly could, someone would almost always do better.

You have to experience defeat yourself in order to learn how to deal with it. Whether it is playing Monopoly with your family or getting good grades at Exeter or vying for the Nobel Prize, you won't consistently succeed until you learn how to lose.

Put differently, you have to lose in order to learn how to win at the game nature has prepared you to play. Life is not one roll of the dice. Life is a game of multiple failures. The people who prevail in life—who become happy in themselves as adults—are the ones who can fail or suffer loss or defeat but never lose heart. We all experience defeat as children, maybe not at Exeter or on the streets of Jackson, Mississippi, but at other places. It is important that we learn to take heart even in the face of disappointment. This is not the whole key to being happy as an adult, but without it the door to long-term happiness usually stays locked.

You can instill this ability in your child in many ways. The best way is to provide the secure attachment early on; that is why *connecting* is the first and most important step in my five-step method, which I outline in Chapter 5.

There are other ways as well. You can model the ability to deal with adversity yourself, in your own life. Children watch and learn from how their parents deal with disappointment, be it in their careers or at an athletic event or even just in being cut off in traffic. You can encourage competition, making sure that your child experiences both victory and defeat, and help her deal with each. You can use humor to deal with the pain, or bits of philosophy, or simply let your children see that you do not give up. You can also tell stories about other people who overcame obstacles (which includes just about everybody). For example, the former CEO of General Electric, Jack Welch, tells of coming home one day and complaining to his mother that other kids were teasing him because of his stutter. His mom replied, "Oh, Jack, you only stutter because you are so smart and your brain is going so fast that your tongue can't keep up with it." Or you can remind your child that Einstein struggled with grade school arithmetic. True examples can help enormously.

You can also teach optimism. You can model it yourself, and you can frequently make such statements as, "There is no problem that we as a team can't solve." Such words may be lost on jaded adults, but they sink in with children. And the more you believe that you can solve a problem, the more likely it is that you can and will.

Furthermore, you can make an effort not to protect your child from all disappointments but rather to be there to help her deal with them as they occur. The best way to learn how to deal with adversity is to deal with it successfully many times over. "Succesfully" simply means that you learn from it and don't give up. You can offer advice that will help your child do better next time and sooner or later achieve mastery. You can provide recognition not only for achievements and successes but also for effort and courage in the face of frustration and defeat. You can quote the words of Rudyard Kipling from his poem "If," words that adorn the tunnel from the changing rooms out to Centre Court at Wimbledon:

If you can meet with Triumph and Disaster
And treat those two imposters just the same

After you quote those lines from "If," explain to your child why and how triumph and disaster are impostors. It may be a tough sell, but this is the creative work of being a parent or a teacher or a coach.

These bits of advice are not random. In the chapters that follow, I will lay out a five-step method in detail that, taken as a whole, confers the ability to deal with adversity as well as to create and sustain joy.

How to Create and Sustain Joy

Just as it is important for a child to learn how to deal with adversity, it is also important for a child to learn how to create and sustain joy.

We usually underestimate the importance of this skill. It is crucial. Millions of adults lead unsatisfactory lives precisely because they have not learned how to create and sustain joy in healthy, reliable ways. The reason millions of adults turn to drugs, alcohol, gambling, and other dangerous ways of finding pleasure is that they have not learned better methods of finding joy in everyday life.

Alcohol and other drugs pose a huge hazard to young people (as well as old) because they offer such an easy, available solution to the challenge of how to find joy in daily life.

How can finding joy be a challenge? Joy sounds simple. Don't worry; be happy. But the ability to create and sustain joy is far from simple. It is at least as complicated—and valuable—as the ability to deal with adversity. Many adults spend their entire lives dealing with adversity, and dealing with it well, but they rarely experience joy. Others only experience joy in ways that are short-lived and potentially harmful, like drinking, using drugs, gambling, or taking dangerous risks.

Let me give you an example. I know a man who worries so much that even when there is nothing to worry about, he worries that he must be missing something. It is extremely difficult for him ever to experience unalloyed joy, because the moment he feels joy, an alarm signal deep within him goes off that says, *"Beware!"* It is as if he were allergic to joy. The only way he ever feels really happy is on the Saturday evenings when he goes out to dinner with his wife and has two martinis.

There is an innovative organization based in Needham, Massachusetts, called Freedom from Chemical Dependence Educational Services, Inc. (or FCD, for short), which sends out trainers to schools around the world to conduct educational sessions for students on how to live a fulfilling life without using alcohol or other drugs. All the trainers are recovering addicts themselves, so they offer an invaluable been-there, done-that perspective. To help in this work, the president of FCD, psychologist and author Alex J. Packer, wrote a wonderfully practical book called *HIGHS! Over 150 Ways to Feel Really, REALLY Good . . . Without Alcohol or Other Drugs.* This book is funny, honest, and written in a style that teens and young adults enjoy.

But of course, we need more than a book. We need to experience joy in healthy ways that we want to return to for the rest of our lives.

To learn how to do this, it is best to start young. To show you how a child might learn this, let me take you to one of the world's leading experts: Tucker, my six-year-old son.

Watching him play is like going to an advanced laboratory of joy. I especially love to watch Tucker when he is playing by himself. Then he is like some Nobel Prize–winning scientist alone in his lab, cavorting among all the experiments he has running at once, thrilled to be able to focus on his myriad projects without interruption.

If I hear Tucker, my scientist of joy, in his bedroom, I will often go to his open door and stand there, listening and watching as he plays. If he sees me, he'll just smile, say, "Hi, Dad," and go on playing.

His room is small, but great scientists don't need much space. There is enough empty floor space for him to orchestrate his imaginary games. He will take whatever material is at hand—and since his floor is usually strewn with stuff, there is a wide selection—and he will make up a game. Maybe he will turn one of my slippers (which has somehow found its way into his room) into a ship, on which he will place his crew of "good guys," plastic figures saved from a Happy Meal at McDonald's or a broken soldier from last year's Christmas or maybe a bottle top from who-knows-where (who-knows-where covers most of our house), and then he will accumulate a few bad guys, from the same sources, and let the adventures begin. Tucker provides the sound effects and the dialogue.

"Whooooooooom! Ker-bang! Ship to chief! Help needed! Help on the way! Watch out, that bad guy is coming in! Shhheeeeee! Womp! Fzzzzzzzzzz! Turn thataway. Straighten her out. OK, now watch it! Whoooooosh!"

He can go on like that for an hour or more. The game will evolve from a battle situation into an exploring expedition to a game of hide-and-seek, all conducted by Tucker with his imaginary players.

As I stand and watch him, and he totally forgets that I am there, I think to myself that this is about the most important "work" he will ever do. He is planting seeds of joy. He is learning how to create and sustain joy, with no more at his disposal than he would have if he were marooned on a desert island. A few pieces of driftwood, some shells, and Tucker would be in heaven. (At least until he got hungry.)

I once heard Jack Welch answer the question What makes a person successful? Welch, who came from humble roots, attended a non–Ivy League school (University of Massachusetts), and has a speech impediment, turned General Electric into one of the most successful corporations in the world. Welch's reply to the question of what makes a person successful was this: "Grab life and live it to the fullest. Whatever you do, grab ahold of life. You only have a short time, so don't be a dabbler. And don't get discouraged by the bureaucrats. Just grab life and live it full and strong."

I could see what Jack Welch was describing in watching Tucker as he played. It is an attitude, not a skill. Another of Welch's dicta was to hire for attitudes, then teach the skills. The attitude leads to the skill, but happiness starts in an attitude. "I am going to go for it" Tucker's playing proclaims. "I am not going to hold back. I am going to play full blast. I am not afraid."

Let me call upon another expert: Lucy, my twelve-year-old daughter. Older than Tucker, she no longer plays on the floor in her room, as he does. But she creates and sustains joy in many ways. Talking to friends is chief among them. On the telephone, in person, via instant messaging (more on monitoring electronics in Chapter 8). Playing soccer. Picking out nail polish and then applying it to the nails on both her fingers and toes. She can be moody, so it is important that she know how to find joy when she gets into a grumpy place emotionally. She has learned this instinctively, by knowing when she needs some alone time, some time with a book or TV, some time on the phone with a friend, or even some sleep.

In the next chapter I describe the forces that tend to combine to create happy children who are on their way to happy, responsible adulthoods. The forces include connectedness, play, practice, mastery, and recognition. That combination, if it is present throughout childhood, tends to result in children who can both deal with adversity and create and sustain joy.

The combination of forces that I describe in the next chapter has circulated throughout Lucy's childhood, and those forces have resulted in a child who is much happier at the age of twelve than either of her parents were then. Although as a parent it makes me nervous to say this for fear of jinxing her, Lucy should be on her way to happiness in adulthood. As evidence of this, look at what she wrote when asked to write a poem about herself for English class in seventh grade:

GLOWING FAIRY

Her name tells of how it is with her.
Her energy is like a flying fairy
Dancing on the moon.
Her creativity is like a sunset
Painting colors in the sky.
Her moods are like the ocean,
Sometimes sparkling and calm, sometimes angry and rough.
Her movement is like a mermaid,
Swimming gracefully through the sea.
Her loyalty is like a mother bird
Protecting its nest.
Her sweetness is like chocolate
Melting in your mouth.
Her kindness is like an angel,
Spreading happiness around.
Her playfulness is like a monkey
Swinging from tree to tree.
Her confidence is like a star
Shining brightly in the dark night.
Her heart is like a glowing fairy,
Spreading light to the world.

Lucy is not a big "star" in any field, from academics to sports to music, although she successfully participates in all of those. She is always an enthusiastic contributor, a joyful presence wherever she goes.

"Yes, but," "Yes, but," "Yes, but," the adults reply. And we all know the many yes-buts. You must wait your turn. You must learn some skills. You must do your homework. You must learn discipline. You must brush your teeth and get your sleep. All true. And it helps if you are a big star, doesn't it? It gives you a "hook" for getting into a prestigious college, doesn't it? Being a star is good, right? Not always. It depends on how you become one.

What matters is preserving that rush of enthusiasm that almost all children feel *and* learning discipline, waiting your turn, acquiring some skills, and brushing your teeth. Let stardom take care of itself.

Too much enthusiasm, vision, and excitement with not enough discipline, patience, and clean teeth leads to frustration. "Why don't people listen to me?" is the refrain of these adults. On the other hand, too much discipline, patience, and tooth-brushing without enough enthusiasm, vision, and excitement leads to joyless competence. "Why don't I take more pleasure in my success?" is the refrain of these adults.

We need to make sure our children both play and brush their teeth.

The ability to create and sustain joy. The capacity to deal with pain and adversity. These are the childhood roots of adult happiness.

A Method That Can Work for All Children

The question of how to instill or acquire these capabilities still remains. I have offered some thoughts in this chapter about learning how to deal with adversity and learning how to create and sustain joy. But you need more. I want to offer specific suggestions and tips as well as warn of certain common mistakes parents and teachers may make.

Moreover, I want to suggest to you a method that can work for all children, regardless of how much money their parents have, how old the children or parents are, where they live, or what genes the children have inherited.

5

THE CHILDHOOD ROOTS OF ADULT HAPPINESS: A REPEATING CYCLE OF FIVE STEPS

If children are provided with the physical necessities of life—and tragically that is not a given for everyone, even in our affluent society—they are remarkably resilient. They grow and flourish, when given half a chance. The program I outline in this chapter, based on research and experience, is my best assessment of what children need, beyond the physical necessities, in order to thrive.

In the five-step program I recommend, each step leads to the next, so a cycle ensues, as shown in the accompanying illustration. The process goes on, hopefully not just throughout childhood but throughout all of life. I will describe the points in the cycle here and then devote a separate chapter to each one.

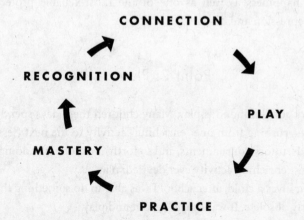

Point 1: Connection

Connection is the most important point in the cycle. It sets all the rest of the cycle in motion. Fortunately nature equips almost all children and parents with the ability to connect. (I say "almost" because some children are born with problems in making meaningful connections with others: these are the children with autism, Asperger's syndrome, childhood schizophrenia, or pervasive developmental disorder. Fortunately we are devising promising treatments for these conditions.)

Connection—in the form of unconditional love from an adult, usually one or both parents—is the single most important childhood root of adult happiness. But it is not everything. As I explain in the next chapter, there are many other kinds of connection that, when combined, form an all but unshakable foundation on which you can build an entire life.

By growing up with a strong feeling of connectedness, a child develops a sense of what Erik Erikson called *basic trust* early on. The child also develops a feeling of security and safety, which, in turn, instills courage and the desire to take risks in the world—whether at six months of age or sixty years.

This capacity to tackle anything that comes along—what I call a can-do, want-to-do attitude—leads to enduring optimism. As I have cited previously, research done by Martin Seligman and others has shown that an attitude of optimism is one of the strongest predictors of adult happiness as well as one of the most reliable protectors against depression and despair.

Point 2: Play

The "work" of childhood is play. Many children these days spend too much time rushing from one "enriching" activity to the next (lessons of all kinds, tutors, tournaments, and so forth), without ever doing the single most enriching activity ever devised: play.

When I was a child, after school I was able to do something that is now nearly obsolete. It was called "go out and play."

As a parent, try never to forget that a child at play is a child at work.

Priscilla Vail, a happy adult who is one of the great experts on learning disabilities in the country, told me that when she was a little girl, she was often left alone, since she was by far the youngest. Her siblings were not around, and her parents were often quarreling. She remembers learning to enjoy her own company and learning how to play alone. She says that talent has been of immense value her entire life.

Play builds the imagination. Play with other children teaches skills of problem solving and cooperation. Solitary play also teaches problem solving as well as the possibilities inherent in solitude. A child who learns to play alone will never be lonely. Play teaches the ability to tolerate frustration, when you don't get it right the first time as you build your building or try to ride your bike, and it teaches the all-important ability to fail.

In addition, when you play in your mind, you daydream. The capacity to dream daydreams is a special talent most children have, and it is a crucial one. We chart our courses in our dreams. Dreams also can lead to or reinforce belief. The stronger your ability to play in your mind—to dream—the greater the likelihood that your beliefs won't begin crumbling as you grow older.

Dreams and beliefs, then, are the fruits of sustained play.

Play generates joy. Play becomes its own reward. In play the child enters that state of mind Mihaly Csikszentmihalyi calls *flow*. In flow humans are at their happiest, forgetting where they are or even who they are. Play, at its best, introduces a child to the world of flow. The more a person can find activities in which he can get into a state of flow, the happier that person will be day after day. We plant the seeds of flow in childhood, in play.

Point 3: Practice

Adults know how important practice is. But how did we learn that? Through experience. Through trial and error. Through . . . practice.

A child who plays will soon learn the power of practice. Rare is the child who can ride a bike on the first try without falling off. But such is the allure of being able to ride that practice becomes tolerable. Frustration becomes bearable. Failure becomes the first step on the road to mastery and success.

Or if you have a piano in your house, your toddler might begin "playing" it by banging on it. When she gets old enough, if she gets lessons, she will find that her playing sounds better and feels better if she practices. She might not enjoy practicing—indeed, most people don't. But she will keep at it because she likes how the final result feels.

Learning anything—from riding a bicycle to playing the piano to speaking Spanish—hurts somewhat. This is because you have to go through a phase in which you see how bad you are at it. A phase in which you feel, and are, inept. Often a phase of marginal improvement despite colossal effort. But with encouragement you keep at it. Finally you see improvement. That leads to step 4, mastery.

With practice comes discipline. Of course, it is not a simple, smooth progression from doing whatever you want whenever you want to leading a disciplined, responsible life. But the best road to getting there runs not through the land of fear and punishment but through the land of connection, play, practice, mastery, and recognition.

In addition, as the child practices, he usually receives some help. This is another important skill that develops as a child practices: he learns how to receive help, teaching, or coaching.

Point 4: Mastery

After a certain amount of practice and discipline, a child will experience the great feeling of mastery. "I can do it!" "Now I get it!" "Wow!" These are the cries of mastery.

Few feelings in life are any better than that. We only experience mastery now and then, but once we have felt it, we want to feel it again.

The roots of self-esteem lie not in praise but in mastery. When a child masters something she couldn't do before—from walking to riding a bike to playing the piano to speaking Spanish—her self-esteem *naturally* rises, whether she receives any praise or not. If you want your child to have a high sense of self-esteem, don't go out of your way to praise her; go out of your way to make sure she experiences mastery in many different ways.

With mastery comes not only self-esteem but also confidence, leadership skills, initiative, and an enduring desire to work hard. You find that you work not because you feel you should but because you want to, in order to experience that unbeatable feeling of mastery once again.

Point 5: Recognition

Mastery leads naturally to recognition and approval by a larger group. When the child takes her first step, mom and dad cheer and probably take pictures or videos. When you ride a bike for the first time, you can join your friends who also ride and gain recognition and approval from a wider circle. Each act of mastery leads to recognition and approval, by an ever-widening circle of people, from parents at first to extended family to friends and classmates to the whole school to your town or business or readership or viewers or whatever your largest audience turns out to be.

It is important not only that others value and recognize the child but that the child feel valued and recognized for who he or she actually is. As Alice Miller pointed out in her classic book *The Drama of the Gifted Child*, many children, particularly the clever ones, can sense from an early age what other people want from them and what they can do to gain the praise of others. So they start to play what can become a lifelong game of people-pleasing, all the while suppressing their true selves, to the point that as adults they have no feeling of who they really are.

To prevent this, children need to be recognized—and valued—for who they truly are.

When who the child truly is coincides with what the larger group values, this not only reinforces her desire to do well—to gain approval from others—but it reinforces her own sense that she matters, that she belongs, that she contributes. If you feel recognized and valued by a larger group, you will feel connected to that larger group. When you feel connected to a larger group, you will want to do right by that group, be it your family, your team, your class, your neighborhood, your company, the kingdom of your God, whatever. This feeling of genuine connectedness to a larger group is the root of moral behavior.

Moral behavior, which all parents want their children to learn and often despair that they are not learning, derives not from lectures and sermons but from this feeling of connectedness to a larger group. Moral behavior—at its best—reflects a desire to do what is right, not a fear of what will happen if you do what is wrong.

Recognition, which leads to social connectedness, not only is the root of moral behavior, it is also a natural validator that what you are doing has worth. This inclines you to want to do more. That is called motivation—which parents and teachers often scratch their heads wondering how to instill.

The five steps, one logically leading to the next, therefore also create other benefits as children grow. These additional qualities, like moral behavior and motivation, grow spontaneously out of the process. Of course, the progress of these steps, like the course of true love, never does run smooth. Still, the basic strategy of following these steps usually leads to many benefits.

The accompanying illustration summarizes the five steps, along with some of the additional qualities each step fosters.

You might think this illustration looks like a shopping list of everything you want for your children. In fact, it is. And it works. But you can't "shop" for what the five-step cycle generates.

One of the mistakes we parents make is "shopping" for everything in that illustration without first considering how the child can grow these abilities naturally within herself or himself.

Take moral behavior, for example. Or self-esteem. I can't tell you how many parents want to *teach* their children moral behavior or *supply* their children with self-esteem. They make them learn the Ten Commandments as a way of teaching them moral behavior, or they praise them up and down all day long to help build their self-esteem.

Ability to Create and Sustain Joy

Ability to Deal with Adversity

Love of Life, Basic Trust
Security, Courage, Optimism
Ability to Deal with Adversity

CONNECTION

Feel Part of Group
Moral Behavior
Reinforced Motivation
Self-esteem
Identity

RECOGNITION

Learn to Create and Sustain Joy
Experience "Flow"
Learn How to Fail
Build Imagination, Confidence
Feel Ease in Chaos
Learn Cooperation

PLAY

MASTERY
Confidence, Leadership, Initiative
Excitement with Learning
Desire to Learn More
Self-esteem, Internal Motivation

PRACTICE
Control
Discipline
Persistence
Ability to Seek and Receive Help

This approach is well-meaning, but it doesn't work. It is artificial. It is like going out to the grocery store and buying some tomatoes, which you then bring home and staple onto a bush in your backyard, and say to yourself, "Look at the beautiful tomatoes I have raised." That bush isn't going to produce any more tomatoes than the ones you have stapled on, which will rot soon anyway.

It is best if you can find a way to raise a tomato plant rather than supplying the finished product and stapling it on. If you can find a way to raise a child so that moral behavior and self-esteem grow naturally from within that child rather than being stapled on, then those qualities will flourish and endure.

We can try to staple on moral behavior, for example, but it never sticks very long that way.

The reason I advocate the simple, bare-bones approach of the five-step cycle is that each step naturally leads not only to the next step but also to the growth of all the items on that "shopping list."

In the next chapter I discuss how this happens.

6

PRESERVING AND PROMOTING THE POSITIVE ENERGY OF CHILDHOOD: WHAT THE FIVE STEPS CAN DO

As the illustration at the end of the last chapter shows, the five-step cycle that I have outlined leads to much more than the five steps themselves.

And when each of the traits or capabilities in that illustration grows from within the child rather than being externally applied, it tends to endure and grow for the rest of the person's life.

For example, instead of "stapling" moral behavior onto a child, it is best to raise the child so that he or she naturally wants to do what is right.

"Not possible," the skeptic (who calls himself a realist, of course) harrumphs. "Humans are naturally corrupt. You can only create moral behavior through clear rules and the fear of consequences."

We need rules and consequences for the people who do not respond to other methods. But the voluntarily moral person—and we all hope our children will become voluntarily moral, not just learn how to fake it—does what is right because he decides he wants to, having weighed the options.

So it is with self-esteem. The child who truly does like who he is feels that way not because he has had self-esteem stapled onto him in the form of compliments and praise but because he has achieved mastery of some kind or another.

Let me give some examples of how the five-step cycle leads to much more than the five steps alone and creates many other qualities that all parents want for their children, such as self-esteem, moral behavior, the ability to deal with adversity, the capacity to create and sustain joy, and internal motivation.

The Five Steps Lead to Self-Esteem . . .

All of us parents want our children to feel good about themselves, to have what we call high self-esteem. But often we put the cart before the horse. We think we can create high self-esteem simply by telling a child that he or she is good. It doesn't work.

While praising children is a fine thing to do—it bolsters a sense of connectedness—studies show that it does not by itself create lasting self-esteem. Self-esteem is usually the result of mastery. After you master a difficult task, your self-esteem naturally rises, just as a muscle naturally gains bulk when it lifts heavy weights. You can no more bolster a child's self-esteem by telling him he is good than you can bulk up a muscle by telling it it is strong. As a child goes through the five-step process, especially after step 4 (mastery) and step 5 (recognition) self-esteem grows naturally, like a muscle that has just bench-pressed a hefty load. Or a tomato plant that has grown strong enough to bear fruit.

. . . AND MORAL BEHAVIOR . . .

Every parent I meet—including my wife and myself—frets over the issue of moral behavior. Particularly these days, when we read not only about school shootings but also about the many milder instances of cheating, vandalism, or disrespect. How can we be sure that our children will grow up to be moral, decent adults? We observe up close how cruel and unempathic children can be; we sometimes wonder how in the world they will acquire a desire to do what is right.

So we give lectures, we take our children to church or synagogue, or we read them stories that have morals in them. Sometimes we get angry. Have you given the tirade in the car about how unappreciative and privileged your children are? I have. It goes something like this:

"I can't believe you are saying you don't want to stop at that restaurant because it doesn't have the right kind of french fries. Here we are, on a long drive so you can go on a wonderful vacation, and you are complaining about french fries? Don't you ever think about anyone except yourselves? Boy, have I done a bad job as a parent. I haven't taught you to be thankful for all that we have. I haven't taught you to be considerate of other people. Instead, I have provided you with so much that you have become entitled little demons. [At the use of such a word, one of the kids usually giggles, then tries to stifle it, fearing I will get angrier.] Well, I am tired of this. As of now, everything is going to change. We will stop wherever and whenever Mom and I deem fit. Do you understand?"

They say they understand, then one of them says he or she is sorry, and the other two follow suit. Then I say I am sorry for yelling, and we make up.

I become a little bit tougher for a while and deny them something or other, then I go back to providing too much. It is an ongoing struggle within myself. Thanks to Sue, though, the kids are not being spoiled too much. My lectures and tirades make some small impact. The kids maybe fear me a little bit—a teensy-weensy bit, as Tucker would say—and I guess this is good. But the roots of moral behavior do not lie in lectures or in knowledge of the Ten Commandments. Those may establish the rules, but they do not provide the motivation to follow the rules.

The most enduring and reliable motivator to do what is right and good is not a belief system but a feeling of connectedness. The child who feels connected to some group larger than himself—be it his family, his team, his town, his class in school, or his group of friends—will not want to harm that group by doing wrong. He will not want to bring dishonor upon himself or his group by getting into trouble. He will naturally want to do his part to remain a respected and valued member of the group. The feeling of connectedness naturally leads to moral behavior, even if the child has never heard of the Golden Rule.

Just as mastery naturally leads to self-esteem, connectedness naturally leads to moral behavior. The ongoing National Longitudinal Study of Adolescent Health, under the leadership of J. Richard Udry at the University of North Carolina and other researchers around the country, has produced very strong evidence that shows how crucial connectedness is in children's lives, not only in helping promote moral behavior but in promoting emotional and physical health in general. We parents make a mistake, albeit a well-intentioned mistake, if we simply "teach" self-esteem or moral behavior. Instead, both will grow naturally if we create a connected childhood for our kids in which each child has the opportunity to experience mastery at various things he or she was previously unable to do.

. . . AND THE ABILITY TO DEAL WITH ADVERSITY . . .

Dealing with adversity is another trait that most parents desperately want to make sure their children acquire. "Life is so hard," parents say to me (and I often say to myself), "I want to be sure he can get up after he gets knocked down." But where does such resilience come from? Certainly not from lectures. It comes from life. Just as the hard knocks come from life, so does the ability to deal with them. Specifically it comes from knowing that you never, never have to be alone.

It is important that your child's reflex response to adversity be to reach out. Too many people—of all ages—pull back when trouble hits. They go into hiding, or they pretend the problem doesn't exist. Most of these people learned this habit when they were children. It is far more helpful if you can learn to reach out to trusted and reliable others when you encounter difficulty rather than retreating to a painful, solitary place.

If you feel connected, you will always be able to deal with adversity. The skills we need to deal with adversity begin not with thoughts or instructions but with a feeling—a feeling of *I can handle this*. It is a feeling of *No matter what happens, I can find a solution;* a feeling of *I have dealt with hard times and come out fine before;* a feeling of *Even when I feel lost, I always have somewhere to turn.* You may call this feeling optimism; you may call it confidence; you may call it faith; you may call it hope. Whatever you call it, if you learn it young, you will probably never lose it. And if you do not learn it young, you probably never will.

I, myself, struggle for it every day. I wish I had been able to learn it better when I was young, but my childhood was too disconnected to let me really steep in it. The greatest hope in my life is that I will be able to give my children a connected childhood, so that they will develop that feeling as strong as steel. So far, they have.

Once again, the optimistic, can-do feeling naturally emanates from the five-step cycle, especially the first step, connectedness. If your child goes through the cycle and still feels defeatist or pessimistic, there are specific steps you can, and should, take to teach the all-important skill of deep and enduring optimism. Martin Seligman's books *Learned Optimism* and *The Optimistic Child* are superb, practical guides.

While I do always tell my children when a problem comes up that no matter what, we will find a way, it isn't just my words that penetrate their fears and fill them with confidence. It is their experience, of having seen bad times come and go, of having felt the strengthening power of the cycle of connectedness leading to play and to practice and to mastery and to recognition.

. . . AND THE ABILITY TO CREATE AND SUSTAIN JOY . . .

Just as the five-step cycle equips a child to deal with hard times, it also equips her to create and sustain joy. I worry that many children growing up today are unable to create joy on their own or unable to sustain it if they do manage, briefly, to create it.

Many parents try to provide their children with experiences of joy instead of trying to equip their children with the ability to create and sustain joy on their own. This is understandable, as we want more than anything for our children to be happy. But these days a parent can seem more like an attendant at a spa than a parent. If we stop and think about it, we know that we want to be teaching life skills, not providing mere entertainment.

As a child goes through the five steps, the ability to create and sustain joy naturally emerges. Play is the key step, but practice, mastery, and recognition solidify it. And connectedness is what sets the whole process in motion.

For example, once you learn to ride a bicycle, you have learned a skill that can provide you with joy forever. You learn it by going through the five steps. The connected child feels bold enough to play and to try to learn to ride. He fails at first, so he practices. Once he has practiced enough, he masters riding the bike. Then he gains recognition from his friends, siblings, parents, whomever.

As you accumulate enough of these experiences, you begin to sense that you can always find such experiences. You begin to make up your own challenges or activities or pastimes. You begin to acquire the ability to get into what Mihaly Csikszentmihalyi calls *flow*. I will speak more about flow later—and have spoken about it briefly already—but this is the state in which we forget where we are and what we are doing and become one with the task.

The ability to create and sustain joy and the ability to get into states of flow are one and the same. Almost any activity, from riding a bike to reading a book to raising a garden, can lead into flow.

But in order to do it regularly, and on demand, you need to have done it before, many times. You need to be in the habit of finding some creative outlet when you are bored. The best way to develop that habit is to go through the five steps many times while you are young.

Whether you go through the five steps in the context of sports or in math class or in getting along with your friends, you learn the same skills: how to get through hard times and create good times.

. . . AND THEY LEAD TO BEING INTERNALLY MOTIVATED

One of the most common issues parents worry about is how to motivate their children. Rewards and punishments—carrots and sticks—remain the basics of the most common systems. These external motivators, while often necessary, do not provide the best kind of motivation.

Ideally motivation springs up from within a person and does not have to be supplied from the outside. You may still deal with carrots and sticks, but if the carrot and the stick come from within a person, that system will last much longer than if the motivation comes entirely from the outside. (Sometimes we actually wish internal motivation *wouldn't* last as long as it does; just ask someone who can't get rid of the sense of guilt that he or she internalized as a child.)

Still, most of the time we prefer internal motivators. The more you run on external motivation, whether you are an adult or a child, the less happy a person you usually are. You may be highly successful—as a child or as an adult—but the more you do what you do out of a fear of consequences or out of a desire to please or impress other people, the less joyful you will be.

Csikszentmihalyi, the great researcher into flow, coined the term *autotelic* to describe the internally motivated person, the person most adept at creating states of flow. Don't be put off by the jargon sound of the term *autotelic*. It is a useful concept. Here is how Csikszentmihalyi describes it:

> "Autotelic" is a word composed of two Greek roots: *auto* (self), and *telos* (goal). An autotelic activity is one we do for its own sake, because to experience it is the main goal. For instance, if I played a game of chess primarily to enjoy the game, that game would be an autotelic experience for me; whereas if I played for money, or to achieve a competitive ranking in the chess world, the same game would be primarily exotelic, that is, motivated by an outside goal. Applied to personality, autotelic denotes an individual who generally does things for their own sake, rather than in order to achieve some later external goal.
>
> Of course no one is fully autotelic, because we all have to do things even if we don't enjoy them, either out of a sense of duty or necessity. But there is a gradation, ranging from individuals who almost never feel that what they do is worth doing

for its own sake, to others who feel that most anything they do is important and valuable in its own right. It is to these latter individuals that the term autotelic applies. An autotelic person needs few material possessions and little entertainment, comfort, power, or fame because so much of what he or she does is already rewarding.[1]

Of course, it is unrealistic to suppose that a child will be internally motivated to clean up his room, brush his teeth, or be on time for the bus to school. But the roots of an autotelic personality lie in childhood.

As a parent, the more you can help a child discover what he loves to do and then encourage him to do it, the more of an autotelic child you will raise. By going through the five steps, children find and solidify what delights them.

On the other hand, if you repeatedly emphasize the crucial importance of certain external goals—like making a lot of money or getting into an Ivy League college or making the all-star team—then you risk draining that child of his own enthusiasms and replacing them with yours or those of society. This is how you create a depressed, although perhaps a materially successful, adult.

It takes nerve, as a parent, *not* to hold up the external goals as the ultimate. Almost all of us parents rely on rewards and punishments, at least some of the time. I know Sue and I do with our kids. But we try not to overdo it. We try to let our children follow their own enthusiasms. The provocative educational commentator Alfie Kohn devoted an entire book to the damage excessive reliance on rewards can do: *Punished by Rewards: The Trouble with Gold Stars, Incentive Plans, A's, Praise, and Other Bribes.*

While I am not as pure as Alfie Kohn, and as a parent I do often resort to what he would call bribes, his fundamental point is true: the less you rely on external motivators and the more "autotelic" you become, the happier you will be. If you overemphasize the importance of the achievements rather than the process of getting there, you run a serious risk of turning your child into a kind of achievement junkie who has no true enthusiasm for anything except more achievement. That is not a recipe for a meaningful or happy life.

On the other hand, over the course of an entire childhood, if you guide your child through the five-step cycle from connection to recognition, he will almost certainly develop an internal motivation to do certain things, whether it be play baseball or play the violin or start a business, and he will almost certainly achieve important goals in the process.

The mistake is to put too much emphasis on any certain goal. For example, some parents believe that getting into Harvard is the secret to a happy life. And so they overemphasize that one goal. It is a Great Parenting Fallacy to exhort, bribe, or command a child to reach a certain faraway goal, like getting into a prestigious college or making it to the Olympics, as *the* key to happiness in life. Many graduates of Harvard, Princeton, or Stanford are unhappy, unsuccessful people today, while many people who went to less prestigious colleges or never went to college at all are now happy and successful.

Much more important than the colleges people attend are the attitudes they develop in childhood. A child who reaches the age of eighteen with a can-do, want-to-do attitude is on his way to success and happiness.

When you experience the cycle of the five steps from connection to recognition, you automatically want to go through the cycle again. You do not have to be scared or bullied or persuaded to do it. You feel motivated from the inside. You do not have to "be motivated," because you naturally are motivated, at least along the lines that count the most.

You are turning into an autotelic personality—even if at age ten you have no idea what the word *autotelic* means.

You can learn the cycle as an adult, even if you did not go through it as a child. You can become autotelic, even as an adult. It is just much easier if you started as a child. But what is commonly called a midlife crisis is often a person's coming to the realization that she has been living her life to please others or out of a fear of others' disapproval. She says, "Enough. I want to play my own game." And so she begins the struggle to find out what *she* wants and who *she* is.

It is never too late to do this. Children who do not do it, do not do it because they are not allowed to. Adults who do not do it, do not do it because they are afraid to. They found their fear in childhood, and it never let them go. Other than abject poverty, fear holds more people back from being happy than anything else.

The best antidote to fear is connectedness, the subject of the next chapter.

7

A CONNECTED CHILDHOOD:
THE KEY TO IT ALL

More than any single factor that we can control, connectedness in childhood is the key to a happy adulthood (and a happy childhood as well!).

A connected childhood does not mean a laissez-faire childhood with no parental expectations or demands. Far from it. It does mean, however, that the *first* priority at home or at school ought to be to create a connected atmosphere in which the child feels cared for, welcomed, and treated fairly.

Recent research bears this out.

For example, David Myers, whom I cited briefly in Chapter 2, is one of the pioneering researchers in the field of happiness (doesn't that sound like enjoyable research?). His studies have determined which factors can predict who are the happiest adults. And if we know what makes for a happy adult, that helps us a great deal in figuring out what our children need in order for them to grow up to become one of those happy adults.

First, the research emphatically debunks one of the greatest myths in the world; it turns out that there is little correlation between being rich and being happy. There is a correlation between living in poverty and being unhappy, but "once beyond poverty, further economic growth does not appreciably improve human morale."[1]

Second, the research identifies "four inner traits that predispose positive mental attitudes: self-esteem, sense of personal control [this refers to a feeling of being able to control your life, at least somewhat], optimism, and extroversion. Dozens of investigations have linked each with psychological well-being."[2] You may think this sounds like a fancy way of saying that happy people are predisposed to be happy, but in fact each of those four traits can be regulated somewhat, if you (or your child) are low in one or more.

The best way to begin to build each of those four traits, short of being born with them, is to lead a connected childhood.

While adults sometimes attribute their happiness or unhappiness to how much they have or have not achieved, high-achieving adults are frequently quite miserable, as are the people around them. This is because their early experiences set them on edge, damaged them, or made them desperate for success. There are many unhappy people in the halls of the very high achievers, and there are many who are there trying to make up for not getting enough connectedness when they were young.

Connectedness is the first—and most important—step in the five-step process I outline. Bear in mind that it is a process in which all five elements work simultaneously. I freeze-frame the process in order to discuss each step individually and to show how one leads to another, but when the film of life is speeding along, they all blend into one smooth process. For example, while you are practicing violin, you do not stop connecting or playing or gaining mastery and recognition. Once you enter the cycle, you can stay in it forever.

The entry point is connection. It begins in the womb, that site of ultimate connection between mother and child. Even there we can see evidence of the next four steps: play, practice, mastery, and recognition. In the womb the baby kicks and turns and tries out the new limbs and organs as they grow; we can call this play. The baby repeats her routine, even as she grows and moves on to the next month of development; we can call this practice and mastery. We do not know if she feels the love and recognition she receives every day from her mother and usually her father and various other people, but there is every reason to suppose that that recognition somehow registers with the baby as she grows in the womb.

Once you are born, you begin a lifetime of connecting with the world. How that happens is the story of your life.

If your life is going to go well, it is crucial that you learn how to connect in many different ways in the world. From those very first moments, the most important work (play?) a parent can do is to connect with his or her child and help that child connect with the world.

What Does the Most Cutting-Edge, Current Research on Adolescents Tell Us?

A groundbreaking study of adolescence is giving us hard evidence—and dramatic answers—about what children need in this country right now. All parents, teachers, and coaches should know about this national study, but few do. One of the most important, comprehensive, and reliable studies of American youth ever undertaken, it is called the National Longitudinal Study of Adolescent Health.

Although it is still ongoing, its first major findings were published in the *Journal of the American Medical Association* in the September 10, 1997, issue; those findings have been reconfirmed since then by subsequent findings.

The study demonstrated empirically, beyond any doubt, the pivotal power of connectedness—and the enormous risk of disconnection.

Let me briefly describe how the study was done; once you see how extensive and detailed it is, you will find its conclusions all the more convincing.

In the first phase of the study ninety thousand students (yes, *ninety thousand*) in grades seven through twelve attending 145 different schools around the United States answered questionnaires in school about their lives, including social and demographic characteristics, education and occupation of parents, household structure, risk behaviors, friendships, expectations for the future, health, and self-esteem.

In the second phase, students were selected from the pool of 90,000 to form a core group who would be interviewed at home. They were selected in such a way that they would represent a statistical cross section of American adolescents; a total core sample of 12,105 adolescents was interviewed. The first wave of interviews, each of which lasted from one to two hours, took place in 1995. The students were then reinterviewed, again at home, in 1996. The topics of the interviews covered all different aspects of the students' lives. While the adolescents were interviewed, a parent, usually the mother, was asked to answer a written questionnaire.

The longitudinal nature of the study provides a chance to see changes over time and tease out what factors appear to be causing which effects.

The study looked at more than a hundred variables in the lives of the students. Among the questions the study sought to answer was what factors might protect students from the negative outcomes parents fear these days, such as violent behavior or extreme emotional distress or suicide attempts or drug abuse or early sexual activity.

The study found that there were two factors that most protected children from negative outcomes. From the more than one hundred factors the study took into account, these two emerged as most significant by far.

The first was a feeling of connectedness at home. If the child reported—and, remember, these adolescents were interviewed live—that he or she felt connected at home, then that child was far less likely to get into trouble than children who reported that they did not feel connected at home. *Connected* was the word that the researchers used when conducting the interviews. It was defined as "closeness to mother and/or father, perceived caring by mother and/or father, satisfaction with relationship with mother and/or father, and feeling understood, loved, wanted, and paid attention to by family members."

The feeling of connectedness at home protected against emotional distress and suicidal thoughts or attempts; it protected against violent behavior; it protected against cigarette, alcohol, or marijuana use; and it protected against early sexual intercourse.

The second protective factor was similar to the first. It was a feeling of connectedness at school. This was defined as the student's feeling that teachers treat students fairly, feeling close to people at school, and getting along with teachers and students.

The feeling of connectedness at school protected against violent behavior; it protected against feelings of emotional distress or suicidal thoughts or attempts; it protected against cigarette, alcohol, or marijuana use; and it protected against early sexual intercourse.

Other factors helped significantly, but none were as powerful as the feelings of connectedness at home and at school. Among the other important protective factors were (in no particular order):

- A parent's presence at key times during the day (in the morning, after school, at dinner, and at bedtime)
- Parents' high expectations for school performance (defined as expecting that the child will graduate from high school and college)
- Parents' engaging in activities with their children on a regular basis
- Absence of guns in the home
- Parental disapproval of the child's engaging in sexual intercourse
- Not having easy access to cigarettes, alcohol, or marijuana
- Lack of prejudice at school, as perceived by the student
- Self-esteem (defined by the student's agreeing to having good qualities, having a lot to be proud of, liking self, feeling loved and wanted)
- Not working at a paid job twenty hours a week or more

The National Longitudinal Study of Adolescent Health offers us irrefutable evidence for making connectedness at home and at school as much of a national priority as high test scores. In fact, the two go hand in hand. While we recognize that academic achievement matters, we have been slow to realize, and act upon, what this study makes dazzlingly clear: the feeling of connectedness counts most.

In another study, this one of college students done by Richard Light at Harvard, the findings were similar. Light spent ten years interviewing college students, gathering empirical data to define what made for a successful college experience. One of the key factors was connectedness, in various forms.

One especially important kind of connection, which many students do not come to college intending to find, is a close relationship with a professor. Light would interview his own advisees at Harvard and ask them when they were freshmen what they hoped to gain from their four years of college. After the students discussed all the obvious answers—gaining knowledge, doing well, preparing for the next step in life—Light would press for more.

The students would pause, puzzled. Light would then offer what he called "the single most important piece of advice I can possibly give to new advisees: 'Your job is to get to know one faculty member reasonably well this semester, and also to have that faculty member get to know you reasonably well.' "

Students were not prepared for how important that advice would turn out to be. But Light's research documents that it was key.

Despite major studies like the National Longitudinal Study of Adolescent Health and the research done by Richard Light, the idea of connectedness has not slipped into the national consciousness the way the awareness of the troubles it can prevent has. Most people know a lot about school shootings. But few people know that a feeling of connectedness at home and at school could have prevented them.

I am amazed that more school officials and politicians haven't identified creating a connected school as a primary goal. Instead, we see an intensive effort in public schools around the country to improve education by mandating higher test scores; passing a standardized test is now a prerequisite for high school graduation in many states. Passing a standardized test is a good thing, but a more powerful predictor of school success later on is social/emotional health. Since it is easier to measure and promote knowledge than social/emotional health, however, knowledge is what gets the funding. But we need to promote *both* knowledge and social/emotional health.

Most school curricula still overlook the crucial role of connectedness in education. If a school gears up to pass a test—and teachers and students alike see their futures on the line, as they do in the high-stakes-testing movement—then connectedness in that school often declines and, with it, social/emotional health. For example, in one Massachusetts school district where the children's scores on the standardized, statewide test were low, the school officials responded by denying the children recess for the rest of the year. The children will stay in and prepare for the next standardized test instead. This policy is, well, stupid.

Let me offer another kind of example. In many schools teachers are forbidden to touch children. Asking an elementary school teacher to teach without touching is like asking an orchestra's conductor to conduct without moving his arms. In order to prevent child abuse by teachers, or to prevent lawsuits alleging such abuse, many schools forbid teachers to give the hugs and pats on the back that would help students feel better at school. Touch is a powerful tool of connectedness, especially in the earlier grades. We make a great mistake when we forbid it.

Forbidding touch is emblematic of a mistake many school administrators and politicians make today as they underestimate the importance of connectedness and make policies geared toward preventing lawsuits rather than promoting something positive.

However, most parents do sense how important connectedness is, even if they are not familiar with the studies that prove them right. Contrary to what you might read in the press, parents by and large are doing a good job of staying close to their children. In a large, national survey of teens, taken in 2001, nearly all of them said that they can confide in someone in their family. They also recognized the danger that arises when this connection is absent, many of them stating that the underlying cause of school violence is parents' not spending enough time with their children.[3]

Connecting versus Expecting: How Much Should You Push Your Children?

While research tells us how deeply connectedness matters, your heart tells you this even more powerfully. Just remember how you felt when you looked at your first baby asleep, the moonlight casting a subtle, silver glow throughout the room, and you gently rocked the cradle in which she slept. Maybe you were so tired that you couldn't feel anything except gratitude that *at last* she was asleep. But from time to time, you also felt something more.

What you felt in your heart right then—call it love, call it total devotion, call it by whatever name you think fits it best—turned you from a mere person into a Parent. You carry that feeling forever now; it is part of who you are.

As you looked down at that baby, your feelings transformed you. You became who you are today, a person devoted, no matter what, to the well-being of your children. As you looked down at your baby back then, you probably dreamed a few dreams.

Let me propose two kinds of dreams you might have for that child. Then tell me which one is more likely to lead to happiness.

In the first dream, let's say you see your daughter getting into the best nursery school in town, which leads to the best primary school, which leads to the best secondary school, which leads to Harvard or some other "best" college, which leads to law school or medical school, and ultimately security and prestige.

In the second dream, you see your child at play, first with you on the floor, then with friends, then on playing fields, then at a workbench, then outside with a kite. You see her talking on the telephone, laughing, and you see her taking a job as an assistant in a fashion design firm, a dream she had since seventh grade. After five years she teams up with a friend, and they start their own business together. You see her holding her breath as she starts this business, but you know she is full of confidence, feeling that, no matter what, she'll succeed.

Obviously I have a preference. I hope you agree that the second example is more likely a beginning of a happy ending than the first.

But the two need not be mutually exclusive. Not at all. You can be a high-achieving student *and* hang out and talk with friends and play. You can be a valedictorian and have a connected childhood; indeed, most valedictorians do. You can go to a prestigious college without being a driven, joyless individual. You can aspire to greatness and also have a disorganized bedroom and no clean clothes because all your clothes are in the hamper. You can like Shakespeare and like Britney

Spears. You do not have to sell your soul, or your childhood, in order to excel.

And yet some parents, good parents, and some children, good children, do just that. They give up on play too soon, and they turn childhood into a grim, zero-sum game. It is easy to get caught up in the great riptide that sucks children out of childhood and into an achievement fast lane as early as nursery school.

Beware of this riptide. It is bad for children, parents, schools, teams, neighborhoods, and just about everyone except perhaps college admissions officers. In the name of giving your child a leg up on the competition, you may cripple him or her instead.

It takes nerve as a parent not to send your child out into this tide. It takes nerve to preserve connectedness as your top priority. But if you do, if you can trust in the power of childhood rather than the power of the résumé, you will be planting the seeds of happiness, as opposed to "drivenness."

However, it is also dangerous not to encourage achievement. I do recommend that you have high expectations for your children. Just not too high. And do not tie your love for your child to your child's meeting those expectations. Research does show that parents who have reasonably high expectations—who expect, for example, that their children will complete high school and go to college—do raise healthier, happier children.

At the opposite extreme from the danger of driving your children too hard is the danger of not expecting enough from them. It is a form of disconnection, called indifference. Just as the riptide of achieve-at-all-costs can ruin childhood and produce a joyless, driven adult, so may the whirlpool of nobody-cares lead to a different kind of ruin.

Studies show that parents who are involved with their children every day, asking about school, encouraging good performance, raise children who fare better than the children of parents who are not involved. Having high expectations for your child is a compliment to the child, a way of saying, "I know you can do it." As long as you keep those expectations in line with the child's capabilities, and you set them for his sake and in line with his interests, not yours, you do him a great favor.

If the child senses that nobody really cares—cares enough to take the time to see to it, for example, that homework gets done—this leads to sadness, loneliness, and low self-esteem, which in turn often lead to a search for forbidden pleasures: tobacco; drugs; alcohol; sex just for sex; dangerous, thrill-seeking behaviors like driving fast, taking dares, or committing crimes. The whirlpool of self-destructive behaviors is full of children who have no one guiding them and expecting that they do their best. These children get together and form an alienated subculture in which they encourage and expect one another to get high, be "bad," and "dis" the world. Their lack of connectedness at home—and the parental expectations that go with it—leads them to find connectedness and expectations, however self-destructive, away from home.

If the disconnected child who feels that nothing is expected of him by his parents does not get into self-destructive behaviors, gangs, or other kinds of major trouble, he usually sets his own expectations so low that he starts a long pattern of underachievement. "Why bother?" becomes his refrain, as he sells himself short over and over again, preferring not to try than to try and fail.

As I have emphasized already, connectedness and achievement should go hand in hand. The connected individual is far more likely to achieve, and achieve in a way that he will enjoy, than the disconnected person.

My own research shows this. In the mid-1990s, the psychologist Michael Diamonti and I did a study of students at Phillips Exeter Academy in New Hampshire. We interviewed students and asked them to fill out lengthy questionnaires. We also spoke with parents and faculty. The study was intensive, taking two years to complete.

We found that the most driven students got poorer grades than the most connected students. In other words, feeling connected to others was a more powerful predictor of academic achievement than feeling driven to do well. We measured "drivenness" by responses to questions like "Do you think that getting into your first-choice college will make a crucial difference in your life?" and "Do you feel that your self-esteem depends upon your grades more than anything else?" and

"Do you feel under intense pressure from your parents to do well academically?" Ironically the students who answered yes to questions like those got poorer grades than those who answered no.

We measured connectedness by responses to questions along the lines of "Do you feel connected to others at Exeter?" and "Do you feel closely connected to members of your family?" and "Do you feel that you are a part of something larger than yourself?" The students who answered yes to those kinds of questions were the students who got the highest grades. They also showed the lowest levels of depression; the highest levels of confidence about the future; the lowest levels of drug, alcohol, and tobacco use; and the highest sense of self-esteem.

The disconnected group, which was a distinct minority, only about 15 percent of the students, showed the highest levels of depression, drug use, pessimism, and low self-esteem.

Interestingly enough, in our study the most powerful predictor of a disconnected student was low grades. At a school like Exeter, where almost every student has the brainpower to do well academically, it is the norm to get good grades. If a student does not, this often indicates the problem is primarily emotional rather than intellectual. Hence, I venture an answer to the chicken-egg question "Do the poor grades cause the emotional disconnection, or does the emotional disconnection cause the poor grades?" Usually the disconnection leads to the poor grades, at least at Exeter, rather than vice versa.

There is a great deal of additional evidence that supports the formative power of connectedness, not only in emotional development but in promoting achievement as well.

It is my sense that most parents know this fact, deep down inside. The challenge to us parents is to act on what we know and not to give in to crazy pressures, and in fact, most parents do not give in. Those who do, those who get crazy, make for provocative magazine articles and upsetting conversation at school gatherings, but they are, thank goodness, in the minority.

I want to reassure you that by providing connectedness, above all, you are doing the right thing and the best thing. You are giving your child the best possible "leg up on the competition." The connected child will achieve, at the level he is supposed to, and will enjoy doing so. He will tend to be optimistic and will be all but immune from depression. He will feel that he is safe and that his life is going well.

Happiness—the feeling that your life is going well—is not an impossible goal. If you want to feel happy for the rest of your life, what can you do? The cynic would say, take drugs or get a lobotomy. But the cynic is wrong.

We have all seen people overcome tremendous odds and find happiness. Remember Shantwania Buchanan. The odds don't get much worse than what she faced. But she had her grandmother and her siblings. She felt she was part of a team, albeit a small one! That feeling pulled her through.

But even if you didn't face much difficulty as a child, happiness does not automatically come your way. You still need to connect.

I know many people who have none of the trappings of material success but who nevertheless lead deeply satisfying lives because they feel connected—for example, to their families or to a mission in life or to a certain institution or to a group of friends or several of these as well as others. Connectedness comes in many forms.

In my own life, I have struggled with depression and a turbulent, traumatic childhood. What has saved me is other people. My "team" is made up of my immediate family, some other close relatives, a number of intimate friends, my work (yes, you can connect with something that you do, much in the same way you connect with a person), and the Presence I call God. Without my connected team, I would be a mess!

If you feel that you are part of a team, life can never totally wipe you out. You might lose all your money, you might suffer severe illness or injury, but if you know that your team—whatever team that might be—believes in you and you in them, then you can never lose everything.

I have heard many wise adults tell me, "We are fundamentally alone. We come into this world alone, and we leave it alone. After all is said and done, each of us is alone."

To these wise people I say, "No. You are wrong." I think what these people are really saying is, "I have been hurt and disappointed too many times to reach out anymore. I can't risk it again." Pride, or the "wisdom of their experience," holds them back. And so they choose the safety of feeling alone, with its occasional attendant despair, over the risk of reaching out. They then use their intelligence to weave a philosophical argument that we are *all* basically alone, essentially to justify their fear of ever reaching out again.

Can't we all understand this? I sure can. I have been hurt many times, in many ways, sometimes after I reached out and left myself vulnerable. Often I have resolved never to reach out again, only later to relent. I relent because I do not do well when I feel alone. Most people don't.

As an adult, I reconstruct my feeling of connectedness and security in my life every day. I have to do this each day because I did not acquire that feeling when I was a child. If you acquire it when you are a child, it can become as much a part of you as your nose and need not be reconstructed every day, as it does for me. But, like many people, I grew up in an atmosphere of insecurity. I never knew what to expect, and I rarely felt safe.

Now, as a grown-up, I work hard to maintain what I need in order to feel secure. I wish security came naturally to me, but it doesn't. Instead, feelings of doubt and insecurity well up each day, and I must dismantle them, by solidifying my connections outside of myself, by turning to my "team." I am thankful that I have a method that works, but I wish I didn't have to rely on it.

The people to whom security comes naturally usually acquired that feeling when they were young. It is a precious gift Sue and I are trying to give our children. My kids are so tired of hearing me tell them that I love them that they roll their eyes at me when I say it now. (Except Tucker. He still comes over and gives me a little hug. I think I have maybe a year of that left from him.)

A feeling of security naturally emerges from a connected childhood. A connected childhood is the most reliable key to a happy life.

Unconditional Love

The starting point in creating a connected childhood is unconditional love—from someone. Usually the unconditional love comes from one or two parents. But it doesn't have to. If a child can find someone— any decent person who is active in the child's life—who loves him or her absolutely and unconditionally, that love is the closest thing to an inoculation against misery that we have.

Stuart Schreiber, who is professor and chair of the Department of Chemistry and Chemical Biology at Harvard, grew up with such love. He always knew that his mother loved him, no matter what. During his young adult years, before he knew anything about chemistry, he was searching about, and the last thing on his mind was academics. In fact, he was considering dropping out of college and going to Colorado to become a ski bum. He was not on the track most parents would wish for their college-age children, but even so, he knew his mother was behind him, 100 percent. His mother's unconditional love had laid a foundation that kept out fear, deep in his soul. He was free to be his own man.

During the time he was considering leaving college, he sat in on a chemistry lecture because his girlfriend was taking the course and she wanted him to come. He went because he liked the girlfriend; chemistry was a subject in which he had absolutely no interest. Until that lecture. What he saw on the blackboard totally captured his imagination. He saw great, beautiful designs, colorful cloud-shaped illustrations of the orbitals of electrons about the nucleus of an atom. "This is *chemistry*?" he exclaimed to his girlfriend, who was busy taking notes. Having a love of design, he was enthralled by the depiction of the atom. So he stayed, and he listened closely, and he imagined more and more than merely what he saw. Now he is one of the foremost chemists in the world.

He told me his mother wouldn't have cared which way he went, out to Colorado or on to chemistry, or in some totally other direction, as long as he was happy. Indeed, he said that if he wins the Nobel Prize one day (which, in fact, he might well do) and he telephones his mother to tell her the news, he knows exactly what she'll say: "Oh,

Stuey, does that make you happy?" And when he tells her that it does, only then will she be glad. He already has the prize that matters most: his mother's love.

A child should not have to work to win love.

But love leads to questions. Back in Chapter 1, I asked some of those questions. First, I asked, What do children need most? And I gave my answer, love. But then I asked, How much love? Love from whom? What kind of love? How much love is too much? Is there hope for the child who does not get any love?

The answer to the question How much love? is, Enough love. Some children need much more than others. You can see it, you can feel it, you can even hear it when a child is not getting enough love. On the other hand, if you smother your child with love and provide too much, you can see that, too. At any given moment, you can probably sense which child needs you the most. Go toward that child. This way, you will provide each child with enough love, as best you can.

Love from whom? Parents. A parent is the person whose love a child needs the most. Of course, substitute parents can do a great job, but as one who relied on substitutes, I can tell you it would have been better if my original two parents had been able to provide the love themselves, in person, day in and day out, instead of getting divorced and sending me to boarding school to find my daily love.

But what kind of love? What kind of love does a child need? Again, you feel this in your bones. You pick up your four-year-old and give him hugs and kisses and cuddles. Your teenager would gag if you did that, so with him or her you offer the same product but with different packaging. Sometimes you show your love by saying no. This is often hard, and unlike the hugs and cuddles, it does not feel good. But it is just as important as any hug ever was. Think of "no" as a special kind of hug.

How you express your love will therefore vary, but the kind of love you express should be, at core, unconditional. Conditional love leads to insecure children, who become insecure adults.

Unconditional love does not mean that you say yes to everything or that you spoil your children. Far from it. Loving parents must set limits and deny requests all the time.

But they never deny their love. They transmit the message, implicitly or explicitly, every second of every day, that their love is constant, unshakable, and totally reliable.

A wonderful children's book called *The Runaway Bunny* captures this state of unconditional love. You might be familiar with this story from reading it to your children, as Sue and I have to ours. The mother bunny tells her little one that no matter where he goes, she will be there. And the book depicts the runaway bunny in many different settings, all around the world. In all of them, mother bunny is right there, too.

The feeling of constancy of love, the feeling that no matter what, it cannot be turned off, nor does it need to be earned—this is the kind of parental love that leads to security in later life.

Recent research has shown how deeply a parent's kind of love influences the development of a child. There is a research measure called the Adult Attachment Interview, or AAI. Using this structured interview, the subject's "attachment style," which is jargon for style of loving, can be reliably deduced from how the subject describes his or her childhood on the AAI. One style is called secure attachment. And then there are three styles of insecure attachment. First, there is the dismissing pattern, in which the person is derogatory or on the other hand unrealistically idealizing about early attachments; second, the preoccupied pattern, in which the person is exceptionally angry or unusually passive in describing childhood attachments; and third, the unresolved, in which the person gives clear evidence that early issues of loss or abuse have not reached any sort of stable resolution.

Amazingly enough, more than a dozen studies have shown that you can reliably predict the attachment style of an infant or a toddler just from the parent's responses on the AAI, even if the interview was conducted before the birth of the child!

This means that if you received conditional love, you are likely to provide conditional love. Or if you were abused, you are likely to commit abuse. Or if you were raised in insecurity, you will likely pass it on.

Unless. Thank goodness, there is an unless. We are not helpless, doomed to repeat what was done to us. Using insight and finding the emotional supports we need in adulthood—perhaps from friends or from a spouse or from psychotherapy or some other source—we can override our unconscious tendency to cripple our children with the same kind of conditional love that crippled us.

Finally, back in Chapter 1, I asked, Is there hope for children who didn't get any love? There is always hope. Always. For everyone. I have never met an adult who didn't get *any* love—in any form, from anybody, ever. But I have met many who didn't get enough. Those who reached out and found substitutes—like Shantwania—usually do well. Those who didn't or couldn't, usually don't do well. They become angry or antisocial or depressed, or they end up in jail or on drugs or burned out. Love can bring them back to a new life, but it is much more difficult to provide love to an angry, antisocial, drug-abusing adult than it is to a hurting child.

So much depends on love.

Bruce Stewart, who is the current head of Sidwell Friends School in Washington, D.C., has been working with children since he started as a teacher in 1960. When I asked him what he thought were the childhood roots of adult happiness, he instantly replied, "Unconditional love." Bruce has had a long time to learn about children. He has seen many students grow up and become parents themselves. He said to me, "*Every single successful kid I have ever seen* had somebody who gave them unconditional love and encouragement. Sometimes it wasn't a parent. Often it was an older woman, such as an aunt or a grandmother. But *always*, there was someone."

In Bruce's case it was his father. Bruce's father emigrated from Scotland to give his children a shot at a better life. He expected his children to take responsibility and do their best, because, as he told Bruce often, "Boy, I crossed the pond for you to have this opportunity." Bruce felt loved unconditionally, but he also felt high expectations from his father. However, he did not feel that the love was conditional upon his meeting those high expectations.

Bruce went to public school in Lynn, Massachusetts, a tough, working-class town with rough-and-tumble kids. Bruce's father expected his children to take responsibility. "We were the ones he held accountable," Bruce said, "not anyone else. It wasn't the school's fault if I did poorly or the textbook's fault or the teacher's. My dad held me responsible, as did my peers."

His father showed his love through actions and example, and his father's example inspired Bruce. This is often the case with dads. They may not shower love on their children with words or hugs, but they show their love for their family through hard work and sacrifice. This, in turn, inspires the children to do likewise. As Bruce related, "My dad had one leg, but he loaded leather goods onto trucks all day to earn a living. We didn't ever have an extra fifty cents, no TV. Dad worked from six in the morning to six at night. How the hell could you let him down when you saw that level of sacrifice? It was up to me to come through."

Many studies have shown that the single most powerful, controllable predictor of how a child will do later on in life is the quality of childhood connections, particularly the parent-child interaction. By a "controllable predictor," I mean any factor that parents can significantly control; this leaves out genetic factors (at least for now) and, to a certain extent, social, economic, and medical factors as well. If you look at what parents can significantly control and give their children, the gift of a connected childhood is the most precious gift of all.

A connected childhood leads not only to emotional health but to success in school as well. Peter Jensen, who is Ruane Professor of Child and Adolescent Psychiatry at Columbia College of Physicians and Surgeons and one of the world's most knowledgeable experts on children, said to me, "What predicts later school success are the social/emotional factors, not the knowledge of colors and numbers. Most of the federal money has gone to support colors and numbers—helping children count to ten or name their colors—because that skill is easy to measure. It is harder to measure the social/emotional benchmarks, but they are more important." You don't need fancy neuropsychological testing to identify the children with problems in the social/emotional domain early on. Just ask any kindergarten teacher which kids in her class she worries about; the children she names are the ones with the social/emotional problems.

The main nongenetic cause of problems in the social/emotional domain is failure to connect at home. Almost every expert in the world would agree that the early experience of a warm, nurturing relationship is a fundamental key not only to happiness but to achievement later on as well.

Fortunately you do not need to take lessons to learn how to connect or how to give unconditional love. Most parents feel it growing within them, even as the baby is growing in the mother's womb.

Never underestimate the importance of the love you feel for your children. That love is the closest thing we've got to God's presence on this earth. It can—and does—change the world every day.

If children get that love—and for many children, that is all they get—it can be enough not only to save them but to propel them into great and happy lives.

On the other hand, there is nothing worse, for a child, than a parent betraying that love—through abuse or neglect. As a psychiatrist, I can tell you—and statistics bear me out—that most of the adults in this world whom we would call "evil" got to be that way because they were abused or abandoned when they were young.

Loving our children is the most important work we do. We are lucky that love can work such magic; we just have to let ourselves do it.

But do *what*, exactly? I am talking about an activity that is extremely simple, primal, natural, and unsophisticated. If you have ever held a baby, or even talked about holding a baby, you know what I mean. Your eyes take on a gentle look, a broad and crinkled smile expands over your whole face, your voice takes on a cuddly tone, and you fall completely into the role of a baby-lover. Each of us can do this if we let ourselves.

Although you do know how to do it, you probably do not know how crucial it is. There is *nothing* you can do—no diet, no trust fund, no exercise program, no vitamin or medicine of any kind, no brain-enrichment program of any sort, no lesson or activity or gift—that can help your child more than the act of loving.

So put it at the top of your list. It is more important than having a clean house. It is more important than laundry. It is more important than being on time for the dentist. It is more important than losing weight. It is more important than making money. It is more important than pleasing other people. It is more important than answering the telephone or checking E-mail.

That does not mean you have to give up everything—like work, laundry, the telephone, and E-mail—in order to do it right. Remember Bruce Stewart's father. He worked twelve hours a day, and he did it right. It does not mean you have to spend vast quantities of time ogling your infant or playing catch with your nine-year-old son. You just have to make sure that the other adults who do spend time with your kids do so lovingly.

The National Institute of Child Health and Human Development (NICHD) has been tracking 1,364 children since their births in 1991. This Study of Early Child Care, which is the most comprehensive such study we have, scared working parents everywhere (like my wife and me) by stating that children who spent more than thirty hours per week in child care tended to have more aggression-related behavioral problems than children who stayed home with mom. However, that was the oversimplified headline that the popular press played up.

This is the problem with "the latest study." Almost invariably what you read in the popular press (the NICHD study was played up in *People* magazine) is a distortion—usually an upsetting, oversimplified, attention-grabbing distortion—that leaves you poorly informed and confused.

In fact, the actual NICHD data, presented at a conference in Minneapolis in April 2001, painted a much more complex picture than what appeared in the press. Kathleen McCartney, of the Harvard School of Education, and one of the researchers involved in the study, clarified the issue by stating, "Parents still play the most important role in their children's development—that's the major predictor of how well children do socially and cognitively. Our second most important finding concerns the quality of interaction between childcare providers and children. When quality is high, children do better on tests of intellectual development, school readiness and vocabulary and have fewer behavior problems." A more accurate headline for the study would have been, STUDY SHOWS THAT HIGH-QUALITY DAY CARE LEADS TO BETTER OUTCOMES FOR AMERICA'S CHILDREN.

You can be a working mom or a working dad and do right by your children, as long as you are serious about the matter of who else is looking after your children.

As you take this seriously—and what parent doesn't?—you care for yourself as well. Not only is the act of loving your child the best gift you can give your child, it is also one of the best gifts you can give yourself.

It is a gift to yourself because when you love a child, when you hold her in your arms when she is a baby, or when you nervously watch her take her first ride on a bike, or when you steal a loving glance at her in your rearview mirror as you drive her somewhere you have no interest in going, not only are you fortifying your child for a lifetime, you are also fortifying yourself. You are fortifying yourself with vulnerability.

You might wonder how vulnerability can fortify a person. It provides you the strength to stop trying to be safe. Acknowledging vulnerability compels you to stop pretending that you are in control or that you know what you are doing all the time or that you are powerful in the face of final forces. When you let yourself love a child, you remove your armor and you willingly become vulnerable.

What makes you so vulnerable is that your love is unconditional. That's the deal. You can't back out, even when the going gets tough. Once you become a parent, you remain a parent forever. And when you offer unconditional love, you can bet the recipient will catch on, sooner or later, and test your unconditionality. Whether it is by crying for hours on end, night after night after night; or by booby-trapping your computer to get back at you for not allowing a sleepover; or by stealing from your pocketbook to finance a trip to the movies; or by wounding you with insults you can barely stand to hear—children of all ages test this love that we never thought could be shaken. And yet we keep loving. We do not smother the screaming baby, we do not evict the computer vandal, we do not disown the pocketbook thief or cease to love the child who has insulted us.

Unconditional love may be a great gift, but what we get back is greater still. We receive the gift of learning to transcend ourselves. We become better than we were.

When you let yourself love, as a parent, when you show up, in the moment, and let yourself love, as you watch the soccer game; or carry the birthday cake, candles blazing, over to the table; or wave good-bye to the group that is heading off in the bus to camp—at all those times, you let die a part of yourself that used to come first. Not only that, you let yourself love totally and completely, knowing all the while that separation will come.

When you allow yourself to love that much, knowing that some-day you must say good-bye, when you show up, cheering and smiling and rooting for the good guys, all the while knowing that time is tak-ing your children away from you and you away from your children, when even then you throw yourself into the moment and say, "I love you so much, I will not protect myself by holding back"—when you do that, you have won the greatest victory of all: you have not allowed time or pain or loss or death to keep you from your loving and loving to the fullest that a human being can love.

Over time the runaway bunny grows up. This is right and good and sweetly sad. When your child finally leaves home for college or a job or marriage, your heart does not break, as perhaps you once feared it would. Instead, it swells with pride, as you shed a tear. It makes sense, now, for this child who once was so little but now has grown tall, to go out into the wider world. You have done a good enough job in raising your child that she or he is ready to leave. You have provided both roots and wings.

When we have a child, we take a leap off a cliff into magical air. We never stand on solid ground again. The updrafts and the downdrafts in this air are like none other. We soar, we glide, then we hit turbulence and hold on tight until the storm breaks and a cool morning breeze lifts us onward. We learn fear that we've never known, joy that we've never felt, and uncertainty that knows no bounds. In that air we know the best in life, even if we collide at times with the worst.

When you love a child, you transcend the worst that life has to of-fer. You stare it in the eye and say, "Loving this child is better than any-thing bad you can throw at me."

For a moment you borrow God's tools and do God's work. Then God leaves you on your own, or so you often feel. But you are never alone. There are parents everywhere, and we all try to be there for one another. We all feel connected, whether we know one another or not.

There Is More to a Connected Childhood Than Unconditional Love Alone

A connected childhood has many ingredients besides unconditional love, and they do not have to be the same from child to child. But they all lead toward the same outcome: a feeling of satisfaction and joy.

There is no one right way to create a connected childhood. There are as many different successful patterns of connection in childhood as there are connected children. But let me give you some guidelines and suggestions as to what the usual ingredients tend to be.

In the accompanying illustration, I name twelve different domains of a connected childhood. If you provide these for your children—and for yourself—the rest of what you want and need in life will follow naturally, to the extent that fate and genes allow. Think of these twelve domains as interacting all the time. There is no hierarchy to them. Unconditional love is the starting point, but once the different domains of connection come into being, they all strengthen one other.

You can see from the array of connections that a connected childhood is like a web or a support net. Just as you need more than one or two lines to make a strong net, you need more than one or two kinds of connection to hold you securely in place. You can survive on one or two, but to thrive, you usually need more than that.

In Chapter 13, I describe each kind of connection more fully and offer practical suggestions on how to set them up in your family's life. The idea here is just to point out the variety of connections that create a connected childhood and a connected life.

THE ELEMENTS OF A
CONNECTED CHILDHOOD

Unconditional Love from Someone,
Family Togetherness

The Individual's Own Self

Friends, Neighborhood, Community

God or the World
of the Spirit

Chores, Work, Responsibility
to Contribute

Institutions and Organizations
(School)

Activities, Sports

Ideas and Information
(School)

Pets

A Sense of the Past

Nature

The World of Beauty and the Arts

8

PLAY: THE SOURCE OF
LIFELONG JOYS

Play sets us free from the tyranny of compulsory boredom. Play leads us to what Csikszentmihalyi calls flow. Play and creativity go hand in hand to create a supremely involved state of mind to which you want to return for the rest of your life. Play is a fundamental key to a life of joy. Don't think that your child will automatically learn how to play just because he or she is a child. Many children these days are not learning how to play.

You can't overestimate the importance of play, especially the kind of play the child makes up on his own or with a friend or group of friends. It is the most important "work" your child can do.

You probably have a good idea of what I mean by the word *play*, but since the *Oxford English Dictionary* devotes six full pages to this one deceptively simple word, and since the meaning of play is crucial to this book, I want to define what I mean by the word.

By *play* I mean any activity in which there is room for spontaneous invention and/or change. You can play as you eat (and many kids do); you can play as you drive (but you probably shouldn't); you can even play as you pee (and many kids do!). The opposite of play is not work; indeed, the best work is playful. The opposite of play is doing exactly what you are told to do. Memorization by rote is the opposite of play; on the other hand, thinking up a mnemonic device to help you memorize a series of items can be very playful.

Don't tell me I am being a Pollyanna when I say that you can play your whole life long. Linus Pauling, who won two Nobel Prizes (for chemistry in 1954 and for peace in 1962), stated when he was an old man, "I don't think I ever sat down and asked myself, now what am I going to do in life? I just went ahead doing what I liked to do."

Of course, he was lucky that what he liked to do coincided with something that was of value to others. Having a successful career really just means that you've found a way to play that other people are willing to pay you for. The roots of this kind of play lie squarely in childhood.

When I watch Tucker play, I see play at its best. His play is full of spontaneous invention and change. He makes up the rules as he goes, he varies the routine constantly, he changes the characters, and he alters the outcome, all according to his whim. Whim and play, by the way, go hand in hand. Trial and error accompany play, as do scrapes and falls. Play is not entirely safe, as the game changes all the time.

But play can be quite structured and governed by rules. For example, when you play the piano, you follow a score. The room for invention and change comes in your interpretation of the score. Or when you play baseball, you follow an elaborate set of rules. The room for spontaneous invention and change comes in how you swing or how you field a ball.

Play deserves more respect than it gets. Playing with images and ideas is what creativity is all about, and creativity advances civilization.

Most children learn play spontaneously, unless they are prevented from doing so by adults who insist that children do exactly what they are told to do. If you only do exactly what you are told to do, you cannot play.

Early childhood should be one of the best times in a person's life, in part because early childhood is when we start to play. If there is any better way to strengthen a brain, or to feed the spirit, than to play, I don't know what it is.

Each of my children had their favorite toys or games when they were young. For example, Lucy loved clothes from the very beginning. I think she would have critiqued her diapers if she'd had the words.

She liked to dress up in different outfits with her little friend Sophie and put on plays in the basement.

I remember buying at an auction when Lucy was four a trunkful of old, used dress-up clothes—feather boas, rhinestone-studded blouses, top hats and a cane, high heels of different styles, scarves and throws of many colors and sizes. It was one of the best gifts I ever gave her. She would sit for hours with Sophie or some other friend trying on one combination after another, one role after another. Now that she is twelve, we still have the trunkful of clothes, although it doesn't get much use these days. Lucy has moved on to Limited Too, the Gap, and Abercrombie & Fitch. But she got her start in that trunk. Her ambition when she grows up? She says she wants to be a fashion designer. She will probably change her mind many times, but her current ambition reflects the five steps I describe in this book. She began with a connection to Sophie; they started to play with clothes; this led to practice; as they became expert in the different combinations and looks they could create, they gained a feeling of mastery over the act of dressing up; and they found recognition from each other, from friends, and from us grown-ups. If Lucy does become a fashion designer, she will have found a form of play that other people are willing to pay her to do, and the roots of that vocation will not be hard to trace.

With Jack, it was puzzles. He was putting puzzles together before he could walk. He simply was born with a strong spatial sense. Early on he could put together a puzzle in a few minutes that would take me a half hour to figure out. It was fun to watch him do it. He would sit on the floor, surrounded by the pieces of the puzzle, and he would look at the pieces for a little while. Then he would pick up a piece and put it down so that it interlocked with another piece. Quickly other pieces would follow, as the puzzle took shape. Jack would have a little smile on his face, as he became totally engaged with what he was doing.

Playing in childhood leads to happiness in the moment, and it leads to happiness many years later.

The reason to encourage children to play is not merely that play is a wonderful end in itself—although it is that. As a child plays, he learns a special skill—the skill of play—and it is a skill that is more useful than any other. The skill of play, of being able to make creative use of time no matter where you are or what you are doing, is the skill that lies behind all discoveries, all advances, all creative activity. If you can play, you will always have a chance to be happy and to do something great.

Maybe because *play* is such a short word, it doesn't get the respect it deserves. Mathematics gets more respect. So does geography. Even brushing teeth. Or maybe play doesn't get respect because it sounds like what you do at recess or when you're goofing off. The fact is, both recess and goofing off deserve more respect, too.

Maybe we should make up new names for play and recess and goofing off. How about if we call them "interacting spontaneously and creatively with your environment"? Would they get more respect then?

I know how play could get more respect. If we could prove that a child who plays gets higher SAT scores and earns more money as an adult than the child who doesn't play, then play would get more respect. Courses in "successful play" would spring up all over the country.

Well, we *have* proved that children who play get higher SAT scores than children who don't. But as with the studies on connectedness, most people don't know about the studies that correlate play with improved mental functioning. As for making more money, I don't know if that study has been done. But I can guarantee you that people are happier as adults if they learned to play as children.

After a child puts away her teddy bears and blocks and dolls, she will find other toys and other games. For instance, she will start to play with words and become an author. Or she will start to play with numbers and become a mathematician. Or she will start to play with chemicals and become a chemist. Or she will start to play with baseballs and become an athlete. Or she will start to play with people and become a leader. Or she will start to play with ideas and become a philosopher. Or she will start to play with emotions and become an actor or an artist or a therapist or a coach or a teacher. Or she will start to play with dress-up clothes and become a fashion designer or with puzzles and become an architect. Whatever the field of interest, if play leads her into it, she will love it and excel.

I don't know if there is a more surefire guarantee of a happy life than acquiring the skill of play. It ranks right up there with receiving unconditional love and leading a connected childhood as the most important childhood roots of adult happiness.

Play and Flow

When you are in flow, you forget who you are, where you are, what time it is, and where you are supposed to go next. You lose self-consciousness entirely, as you become one with the activity you are doing. Maybe you are skiing, maybe you are playing the piano, maybe you are arguing a point in a heated debate, maybe you are gazing into a fire, lost in a daydream. Whatever the activity, it has captivated your mind so that "you" disappear and are replaced by you-in-action, you-skiing, or you-playing-the-piano or you-debating or you-lost-in-thought. The observing, self-conscious part of you has for the moment vanished.

This is why people become aware of their experience of flow only in retrospect. When we are happiest, when we are in flow, we do not realize it at the time. It is a paradox that we do not recognize happiness as it is happening and only remember it after the intensity has disappeared.

In any case, the more chances you create for yourself to experience flow, the happier you will be. You will also be more successful if you spend a lot of time in flow, as people are at their most effective in these highly concentrated states.

You might wonder how flow is relevant to play. Well, play is the childhood version of flow. When Tucker is wrapped up in some imaginary intergalactic battle with his action figures, as I described in Chapter 4, he is in a state of flow. He forgets where he is, he forgets who he is, and he becomes one with his game.

I can see in Tucker's play the basic steps Csikszentmihalyi has found to comprise flow.

First, to reach a state of flow, the challenge inherent in the activity should match the skill of the person involved. Too much challenge and you feel frustrated and defeated. It is like playing tennis with a far superior opponent. Too little challenge and you feel bored, like playing tennis with someone who has never played before. Children naturally match the challenges of their play to the skills they bring to it.

Second, you know what you are doing from moment to moment, and you control your steps. When Tucker plays, he is in complete control, and he is doing exactly what he tells himself to do. He can't get lost or feel overwhelmed.

Third, you get immediate feedback on what you are doing. In a tennis game, I see what kind of shot I made right away. In writing a book, as I am doing now, I can see what kind of sentence I have written as soon as I finish the sentence, and then I can compare it to some internal standard that gives me my feedback immediately (often to my dismay!). Even if I miss the shot in tennis or write clumsy sentence in this book, the immediate feedback keeps me in the state of flow, because I get another chance right away. When Tucker plays, he instantly sees the result of whatever he is doing, either by himself or with a friend, and he or they can make adjustments on the spot.

When children play, they naturally drift toward kinds of play that lead into flow. As a parent, all you need to do is keep their energy moving that way. Sometimes you need to set up barriers, like a barrier between your child and the television or the Nintendo, as these passive kinds of play do not promote flow.

According to Csikszentmihalyi, in order to learn flow, children should turn off the television and turn on their minds. "One learns to experience flow," he writes, "by getting involved in activities that are more suited to provide it, namely, mental work and active leisure."

He then goes on to say, "It is not enough to be happy to have an excellent life. The point is to be happy while doing things that stretch our skills, that help us grow and fulfill our potential. This is especially true in the early years: A teenager who feels happy doing nothing is unlikely to grow into a happy adult."

The goal of play, then, is to stretch the mind and expand your repertoire of ways to create joy. Csikszentmihalyi's research also establishes how crucial connectedness is for the development of play and flow. His research shows that the people who are best at finding and maintaining flow also spend "a significantly higher amount of time interacting with the family—on the order of four hours a week—compared to the others. This begins to explain why they learn to enjoy more whatever they are doing. The family seems to act as a protective environment where a child can experiment in relative security, without having to be self-conscious and worry about being defensive or competitive."

This is precisely the point I have been stressing about the relationship between connectedness and play. You create a safe environment first; play naturally follows. The only truly dangerous learning disability is not dyslexia or attention deficit disorder (both of which I have myself) but fear. Fear, and its cousins shame and embarrassment, are what hold children (and adults) back from doing their best and from learning new skills. Fear inhibits play. Fear can prevent flow. So as you reserve time for your children to play, be sure you preserve the feeling of safety and connectedness along with it.

Play Need Never End

The child who plays early continues to play, and with some luck as an adult he will find a kind of play that people are willing to pay him to do. Look at the adults you know who are happiest in their work. Most of them will describe their work as a kind of play—serious play, perhaps, and challenging and exhausting play, even painful play at times, but still, at its core, play.

With that in mind, let me help you parents manage a difficult transition in your children's lives. This transition is easy for children but hard for many parents. It is when your child leaves his toys behind. You are saying good-bye to a certain little buddy that you will never see again, except in memory. I remember Lucy playing with her dolls, which are now all gone. I remember Jack playing with his LEGOS, which he is starting now to leave behind. And now, when I look at Tucker at play in his room with his teddy bears and toy soldiers and superheroes, I get a lump in my throat, realizing the time is brief when he will play so unselfconsciously. These transitions are proud moments for our children, but they can make us parents pretty sad.

A. A. Milne wrote a poem about this transition in *Now We Are Six*. In this poem, "Forgotten," Milne imagines how a child's toys, the "Lords of the Nursery," might feel as they wait for the little boy who used to play with them to come back. Where has he gone? He has grown up, sad to say.

> Lords of the Nursery
>   Wait in a row,
> Five on the high wall,
>   And four on the low:
> Big Kings and Little Kings,
>   Brown Bears and Black,
> All of them waiting
>   Till John comes back.
>
> Some think that John boy
>   Is lost in the wood,
> Some say he couldn't be,
>   Some say he could.
> Some say that John boy
>   Hides on the hill;
> Some say he won't come back,
>   Some say he will. . . .
>
> Slowly and slowly
>   Dawns the new day . . .
> What's become of John boy?
>   No one can say.
> Some think that John boy
>   Is lost on the hill;
> Some say he won't come back,
>   Some say he will.

What's become of John boy?
    Nothing at all,
He played with his skipping rope,
    He played with his ball.
He ran after butterflies,
    Blue ones and red;
He did a hundred happy things—
    And then went to bed.

But as sad as I feel when I realize that Tucker will soon leave his toys behind and follow Jack and Lucy into older years, I also take heart, because Tucker is learning how to play now in such a way that the skill will grow from year to year rather than disappear. The toys will change, the games will change, but the mental activity of creative, imaginative play that Tucker learned from ages zero to six will only grow.

Even though, as Tucker said, he cannot control his heightness because he has to go up, up, and away, he will take with him the good work he did with those toys. He will take with him the ability to play.

Those toys lined up against the wall should be proud. They gave that little boy a gift more precious than any wage he'll ever earn.

And so, parents, take heart. You have done your work well if your Lucy, Jack, or Tucker knows how to play. And I would say to the toys in your child's room, "Good work, you magnificent, tattered, brave, worn-out toys. Don't be sad. You built my child's imagination so strong and big that now that child can do anything, thanks to you. Don't be lonely, be proud. More children will come along. I'll take you out to a yard sale and find some for you soon."

The connection between childish play and adult happiness is crucial. One of the best ways to predict if an adult is happy or not is to see if he or she can play. Adults who can play tend to be resilient and be full of joie de vivre. Adults who cannot play may be successful in their driven way, but they are likely to be low on happy moments.

They are also low on innovative or creative moments. In the business world these days, everyone wants to hire people who can "think outside the box." If that's what they want, they ought to hire children, or the next best thing—adults who still know how to play.

Adults who can't play are in trouble, not only in their pursuit of happiness but in their pursuit of excellence as well. Let me give you an example of the kind of problem they can encounter.

One of my jobs is to serve as a consultant to the chemistry department at Harvard. For several years I met on a monthly basis with Professor Jim Anderson when he was chairman of the department. Sometimes we would discuss what makes for a successful graduate student or postdoctoral fellow in chemistry.

Jim explained to me that there are two groups of students, those who can work (or, in my terms, play) on their own and those who cannot. Everyone who applies to the graduate program at Harvard has top scores and a bundle of honors and prizes to back them up. But many of these top students will not make good scientists. What separates the ones who will become top scientists from the ones who won't is the ability to play.

When you enroll in graduate study in chemistry, the rules change. Suddenly you have to discover new knowledge, not just master what is already known. Suddenly you have to design and run your own experiments, not just follow the directions in a lab manual. Suddenly there are no more tests to ace, just a lab bench silently awaiting a new experiment and the world of undiscovered knowledge daring you to find a way to penetrate its walls.

Some students jump for joy at this. "Let me at it!" they exult. At last they have found what they've been waiting for. They have found their field of play. It will be hard, serious, exhausting play; they will stay up late into the night, and they will get bad results more often than not. They will bang their heads against the walls of undiscovered knowledge and come up empty again and again. Sometimes they will curse their luck and worry that they will never find anything of significance. But they will love what they are doing anyway, because they will be following the force of their own curiosity. They will be doing what they've always wanted to do. The true scientist is not the bespectacled nerd of popular stereotype; he or she is more like Indiana Jones, taking great risks, hunting down the Lost Ark. This is the scientist: an adventurer finding a way into unexplored worlds.

Other students, those who cannot play, collapse. With no more tests to take, with no more A's to get, with no one telling them what to do, they don't know where to turn. Without instructions they are at a loss. They don't know how to generate their own questions and hypotheses, nor how to design their own experiments. They never become true scientists.

This same distinction holds in most fields. The people who break new ground in literature or history or technology or business often were not the top students in school but rather were itching until they could get out of school and mix it up with life—play, to use my term—according to where curiosity and invention led them.

You can go back to childhood and find the same two groups in school. Some children need to be told what to do or have a television or a computer game lead them along. They can't make up anything on their own. Other children can play even in an empty room. No toys. No furniture. Nothing. But they invent imaginary figures and soon fill the room with creative play. It is much easier to convert a *child* who can't play into one who can than it is to convert an adult who can't play into an adult who can.

Some children do not learn how to play as well as they might. It is not because they are confined in authoritarian environments but because they spend too much time interacting with video games, computers, and televisions, which are restrictive in their own way. In a remarkable article, entitled "Why Johnny Can't Play," published, of all places, in *Fast Company* magazine, Pamela Kruger reported on research done by, of all people, a market-research executive.

What's the matter with kids today? Says market-research guru Ted Klauber: Their lives are so busy, so structured, and so infused with digital technology that they have no time for fun.

Ted Klauber is fiddling with a projector, trying to find just the right video clip to illustrate his point. Klauber, 42, a New York City–based senior executive at advertising giant FCB

Worldwide, has spent the past year researching the relationship between kids and technology. He could talk for days about how kids today are different from those of previous generations and about how FCB's clients should respond to that change.

But he knows that the most articulate voices for his ideas belong to the kids themselves, as well as to their parents. So Klauber turns off the lights and shows his clip. First a group of young boys from London rattle off a seemingly endless list of after-school activities that the week has in store for them. Then the mother of a boy in Singapore describes the four classes that her son takes every Saturday. "It's incredible when you think about it," says Klauber, senior VP and worldwide director of Mind & Mood, a proprietary tool of FCB. "When I was a kid, I'd roam around on my blue Schwinn for hours. These kids have daily to-do lists. Some of them have only twenty minutes of free time a day."

When Klauber started this project, he had no initial hypothesis—only a commitment to exploring an infrequently asked question: How is digital technology (and the lifestyle issues that go along with it) affecting young children's "sense of fun, play, and thinking"? After conducting forty in-depth workshops with kids (ages six to eleven) and their parents from several countries—including Brazil, Germany, Mexico, and the United States—Klauber arrived at answers that are both refreshing and alarming.

Among his seven primary findings: The obsession among parents with efficiency and productivity has trickled down to even the youngest of kids. Playtime has morphed into what Klauber calls a "digital wonderland"—a fast-moving, goal-oriented zone that affords "little time for aimless fun." Kids today are focused on competition, on efficiency, and on results. One consequence of this development is that their imaginations are beginning to atrophy: Play is all about the destination, rather than the journey.

"When parents talked to us about their childhoods,"

Klauber says, "they had a sense of wonderment. They remembered building forts out of pillows and blankets. They remembered making up elaborate stories. But because kids today have so little free time, and because they're always surrounded by media, they don't explore what's off the beaten path. They want their fun to be quick and easy. The art of being bored is lost." . . .

There's no question that Klauber's findings are causing some of his clients and colleagues to rethink their ideas about kids and their needs. For instance, after listening to Klauber's presentation, an executive at Mattel took a leave of absence to devote more time to her children. One FCB executive was so moved by the findings that he left work early to talk to his wife about how they could make their kids' lives a little less structured.[1]

This warning has been sounded by experts from diverse backgrounds. One of the most authoritative is the Alliance for Childhood, an interdisciplinary group of teachers, scientists, doctors, parents, and others concerned with children. The alliance published a monograph entitled *Fool's Gold: A Critical Look at Computers in Childhood*. Another expert on children, Dr. Jane Healy, cautioned against looking at computers as a pedagogical cure-all in her excellent book *Failure to Connect*. And Dr. Susan Villani, from Johns Hopkins, published an article in the April 2001 issue of the *Journal of the American Academy of Child and Adolescent Psychiatry* reviewing all the studies that have been done in the past decade on the effect on children of the various electronic media (television, videos, DVDs, video games, Nintendo and the like, computer games, the Internet).

The consensus of the experts is clear on two points: First, some media is fine, but too much is bad. Second, parents should monitor the content of all the media into which their children delve. Some Web sites are toxic waste dumps, just as some movies and even some books can be. Parents need to know not only *how much* but also *what* their children are watching.

Certainly one of the most dramatic ways in which childhood has changed is the emergence in this generation of the Internet, E-mail, chat rooms, instant messaging, and video games, to go along with television, which the previous generation also grew up with.

The media themselves are not destructive unless, as the Klauber study points out, the electronics crowd out everything else or the content is toxic.

It is entirely possible to play constructively with a computer or on the Internet. Indeed, some of the most playful people are the designers of computer technology, especially computer games.

But there is a huge difference between designing such a game and playing one. The designer is creative, the player minimally so.

So when it comes to electronics, be careful.

We need to preserve and protect for children what I call "the human moment." I am such a champion of its formative power that I wrote a book about it called *Human Moments*. The human moment—as opposed to the electronic moment—is any moment when you are engaged with other people, live and in person. Playing with a friend in the backyard is a human moment. Family dinner is a human moment. Talking in the car as you drive somewhere is a human moment. Reading aloud is a human moment.

Human moments are far richer than electronic moments, because you get enormously more information in person than you can possibly get electronically. You get body language, tone of voice, facial expression, timing of words and sentences—none of which comes across if you are not present personally. Human moments are also safer, in that you cannot be anonymous, and you are much less likely to be misunderstood or to take foolish risks.

Human moments provide the best context for play. That is not to say electronic play is bad. But if it comes to *replace* the human moment, then that is a bad effect.

However, you do not have to be with someone else in order to play. As I sit here alone writing this book, I am playing. Granted, it is disciplined play, but it is play nonetheless, as I am trying this word and trying that, experimenting with this sentence, experimenting with that. I am juggling words, as a juggler juggles balls or pins. For me this is play, because I love to do it, even though I agonize over it often. Most people who practice a craft feel this way. It is play, albeit often difficult play.

Many adult forms of productive play find their roots in childhood. My love of words goes back to family dinners during which my aunt, uncle, and cousins (I spent more time at their house than at my own) would play word games like Ghost. In Ghost the first player offers up a letter of the alphabet chosen at random. Let's say it is a *t*. The next player then must add a letter before or after the *t* without completing a word. The game proceeded from player to player, each person having to add a letter before or after the existing combination of letters. You lost the game if you completed a word, but you could also lose the game if the next player challenged you to name the word you had in mind and you were bluffing, having no actual word in mind.

My family played this game so often at dinner that we got good at thinking up difficult combinations of letters. To *t*, for example, I might add the unexpected letter *b*. This meant that I was maintaining I knew a word in which the combination *tb* could be found. If you are new to the game, you might not be able to think of any such word. In fact, there are quite a few, like *bootblack*, *batboy*, *hatbox*, and *flatbed*.

Difficult combinations of letters abound in English. That's because there are so many compound words. But not all the difficult combinations come from compound words. For example, can you think of a word in which the combination *uu* appears? I know of only one: *vacuum*.

Playing these games helped develop a love of words in me. My interest probably began with a genetic predisposition toward play with words; had I not had those genes, the games likely would have bored me. But since I had the genes, the games drew me in and spurred me on. In school I was one of those rare birds who actually liked grammar. In fact, I still like to think about grammatical issues, and while I don't know all the rules—far from it—I enjoy trying to reason them out. Just as a baseball fan might have a book of statistics nearby, I am never far from a dictionary or a copy of Fowler's *Dictionary of Modern English Usage* or Strunk and White's *Elements of Style*.

You can find out what your child is genetically predisposed to enjoy by noticing what she is drawn to play at. Lucy was drawn to clothes; Jack, to puzzles; Tucker, to action figures and making up stories about them. Once you start to play with something you have an innate predisposition to enjoy, then you will start to play it more and more. You will do what is called "practice" (which is the next element in my series of five), but the process will not be onerous because you will want to improve.

Some of these activities have more value than others. Many children enjoy Nintendo, but the value of becoming expert is limited. On the other hand, if your love of Nintendo leads you to learn about electronics or computer science, then its value increases a good deal.

We parents witness the messy beginnings of talent and should always be on the lookout for enthusiasms of any kind. Messes can be good. Messes often indicate an enthusiasm. There is a story that Steven Spielberg painted his kitchen yellow using egg yolks as paint when he was a child. I don't imagine his mother said, "Oh, Stevie, how creative. You are a genius in the making." But she might have consoled herself, as she hounded young Steven to clean it up, that this was not the doing of an unoriginal mind.

In childhood, talent usually shows up in play. If you want to find out what your child might have a gift for, look at her play.

Play is almost always imperfect, chaotic, excessive, undisciplined, and annoying to various adults. While we parents have to hold our children responsible for cleaning up, apologizing, and making whatever repairs seem appropriate, we should try never to kill the enthusiasm and creativity behind the making of the mess. We can kill it with ridicule or inappropriate punishment or anger or guilt.

One of the most common arenas for children to learn how to play—and then to practice, achieve mastery, and gain recognition—is in youth sports. Once the exclusive domain of boys, this world has opened up to girls as well, so that both sexes now participate at all levels.

Youth Sports: The Perfect Place
to Play . . . but Be Careful!

There are about thirty-five million children in the United States between the ages of three and fourteen who participate in organized
youth sports. At their best, organized sports are the ideal forum to go
through the five steps toward adult happiness that I outline in this
book. But by injecting youth sports with too much pressure from
adults—by turning them into work rather than play—we can ruin
them for kids. If you don't think this is a problem, consider the following sad statistic: 70 percent of the children in youth sports stop playing sports by the time they turn fifteen.

At its best, a team allows a child to connect with a group of her
peers as well as an adult mentor, called the coach. In this safe atmosphere of connectedness, the children begin to play, whatever the
sport might be. As they play together, they have fun. This should be
the immediate goal: fun. Many parents, teachers, and coaches don't
realize that fun sets off a cascade of positive events. If you make having fun the goal for your child in youth sports, and your child achieves
that goal, then it is likely your child will also achieve all the rest: practice, discipline, mastery, and recognition, as well as teamwork, sacrifice, and the other intangibles that sports can so wonderfully instill.

As Al Skinner, the successful and dynamic basketball coach at
Boston College, said, "The purpose of youth sports is fun. If it's fun,
they'll practice more and improve, and success will follow."

Al Skinner gets it. Many well-meaning parents do not. By making
victory or stardom or discipline the *first* goal, you can kill the fun—
and the benefits of the sport—for the children.

Play that is fun leads to practice, as Al Skinner pointed out, and
practice leads to mastery. Mastery then leads to recognition by other
members of the team and other people as well, which in turn leads to
a deeper connection, more play, more practice, more mastery, and
more recognition. More victories ensue, but they are a by-product of
the process, not its first goal.

Youth sports highlight a mistake all of us parents can easily make.
In our concern that our children do well later in life, we can lose the

nerve it takes to let them have a childhood. We can cease to trust in the process of childhood and in our child's ability to become whatever he or she is meant to become. Instead, we can start to impose our own predictable, prefabricated vision of success. We can demand high achievement now—victories and awards in sports, top grades in school, or high-status activities that look good on a résumé regardless of whether the child has an interest in or aptitude for them—believing that high achievement now is the best guarantee for a successful life.

When I say "trust the process of childhood," I do not mean we parents should take an indifferent approach. I mean we should do what I outline in this book. Let children be children. Let them play and have fun before they take on the pressures of the adult world. Indeed, playing and having fun when you are a child is the best way to learn how to take on the pressures of the adult world later on.

If you trust in the process I outline and recognize play and fun as essential elements of the process, if you allow a child to be a child first and become an adult later, something amazing happens. The child becomes who he or she is meant to become. Not who you or I want the child to become but who the child wants and is meant to become.

The best preparation for dealing with intense pressure in adult life, for actually enjoying pressure in adult life, is not subjecting a child to pressure before he or she is ready. Just the opposite. It is giving him or her the chance to develop the muscles of confidence, optimism, and hope, which can only be built slowly, on a unique, lazy summer morning, a long morning we call childhood.

At the end of selected chapters about the five steps, I offer some tips related to the particular step discussed in that chapter. I offer the tips on creating connectedness at the end of each section describing a specific kind of connectedness in the extended chapter on connectedness, Chapter 13.

Here, then, some tips on play:

• Understand what play means and how important it is for children (and adults). If you don't stop to think, you might make the common mistake of assuming that a child who is going through the motions at basketball practice is playing while a child who is sitting under a tree with a friend is not. The child at basketball practice may be just listlessly doing what he has been told to do, while the child beneath the tree with his friend may be dreaming up the most amazing spaceship ever invented.

• Make time for play. You may have to carve the time out of the hardwood of the daily schedule, but do it. Children (and adults) need free time to play. They need time when nothing is on the agenda. They need time when they are not expected to be anywhere, doing anything.

• Limit electronic time. You may set aside free time only to see your children fill it with Nintendo or chat rooms or instant messaging. My advice is to limit this time, not forbid it. In our house the rule is one hour per day of what we call "electronic time" (television, video, computer, and Nintendo) during the week and two hours on weekends. With the rest of their free time, we ask our children to amuse themselves, find a friend, devise a game, read a book, or in some other way use their imaginations to entertain themselves. Little do they know that this time is perhaps the most important time of their entire day.

• Don't overschedule your children with enriching activities that obliterate their time for unstructured play. Make sure they have time for just hanging out. We can give our children too much of a good thing if we are not careful. Too many lessons (violin, soccer, computer skills, Hebrew, and so forth). Too many exciting, preprogrammed activities. The next thing you know, you create a kind of high-stimulation junkie, a child who cannot think up anything on his own.

• Sports are great arenas for play, but don't turn youth sports into a pressure-packed, hypercompetitive drama. Youth sports—and all athletics in childhood—ought to be a place to have fun. It ought to be a place to plant the childhood roots of adult happiness, not adult rage or regret. It ought to be a place to learn about teamwork and team loyalty, cooperation, compromise, sacrifice, how to deal with people who are more talented than you and less talented than you, how to win and lose gracefully, and other life lessons. The win-loss record of the team is the least important item on the list.

• Relearn how to play as an adult. Go out in the yard or sit down on the floor, and let yourself go. Make funny noises. Do a somersault (when was the last time you did one of those?). Be silly (that is, playful). Make up a game (it's easy to do, once you let yourself go). Not only will your children love this, but relearning how to play will also help you in all aspects of your own life, especially love and work.

• Try to find a place where your children can be left alone to play. The most obvious is a backyard with a fence, if you have one. Or a neighborhood, if you have one. The old-fashioned neighborhood used to come equipped with moms and grandmas looking out their windows, keeping half an eye on all the children in the neighborhood so that everyone was safe. Such neighborhoods have been supplanted by the modern neighborhood of play dates and friends who live far away. So you have to get creative to find the places where the kids can feel somewhat on their own but still know they are safe. Maybe a park. Or a camp. Or a team. Or a party where grown-ups are nearby.

• Make sure your child's school understands the value of play. Try not to let your school eliminate recess, as some schools are doing in order to provide more time for studying, so as to raise standardized test scores. Make sure your school realizes that children need to play and exercise regularly for their minds to be in the best shape to learn.

• Keep your family alive with humor. Humor is play. Where you find kids laughing, you find kids playing. Studies show that where you find laughter and play, you do not find much depression, anxiety, or fear.

• Now make up a tip yourself. What is one practical way you can think of to encourage play in the lives of your children, yourself, and your family? Maybe you could go hide something right now and at dinnertime announce that after dinner there will be a game to see who can find the hidden thing. Or maybe you'll go buy a ball you don't have. Or maybe after dinner say, "Let's all go outside and lie down on the grass and look up at the sky." (I'm assuming it is summer. But you could go lie down on the snow as well.) Or maybe make up a word game you want to play at dinner. Or go play catch with your kids. Or take them bowling; when was the last time you did that? Or maybe take up fishing. That is the one I am going to do this summer. I am a rotten fisherman, but recently all my kids went fishing and really liked it. So this summer when we go off to our rented cottage on Lake Doolittle, I am going to get us all simple rods and go fishing, even though I barely know how to fish. This is one of the treats of play: you don't have to be an expert to have fun.

9

PRACTICE: THE WAY FROM
PLAY TO MASTERY

Ugh.

That is our typical reaction to the word *practice* as well as its cousin *discipline*.

I want to give you a totally different philosophy about practice and discipline in this chapter, one that will allow you to use those words with your children with enthusiasm rather than by drearily intoning the old "If you want to succeed, you've got to work hard" lecture.

The scientific studies into what makes for happiness both in childhood and in adulthood always emphasize that it is crucial to feel that you have control over yourself and your environment. The best way to develop that sense of control is through practice. Soon you learn that practice leads to mastery, which shows you that you can control your life, at least somewhat.

Furthermore, structure and discipline unlock the door to talent. How many adults have kept their talents locked up because they never developed the structure or discipline to develop them?

Structure and discipline also unlock the door to free time. If you can get your homework done in an organized, timely fashion, you will have more time to talk on the telephone or play outdoors.

But how do you sell these ideas to your children?

If you present the issue as a means of gaining freedom and developing talent rather than submitting to drudgery, you may present it more persuasively, not to mention more accurately.

Adults can act like killjoys when we approach the issue of practice and discipline. We can wring our hands and almost apologetically plead with our children to clean up their rooms. Or we can read the more hard-line parenting books, roll up our sleeves, and in the name of not spoiling our children, turn our homes into a juvenile version of boot camp.

Neither of those approaches works well. What I have tried to do in my own life and in the lives of my children is to see discipline not as a grim necessity of life, sounding a death knell for the carefree joys of childhood, but as the powerful, liberating tool that it actually is.

It is important for parents (and teachers and coaches) to have an infectious, positive attitude about practice and discipline. Otherwise, you will take on the role of killjoy, sermonizer, or punisher, all less than optimal roles.

You can feel enthusiastic about encouraging practice and discipline if you understand and believe one basic fact: practice and discipline build the bridge between play and mastery. Children may not understand this intellectually, but they experience it all the time. So do adults.

When you play, you usually find something that you like to do. Since you enjoy it, you tend to want to do it over and over again. This may be playing patty-cake or peekaboo with mommy as a baby or basketball as a ten-year-old or writing in your diary as a teenager or driving a car soon after you get your license. When you do something over and over again, it is called practice or discipline. Over time this leads to mastery. So practice and discipline build the bridge between play and mastery.

It is better simply to set the process up, over and over, than to lecture. Let your child connect with others and play, let him find something he likes and practice it, and let him then taste mastery and receive recognition. As this process repeats, the roots of practice and discipline start to grow. The child need never even be subjected to the word *discipline*, let alone be subjected to any lectures on the topic.

Lecturing children (or adults) about the importance of practice and discipline may make mom and dad or the CEO feel that they are doing their duty, but it can easily backfire. The child may listen, then want nothing more than never to practice again.

Practice can grow naturally out of play. The kinds of practice and discipline that endure derive more from enthusiasm, desire, and devotion than guilt, fear, or mindless obedience.

It is often noted that the word *discipline* derives from the same root as *disciple*. Just as the disciples of Christ chose to sacrifice everything they owned to follow Christ, not out of fear or guilt but out of enthusiasm and excitement, so the happily disciplined child or adult practices and makes sacrifices not out of fear or guilt but out of desire and enthusiasm.

Let me use myself as an example. In many respects I am not a disciplined person. I can eat too much, drink too much, sleep too much, lose track of my finances, lose weight only to gain it back, waste hours watching TV, forget to return phone calls or E-mails, lose track of the time and be late, forget to pay parking tickets, lose items I need (especially pens and umbrellas; Freudians, have a field day!), start projects and fail to complete them, and stare blankly into space instead of doing something productive.

I qualify in these respects as an undisciplined person.

On the other hand, I am disciplined in the areas I love. I am disciplined in preserving plenty of time to spend with Sue and my children. I am disciplined in taking care of my patients. I am disciplined in my writing of books. I am disciplined in the lectures and seminars I present. I am disciplined (although not very good) in how I play squash. I am disciplined in setting aside certain hours for dates with specific friends so I don't lose contact with them. I am disciplined, although far from perfect, in attending church.

How can I be so undisciplined and so disciplined at the same time?

The fact is, I am disciplined in what I love and undisciplined in what I don't love. I love my family, I love writing, I love the practice of psychiatry, I love giving lectures and seminars, and I love my friends and squash and church. Discipline that lasts usually begins in the love of an activity and the desire to get better at it or at least to do it again.

Connection leads to play, which leads to practice, which is discipline. If you build discipline from the bottom up, from connection through play into practice, on to mastery and recognition, then you can create a disciplined individual, even within a person like me who is undisciplined in so many ways. If, on the other hand, you rely too much on top-down discipline, a do-this-because-I-told-you-to mentality, it won't translate into much good beyond obedience, if that.

I can hear you saying, "But what about brushing teeth and cleaning up your room? Nobody does that out of love!"

In fact, they do, just not when they're children. Self-care—brushing teeth, cutting hair, cutting your nails—eventually comes to be an expression of caring enough about yourself to want to take good care of yourself. Cleaning up your room can be a kind of self-care, or it can come from a love of order. Some people really love order. They feel good when they clean up their rooms. Others don't care. They tend to be the people who do not clean up their rooms as children or as adults.

So then I hear you asking, "What happens when what I love—order—does not coincide with what my child loves, namely, disorder? How do I instill discipline based on love and enthusiasm then, good doctor?"

Well, then you rely on the traditional concept of discipline. "You have to do this because I am telling you you have to do this." Every parent must say that many times. However, discipline that lasts tends not to derive from doing something that someone else wants you to do.

Lucy, Jack, and Tucker do not love order, at least not yet. They do not yet clean up their rooms without being asked to do so. Sue and I command them to clean up their rooms if too much clutter accumulates. We help Tucker more than we help Lucy, and Jack is in between.

Lucy, Jack, and Tucker were not born saying "please" and "thank you." Sue and I had to teach them that, and we still have to remind them. Lucy, Jack, and Tucker were not born knowing how to shake hands firmly and make eye contact upon meeting a new person. Sue and I had to teach them, and we still have to remind them. The same for table manners, appropriate dress, getting organized in the morning for school, doing homework, and so on.

I am not suggesting you abdicate your role as the teacher and enforcer of politeness, neatness, punctuality, responsibility, and so forth. I am not proposing some radical, permissive regime. Not at all. I get after my children all the time to do the things I have mentioned and more. However, I am stating that in the context of a connected childhood, certain kinds of practice and discipline naturally develop as a bridge between play and mastery.

It is our role as parents to encourage and, if that fails, to demand adherence to certain standards of behavior. Over time these standards become habits, like using a fork instead of fingers to eat when you go out for dinner or saying "please" and "thank you." These small points comprise the large virtue we call civility, and it is not a virtue that comes naturally to most children. It is a key to getting along with other people, which in turn is a key to happiness throughout life.

In teaching these various small points, you do need structure. You need rules of the house, rules of the dining room table, rules in games, rules of all sorts. You also need schedules. A time for this, a time for that. And you need rituals: shake hands and make eye contact, say "thank you" when you leave someone's house, wash your hands before you eat. None of these structures is rooted in enthusiasm, love, desire, or excitement, but a happy life almost always contains at least a measure of structure.

Children actually do love structure. As Dary Dunham, who has been teaching young children for thirty-five years, said to me, "Structure provides freedom. Children want to know that there are rules and timetables and right ways and wrong ways. I see it over and over again, when a child gets structure in his life, he becomes happier, healthier, and more successful at everything he does."

So there is a measure of discipline—in the form of structure, rules, schedules, and rituals—that has to come from the top down, from the person in charge, and must be enforced, not merely recommended; it generally will not evolve from the bottom up.

But at the same time, I urge parents to realize that structure is but a part of the larger tool of practice and discipline and that not all hard work is drudgery. Indeed, most disciplined work that lasts for very long derives from a love of the work, which motivates the individual to make the sacrifices and endure the pain.

Let me give two more examples, these from the lives of two of my children.

When Jack was eight years old, he started to enjoy soccer a great deal. He had played it since he was six, but he didn't really care about it until he was eight. Then, perhaps because his close friend Noah loved soccer, Jack started to play harder.

At the same time, he started to become short of breath. After he'd run the length of the field, it would take him longer than the other kids to get his wind. I didn't know about it at the time, but some adult told him that if he tried harder, he would not get winded so easily. So Jack pushed himself as hard as he could and still got short of breath more easily than the other players.

One evening as I was driving home, I saw a little boy running down the sidewalk. As I drew closer, I saw that the little boy was Jack. I slowed down my car, rolled down the window, pulled up alongside Jack, and asked him what he was doing. Without stopping his running, Jack, panting, replied, "I'm running laps around the block to try to build up my endurance."

After he finished running, he came inside and told me the whole story of how he'd been losing his wind more easily than the other kids. We took him to the doctor to see why he was getting short of breath. The doctor scared the daylights out of me by doing a test for cystic fibrosis, which thank goodness was negative. But the other pulmonary function tests showed that there was a problem: Jack had asthma. All the while he had been pushing himself, he was living with undiagnosed and untreated asthma. Once we got the asthma treated, his wind improved tremendously.

I will never forget the sight of Jack, age eight, running laps on the sidewalk around our block even though he was struggling to catch his breath. Here was this boy so determined to get better at soccer that he was pushing himself even in the face of a medical problem that would have kept many kids from playing soccer at all, let alone running laps after practice. No one had told Jack to run laps. He simply had heard that if he tried harder, he would get better. So he tried harder. That's discipline, deriving from a love of the activity and a desire to get better. That is the kind of discipline that lasts.

In Jack's case, we had done nothing specifically to "instill" such discipline. Rather, it arose naturally from his desire to get better at soccer, which arose naturally from his being allowed to play it, which arose naturally from his feeling connected enough to dare.

Of course, he does not exhibit a similar discipline when it comes to cleaning up his room. For that, we have to request, and require, that he do it.

To give a different example, Lucy has been playing violin for six years. She started taking lessons when she was six years old because her best friend at the time was taking lessons. Sue and I resisted offering Lucy lessons because we thought she simply wanted to play the violin to be like her friend. However, when she persisted in asking and promised she would stick with it, we said OK.

Now that she is twelve years old, she really likes violin. However, she really dislikes practicing. Unlike the example with Jack, in which the discipline arose naturally from within him to run extra laps, in Lucy's case we have to prod her to practice. She is always glad once she has done it, and she truly enjoys the violin. We ask from time to time if she wants to give it up, and she always says no. However, she also often says no when it is time to practice. At that point, we urge her to do it. She needs prodding from us to do what in the long run she is glad she has done.

In this instance Sue and I are acting sort of like football coaches. Football players volunteer and compete to get on the team, but they often hate the drills and repetitions of practice. The coach sometimes has to hound them. Each player is free to quit the team, but as long as he wants to play, he must put up with the coach putting him through his paces at practice.

Here the discipline needs a prod from the outside. Lucy is free to quit the violin, but as long as she wants to continue—and it is clear she really enjoys being able to play—Sue and I feel that we should help her by making sure that she practices.

Practice builds the bridge from play to mastery, but it builds it more slowly and painfully the more difficult the task. For a parent, teacher, or coach, it is a difficult call sometimes to decide how hard to push from the outside and how much to leave up to the child.

As long as you—the parent, teacher, or coach—are sure you are not pushing the child because of your own selfish motives, then external encouragement, even demands, can help a child reach difficult goals he really wants to reach.

In general, as long as the child continues to express interest and shows at least minimal aptitude, she may implicitly be asking you to help her practice and request that she do it.

Once the child—or the adult, for that matter—begins to taste mastery, the need for prodding from the outside diminishes, although it doesn't disappear. The beginnings of mastery, like the first few pounds you lose when you go on a diet, provide the best motivation of all.

I offer below some tips that you might find helpful in developing in your child habits of practice and discipline in such a way that these become the keys to happiness that they truly can be.

• Think back to your own childhood. What worked and didn't work for you? Don't make the same mistakes that were made with you with your own children. But do try to do what worked well.

• Loosen up. Remember, messes are part of childhood. Messes can be good. Order should not be the top priority in childhood. Don't apply the same standards to your children's play space that would apply to your employees' desks.

• Present discipline as a ticket to free time, mastery, and success, which, in fact, it is. Think of ways of explaining this to your children in words that make sense to them. You should first think it through enough to believe it in your own heart, though, or you'll sound like a used-car salesman.

• Explain to your children how the successful people they admire only reached their goals through hard work. Then explain to them that those people worked hard, not because they were extraordinarily virtuous but because they enjoyed the feeling of mastery so much that they wanted to feel it over and over again. Lead your child to that feeling. Once she tastes it, she will want to taste it again.

• Try to separate your own hang-ups about practice and discipline from what you pass on to your children. If you are a neat freak, realize that you go overboard on this issue and try not to inflict it on your family. On the other hand, if you are congenitally sloppy, try to acknowledge this as a problem and work on it rather than letting your mess engulf the house and allow your children to believe that this is acceptable.

• Offer specific pointers on organization and help your child set up an approach that works for him or her. If time management is a problem, work with a written schedule or an alarm watch or some other device. If practicing an instrument is a problem, try to figure out what is getting in the way rather than just nag. Ask the music teacher, or the teacher in whatever area presents the problem, for help as well. Help your child develop the ability to prioritize and to plan. This does not come naturally to many children, so if you can teach some of the tricks you have learned along the way, from flash cards to lists to other kinds of reminders, your child will likely pick up on them. Remember, one of the great tools we parents have, and often forget we have, is that our children imitate what we do.

• Reinforce at home what is being done at school, on the playing field, at the lessons, or wherever the activity may be. Try to communicate with the other adults who are working with your children so that you are all using the same approach to discipline and practice, if possible.

• Don't use words like *lazy*, *slacker*, *loser*, and so forth. Lots of people give up on themselves too soon, thinking they just do not have what it takes to acquire discipline. The key to becoming disciplined is believing it will be worth the pain. Better to give encouragement than to invoke negative adjectives.

• Don't be afraid to require your child to do what is asked, from homework to chores to manners. At times you simply have to insist. You can do it with humor, but you do need to do it. Children want limits, and they will push until they get them.

• Don't scare your children away from anything by saying it takes "so much discipline" or "years of practice." All this does is instill a sullen sense that the task is insurmountable. I almost did not apply to medical school because I had been told how arduous an ordeal it was and how much discipline it required. Since I liked to sleep late, I thought I lacked the discipline to become a doctor. What nonsense. Anybody can learn to get up early. If you want to do something, you can do it. That is the attitude you should instill in your children.

10

MASTERY: THE GREAT MOTIVATOR

As you cross the bridge you arduously build through practice and discipline, you arrive at the wonderful world of mastery.

Once you have been there, you want to go there again. Once you feel mastery, you want to feel it many times. Do you remember the first time you did something you didn't think you could do? For me it was riding a bike. My cousin Jamie taught me how. I'll never forget how I felt when he let go of the bike for about the tenth time and *this* time I got it. I didn't fall off. I rode and rode and rode, right on into my adult life.

The feeling of mastery, and the wish to experience it again, transforms a child, or an adult, from a reluctant, fearful learner into a self-motivated player. One of the great goals of parents, teachers, and coaches should be to find areas in which a child might experience mastery, then make it possible for the child to feel this potent sensation.

Mastery is the great motivator, because people like to do what they do well. "Duh! Dad," my daughter would say. But often we forget this crucial, obvious fact and assume that it is bad attitude, laziness, ineptitude, or stupidity that keeps a child from becoming enthusiastically involved.

What holds children back the most is a fear of messing up. It is a feeling of I-can't-do-this-and-I-don't-want-to-look-foolish. Fear is the great disabler. Fear is what keeps children—and adults—from realizing their potential.

The more you have felt mastery, the less likely it is that you will give in to fear when you approach a new activity or task. The more you experience mastery, the stronger the emotional muscle called confidence will grow. The best antidote to fear, timidity, and self-doubt is the feeling of mastery. Not only is mastery the great motivator, mastery is also the great builder of self-esteem. The memory of mastery is what keeps us coming back to try again, even if we initially fall short of our goal.

The mistake that parents, teachers, and coaches often make is to try to demand mastery rather than lead children to it.

My definition of a great teacher is a person who can lead another person to mastery. The best parents are great teachers. If there is any greater joy than achieving mastery yourself, it may be the joy of leading a child to it.

As parents, we get the chance to do this in many ways every day. All the minor tasks we take for granted—from telling time to tying a shoe to putting on nail polish—are new and at first impossible for our children. For a child any of these tasks can begin as a source of frustration and even shame but with a parent's guidance can turn into a source of mastery and joy.

I'll never forget teaching Lucy how to snap her fingers. She watched me do it, then she practiced off and on for a few days, and within a week or so she became an accomplished snapper. It seemed like months before Lucy stopped snapping her fingers all the time.

Each time you go through the cycle and reach mastery, you add another strand to your child's growing muscle of confidence and self-esteem. In the body we call happiness, that is the most important muscle.

It is easy for an adult to guide a child through this cycle; all it takes is patience and time.

It is also a lot of fun.

Let me tell you a story.

Years ago Jack and I were home alone on a rainy Saturday afternoon. I can't remember where Sue and the other kids were. Jack and I looked at each other, wondering what to do. Out of nowhere, I proposed bowling. Jack was about five, and he had never bowled, even though there is a bowling center called Lanes and Games not far from our house. "Great!" Jack said to my proposal, having at least bowled plastic balls toward plastic pins on the living room rug before.

Where I grew up, on Cape Cod, candlepin bowling was the norm, so I like bowling with the little balls at the tall pins. Scores are low, but the game is fun. At Lanes and Games, they fortunately offer both candlepin and tenpin bowling. Jack and I chose candlepin. One of the pleasant aspects about teaching young children is that they will go along with whatever you propose in the areas where they do not yet have experience or preferences.

I showed him how to roll the ball down the alley by first doing it myself. When he picked up a ball—in candlepin bowling the balls are about the size of a grapefruit—it was a little too big and too heavy for his hand, so he used two hands and sort of slung the ball sidearm down the alley. It bounced a couple of times and rolled off toward the gutter. At these lanes they have rails along the gutters for children's bowling, so the ball doesn't go into the gutter but instead bounces off the rail and eventually hits some pins. (Those gutter rails provide a good, practical example of how you can set a child up to succeed.)

Jack cheered. He wanted to roll another ball right away. This time I showed him how to hold the ball with two hands, bend over, and roll the ball from between his legs.

Jack tried a few that way, as I continued to roll my balls the grown-up way.

The next thing I knew, Jack picked up a ball in one hand, cocked his wrist so as not to drop it, took three strides up to the line, and rolled the ball as closely to the way I did it as he could.

I'll never forget that sight. Here I was, imprinting a style of bowling on my young son, simply by bowling with him. It touched me deeply that he wanted to do it like me (believe me, no *adult* bowler would ever want to bowl like me!) and that I had the ability to so inspire him.

This is just one of the joys of leading children to mastery: they appreciate our talents even in those areas where we lack talent.

Now, four years later, Jack loves to bowl. He still bowls a bit like me, only he has smoothed out his style and turned it into his own. At the age of nine, he is a much better bowler than I am.

If you plant the seeds early, the skills will grow, even if you lack the skills yourself.

Try not to decide, yourself, what you want your child to excel at. This is understandable—we naturally hope our children will share our enthusiasms—but it is a mistake to force the matter. Instead, plant many seeds. Then see what grows. No matter what grows, mastery will bring confidence, self-esteem, and internal motivation with it.

Mastery versus Achievement

It is important to distinguish between mastery and achievement. Mastery is a feeling. Achievement is a benchmark.

Usually a feeling of mastery accompanies an achievement; in this way mastery and achievement go hand in hand. But sometimes they do not. Some children and adults ring up achievements without gaining the feeling of mastery because they short-circuit their way to the achievement. For example, if you take an easy course in college for the sole purpose of getting an A, you will not feel much mastery, although you may ring up the achievement of a high grade to put on your record. Or if you simply do the minimum amount required to complete your science project, you will not feel much mastery, although you will have achieved the goal of completing the project.

But the problem can grow more insidious than that. Some people do not feel mastery even when they achieve something extremely difficult. This is because their capacity to feel mastery has been blocked by excessive criticism and excessively high expectations. While it is good to challenge children to do their best, it is destructive never to let them feel that they have done something masterfully.

While you may think this is a rare problem, as you grow gray hairs just trying to get your children to do their basic homework, I know many high-achieving adults who are psychologically *unable* to feel pride or mastery in what they do, even though the rest of the world deems their work superb. The problem goes back to a parent or a teacher or a coach whom they could never, ever satisfy. Like many talented people who believe criticism much more readily than they believe praise, these people internalized the relentless criticism of their unpleasable master and became unpleasable themselves. This is one of the cruelest ironies of high achievement: sometimes it induces not well-deserved pleasure but only greater demands and more intensive self-criticism.

But for most people, if you just work hard and do your best at some activity that is challenging to you, you will feel mastery. To continue to feel it, you must then raise the bar.

For example, once I learned how to ride a bike, my feeling of mastery peaked, then gradually subsided over the following weeks. In order to feel it again, I had to try something new on my bike, something that required more work, like riding with just one hand, then riding with no hands, then standing up on the seat as the bike was moving (I never did master that!).

The feeling of mastery is its own reward. On the other hand, you can achieve a lot, as many people do, but feel little satisfaction or mastery. But a feeling of mastery can accompany what looks to other people like not much. I experienced a great feeling of mastery in medical school when I learned how to draw blood. It was no big deal to all the other people at the hospital who knew how to draw blood, but it made me feel just grand.

If you can encourage your children to do their best, mastery will follow, and with mastery will come motivation to do more as well as a growing sense of self-esteem. Happiness depends on a lifetime not of achievement but of gradually increasing feelings of mastery.

Mastery and Optimism

The five-step process I am outlining builds many powerful psychological beams and girders. One of the most important is the mental habit of optimism. Repeated experiences of mastery help build an attitude of optimism.

Research shows that if you can raise your child to be optimistic, that will increase his chances of becoming a happy and confident adult. The obvious question is, *how* do you raise your child to be optimistic? While you may be genetically predisposed toward optimism, as my mother was, or pessimism, as my father was, you can also be encouraged—indeed, *taught*—when you are young, to grow toward optimism or toward pessimism. Thanks to my mother's genes and her teachings, I have a stronger bent toward optimism, despite the pessimism I inherited from my father.

Research has demonstrated that optimism is one of the strongest predictors of adult happiness. Sometimes we think of optimism as a superficial quality, when in fact it is anything but. Optimism is tough, much tougher than pessimism and its weak cousin cynicism, because it has to be in order to survive. If optimism weren't tough, it would wither after just a few setbacks. It takes much more courage and creativity to maintain an optimistic stance than to wilt into pessimism and cynicism.

Pessimism is like a tar baby: the more you touch it, the more it sticks to you. The same goes for cynicism. Try not to touch your children with pessimism and cynicism, even if you are coated in them yourself. Try not to pass negativity on. It is a curse.

The research shows that to some extent optimism is inherited genetically. However, you can still do a lot as a parent to encourage the development of optimism as a learned way of viewing life. Optimism is a habit you can acquire, even if it does not come naturally to you. If you train yourself, and your children, not to globalize or catastrophize bad events, you will learn to keep bad events in proper perspective. If you teach them an explanatory style that reflexively interprets events in a more upbeat than downbeat way, you will be giving them a huge gift that can last the rest of their lives. It helps enormously not only in dealing with bad events but in freeing up energy to create good events.

Optimism is a trait that can endure, and indeed grow, over a lifetime. Optimism does not refer to a silly or blind denial of the negative aspects of life but rather to the practice of finding solutions to problems and a tendency to believe that there always is realistic hope, no matter how bad things may get.

Martin Seligman, the major researcher in the field of optimism, states:

> Even though optimism is unquestionably heritable in minor (less than fifty percent) part, this does not mean that optimism genes exist, or that the right childhood experience is not crucial to forming optimism. As parents and teachers, you should remain alert to the fact that lots of success for your child will lead to optimism. You should go out of your way to help your child follow up one success with another, and another. The right coaching from you will support and maintain his optimism, and the right crucial experiences will set his optimism in concrete.[1]

While Seligman's research showed that optimism can be learned, and learned at any age, it is best learned young. If your child develops a mental attitude that no matter what happens, he can find a way to a good outcome, that attitude becomes a self-fulfilling prophesy. On the other hand, no matter how intelligent and creative your child may be, if he develops an attitude that things never work out well in life, then things usually don't. And even if things do happen to work out, the person rarely enjoys the good times, because he is pessimistically waiting for the next bad thing to happen.

If one of the great gifts a parent can give a child is the gift of optimism, how can we make sure that we give it, especially if we do not possess that gift ourselves?

You can begin to build an optimistic attitude through your positive connection to the child. Even if you did not get such attention when you were a child, you can still give it to your children now. You can give them what you didn't have. And if you were lucky enough to get it yourself, then make sure you pass it on. Connectedness does not happen automatically. You have to take the time to water the garden.

The child who feels closely connected and unconditionally loved develops a feeling of basic trust and security, which naturally leads to a feeling that it is safe to try new things. This leads to play, which in turn leads to practice, which leads on to mastery. Repeated experiences of mastery lead to optimism and confidence. But if the connectedness is not there in the first place, it is less likely that the crucial experiences of mastery will happen as often.

As problems arise—and life is all about problems—the connected, secure, optimistic child tackles the problems with a sure sense that they are solvable. Rather than give up, the optimistic child tries again.

C. R. Snyder, Ph.D., a professor of psychology at the University of Kansas in Lawrence, wrote an excellent book called *The Psychology of Hope: You Can Get There from Here,* in which he states that three elements contribute to hopefulness and optimism in children. First is a goal. Second is willpower, or the energy needed to go after the goal. And third is what Snyder calls *waypower,* or the inner feeling that you can find a way, even many ways, to reach the goal you have in mind.

Goals come naturally to children. *I want a cookie,* or *I want to be an astronaut someday.* Willpower and waypower, however, depend on connectedness, play, practice, and past experiences of mastery. The more connected a child is, the more likely the rest of the steps will naturally follow.

Of all the tests that my daughter Lucy has taken in her young life, the one that I cared about most was one I gave her myself. It is the test from Martin Seligman's book *The Optimistic Child* that measures how optimistic or pessimistic a given child is. Developed by two of his research assistants, Drs. Nadine Kaslow and Richard Tanenbaum, this test has been taken by thousands of children and has been statistically validated. It is a more reliable measure than your intuitive assessment alone. It is intended for children of ages eight to thirteen, and the test takes about twenty minutes to give.

One day I asked Lucy, then age twelve, if I could ask her some questions that would help me understand what kind of outlook she had on life. She said, "Sure." She lay down on the floor, doodling on a piece of paper, as I asked the questions from Seligman's book. I was the anxious one in the scene; Lucy thought the whole process was kind of funny.

I was anxious because it mattered a lot to me that Lucy be developing the habit of optimism. I knew that this would help her immensely in life. She was and is an upbeat girl, but I wondered if that attitude might just be a front she put up. I wondered if underneath she might be pessimistic, especially given my family's history of depression. So her score on this optimism test mattered much more to me than her IQ, grades in school, or any other academic measure.

Once we finished the test, it took me a while to score it. Kaslow and Tanenbaum, true to their training as researchers, have filled the test with subtests and subscores and various acronyms, like PMB (permanent bad events) and PVG (pervasive good events) and HoB (hopelessness, bad events), which I had to score separately. This kept the final tally a secret from me as I did the arithmetic. Lucy lay on the floor doodling while I scratched numbers on a piece of paper.

Finally I arrived at her score. When I looked at what it meant, I jumped up and gave Lucy a giant hug. "You're optimistic!" I declared. "Not only are you optimistic, you are off-the-charts optimistic!" Lucy looked at me as if to say, What's the big fuss? But she humored me by smiling and saying, "That's nice."

According to the extensive data Seligman has collected, Lucy's very high score in optimism correlates with resilience and success and makes her all but invulnerable to depression.

You may have provided a close and nurturing connection for your child and still see him develop a pessimistic attitude as he grows older. That does not mean you have failed. It is because there are other factors at work that you can't control—most notably, genetics, what teachers, peers, and coaches say and do, and the culture in which you live. But even if those forces are working against optimism, you can still encourage the growth of an optimistic mentality.

As a parent you promote optimism in your child not only by creating a secure connection but also by modeling optimism yourself. This does not mean you have to go around whistling a happy tune, quoting Norman Vincent Peale, and sticking happy faces on your car's bumper. But it does mean you should try to avoid certain negative mental habits, like globalizing one negative situation as being representative of all of life or catastrophizing one problem into a sign of utter disaster or selecting one shortcoming in yourself as being an indicator that you are completely useless or taking one setback as an omen that nothing but setbacks lie down the road.

Instead, model and teach rational optimism for your children, not to mention for yourself! If you are by nature a pessimist, take being a parent as your opportunity—indeed, your mandate—to practice becoming an optimist. The best manual on how to do this is Seligman's book *Learned Optimism.*

Optimism need not be mystical or irrational. Indeed, optimism can be utterly rational. Rational optimism leads you to try to solve a problem rather than get mired within it. Rational optimism leads you to try to see the real opportunities embedded in every problem or catastrophe. Rational optimism guides you to put a boundary around a problem rather than allow it to take over your whole life. Rational optimism means that when you lose your job, you do not say to your family that you are going broke but that you have had a setback, that the family will have to tighten its belt for a while, but that you expect to find work sooner or later, as most other people in your situation have also found work. You appeal to reason to give you hope rather than allowing irrational pessimism to take you over and submerge you in depression.

Children learn from how you react to problems. This is their non-genetic inheritance. Children learn from your explanatory style, and in this sense they inherit your attitudes and behaviors, even if they did not acquire them from your genes.

In the cauldron of childhood, when a person's feelings and attitudes are most fluid, you can shape those attitudes so that when they harden later on into adult feelings and attitudes, they will be strong enough to withstand adversity as well as create and sustain joy.

The feeling of mastery leads to optimism, which is at heart a feeling of I-want-to-do-it-again, whatever "it" may be.

Sometimes you can experience mastery but still feel deflated. At some point you need recognition and approval from others, which is the fifth step in the process I describe and is the subject of the next chapter.

But first, let me offer a few tips on developing mastery. As with all the bits of advice offered in this book, these tips are meant to stimulate your own thinking and not be followed cookbook style.

• Be sure that you and your child know the difference between achievement and mastery. Achievement is a benchmark, while mastery is a feeling. The two can go hand in hand, but don't forget to look behind your child's achievements and make sure a feeling of mastery is also there. Achievement without the feeling of mastery is thin gruel; it offers little sustenance.

• The feeling of mastery is the great motivator. I play golf three or four times a year, instead of never, because in every round I make at least one masterful shot. The feeling I get when I hit that one good shot overrides the bad feelings from all the flubbed shots and motivates me to come back again. The more you can lead your child to experiences of mastery, the more internally motivated your child will become.

• Try to set up your child to experience mastery in as many ways as you can. Learning how to walk is a great moment of mastery. Learning how to talk, to read, to add and subtract—all these bring with them the feeling of mastery. Your job as a parent—or as a teacher or a coach—is to facilitate these moments.

• Don't expect praise to take the place of the experience of mastery. Sometime adults believe they can instill self-esteem simply by offering praise. It doesn't work. Self-esteem and confidence come from the experience of doing something well yourself.

• Explain that pain and frustration precede mastery. Don't present this fact as a lecture; then your child can dismiss it as just another parental riff. Instead, offer it as a point of information, a curious fact of life you want your child to know. We purchase the pleasure of mastery with pain. So when your child complains about how hard something is or how frustrating it is not to be able to do it better, say, "It is actually really good you are feeling that way. That means you are stretching yourself. And that means you are getting better. Soon you will feel some satisfaction. Just keep at it. You'll see."

11

RECOGNITION: THE BRIDGE
FROM LONGING TO BELONGING

Although mastery is its own reward, another crucial element reinforces mastery while also leading on to a wider feeling of connectedness. That element is recognition, the feeling of being valued by others, especially others whose opinions the person respects.

Charles Ducey of Harvard University taught me the phrase "from longing to belonging," and while he said self-effacingly, "It is too cute by half," I think it pinpoints perfectly what recognition, when properly given and received, can do.

Think back. Can you remember when a really demanding teacher said to you, "Good job," and you felt yourself float up about ten feet into the air? Or do you remember one teacher who gave you a specific compliment on a specific day that inspired you to do some of your best work that year? Maybe it was in third grade or fifth grade, maybe tenth grade. But most adults can remember one teacher or coach who inspired them to do excellent work—and to feel really good about themselves—simply by offering strategically placed bits of recognition.

Indeed, an adult's major field of interest is often originally determined not by innate talent or curiosity but by some recognition a teacher or coach gave her when she was young. That bit of recognition then so inspired and motivated the child that that teacher's subject or that coach's sport became the child's passion—and the passion lasted the rest of her life.

Recognition can be seemingly trivial, like being asked to shake out the erasers one day or being placed at the front of the line for lunch. Giving a child responsibility, especially when it is unexpected, can be the first step in the making of a president of the United States or a major CEO.

Parents, teachers, and coaches can exert a tremendous positive influence through the recognition they offer. We adults too quickly forget how much it meant to us back then—but it meant the world to us, and to children today it still does.

It also matters who provides the recognition. You might think that I could have hired a bowling teacher for Jack and Jack would have achieved the same skill at bowling, maybe even better. But of course, it was more than a skill that I wanted Jack to acquire. I wanted him to acquire a memory of doing this with me, I wanted him to acquire a feeling of teamwork with me, and most of all I wanted him to know I wanted to be there. I wanted him to feel recognition from someone he loved.

Recognition can make the difference between joyless achievement and joyful mastery. Once you know that what you have done matters to people who matter to you, then what you have done becomes more uplifting to you. You feel more closely connected to the people who have recognized you. Just as practice builds the bridge from play to mastery, so recognition builds the bridge from mastery back to connection.

When you learn to do something well and someone else values your having done this, you feel a sense of pride within yourself but also a feeling of connection outside yourself, a connection to the person who recognizes what you have done and to the larger group that person represents.

For example, when I learned to ride my bike and Jamie, my cousin, praised me for it, I felt more connected both to him and to the world of bike riders he represented. I could proudly take my place in the world of people who could ride a bike.

However, be careful with how you provide or seek recognition. Recognition is so powerful, it can become dangerous. Some children (and adults) hunger for recognition like a drug they can't live without.

This is because they are using the recognition not to connect with the larger group but to *separate* from it, to rise above it. They crave praise and recognition not as a means of connecting but as a means of proving they are better than others, a means of disconnecting from them.

This is the great danger of praise and recognition, especially in a competitive world like ours. If a child or an adult needs recognition solely as a means of rising above others, the person can become what mental health professionals call a narcissist: he can feel pleasure only when others admire him, and his appetite for admiration becomes insatiable. Such a person can't truly love or give other people positive feelings. The narcissist is desperately unhappy, even if he achieves at a very high level, as many do.

He is unhappy because he is so alone. The moment he feels close to someone else, he feels he must gain that person's admiration and adoration; he then gives a beautiful performance in order to suck out of that person the admiration that that person has to give. Once the person is sucked dry, the narcissist loses interest and moves on to another prospect. Like emotional vampires, narcissists live off of the lifeblood of other people.

But do not think that all praise leads to narcissism. Perhaps because recognition can be so dangerous, we sometimes teach our children that it is wrong or "selfish" to want or enjoy any praise. After all, we don't want our kids to become narcissistic little monsters. But all children, like all adults, need a certain amount of praise.

If we puritanically discourage a child from taking any pride in her achievements, and if we teach her that it is "unseemly" to enjoy praise, then we send her a message almost as dangerous as what we are hoping to avoid. We send her the message that it is shameful to feel good about what you do or to enjoy the praise of other people.

This child is the opposite of the budding narcissist. This child is on her way to a life of low self-esteem, passivity in relationships and work, and very little joy in anything that she does. Pincers of guilt will pluck out any tendrils of pride that might try to grow inside her, leaving her a barren inner landscape devoid of anything pretty at all.

These two miserable extremes are not rare. But both can be avoided.

The crucial differentiating factor between the narcissist's unremitting appetite for praise and the normal person's healthy enjoyment of mastery and praise goes back to connectedness, the first factor in the five-step cycle. If a child (or an adult) feels comfortably and securely connected in the world, then he will not need to hoard recognition and praise, as a starved person would desperately hoard food; instead, he will want to bring it back to his group proudly and share it. He will use the praise not to separate from the group but to contribute to the strength of the group. He will be proud that he is pulling his weight, maybe even more than his share of the weight, not so as to go off and be alone and above it all but rather to enjoy his connection with the group and increase the chances that the group will prosper and endure.

The group may be a family, a team, the fifth grade, the world of people who can ride bikes or bowl, or any group of which a person feels a part. One reason that narcissism is so rampant among both adults and children today is that so many people do not feel a part of any group at all. They feel disconnected. Disconnected people can turn to achievement and recognition like drugs. Every day—every hour, even—they need a "fix." If they do not get one, they become angry or depressed or both. Instead of reaching out to others for help, they then use their often considerable talents to take revenge upon those who have not given them what they want, their fix of praise and recognition, by achieving even more in the hopes of making that praise and recognition unavoidable. "I'll show them" is their refrain. They dream of being able to lord it over what soon becomes, in their minds, the entire world. They entertain fantasies of being all-powerful, of being Bill Gates or Tiger Woods, not as a means of giving back or joining in but as a means of taking revenge and receiving coronation.

The other extreme, the joyless adult who learned as a child that it was wrong to take pride in anything, is less flamboyant than the narcissist, and so her plight may not be detected, even as a child. These people suffer in silence. They smile when they should, they say, "Thank you," when praised, and they never put up a fuss or go off in a snit to pout. If only they would, we might discover how unhappy they are.

Instead, they defer to others as a matter of course. They pick up on what others need, and they provide it. They please others, not to gain admiration or recognition but because they would feel guilty if they did not. They would feel as if they had let that person down. While the hunger for recognition and praise is what drives the narcissist, the fear of not pleasing others is what drives the joyless individual. This person feels intensely uncomfortable when noticed or singled out in a positive way, so she quickly defers to someone else. She feels ashamed and unworthy at being praised.

Such intense discomfort with feelings of praise makes positive self-esteem, one of the key ingredients to happiness in life, all but impossible. This person feels that it is *wrong* to feel good about who she is. She is the opposite of self-centered: she practically has no self on which to center; she intentionally negates her sense of self.

Such an attitude gets its start in childhood. Like the narcissist, this person never learned how to deal with recognition in a healthy way. Such is the power of recognition that if it is not handled with care, it can twist a psyche into a permanently painful shape.

The way to prevent both of the painful shapes I have described is to provide healthy connections, especially a connected childhood. It is all but impossible to find an adult narcissist or an adult self-negator who tells you he or she had a warmly connected childhood.

But if you provide as connected a childhood as you can, then praise and recognition will not become addictive drugs or feared substances. Rather, they will expand and deepen the growing feelings of connectedness. Recognition then makes the child feel that she belongs to the group, because she is doing something that the group values. It will make her more inclined to do for others, rather than lord it over others or negate herself, because she feels joined to them, convinced that they like her and she likes them, and that it is OK to like and be liked.

Learning how to deal with recognition is particularly important for adolescents. The main reason so many teenagers can be sullen, ungrateful, angry, and rejecting of adults is that they feel disconnected from the adult world. They feel they do not belong. They are no longer little kids, who can ask to be taken care of, but neither are they independent adults who can make a living and come and go as they please. They are caught between these two worlds. Often their only source of connection is their peer group. This is why peers exert such a crucial influence upon adolescents.

As an adolescent gains recognition from the adult world, by earning a wage at a job or by receiving awards from a school or simply by being complimented on doing a job well, the adolescent feels more connected to the larger world he is about to enter. The praise and recognition in this way build a bridge to the connection to the adult world the adolescent is (secretly) hoping to feel.

Let me give you an example from my own life. When I was in the twelfth grade, I was feeling pretty inept as a person. My twelfth-grade English teacher, Fred Tremallo, handed back a short story I wrote early in the year with a comment, "Why don't you turn this into a novel?"

A novel? I thought to myself. *I can barely write a three-page story.* When I asked Mr. Tremallo if he really meant that I should try to write a novel, he simply nodded, yes.

I admired Mr. Tremallo. He was one cool dude. He had a mustache and used to be in the Secret Service. He also was a published writer himself. If he thought I could write a novel . . .

I also felt a taste of what the narcissist might feel as well as the self-negator. I felt, *He thinks I can write a novel? Wow, I must be really special!* But I also felt, *Why me? I'm not good enough. Why does he have to lay this on me?* Most of us have partaken of the two extremes now and then, enough to know of their dangers and habit-forming potential.

What kept me from getting stuck in either extreme was my upbringing. I had been raised imperfectly, as most of us were; but I had been raised skillfully enough not to get stuck in either trap recognition can set.

So I did what I had learned to do. I did my homework, as asked. I slowly started adding pages to my three-page story. Page by page, the manuscript grew. Mr. Tremallo penned comments all along the way. He offered encouragement as well as many corrections and criticisms.

By the end of the year, I had done something that I thought at the beginning of the year was flat-out impossible. I had written a three hundred–page novel. To my amazement it won the Senior English

Prize, still the prize I value most of any I have ever received (which aren't all that many!).

The project began in my connection with Fred Tremallo. Then, it led to play (writing), discipline and practice (Fred's comments, my continued writing), a taste of mastery, followed by recognition, the prize.

When I received the prize, I felt as if I belonged. I felt as if I could hold my head up high among my peers. I had found something that I could do well. The recognition I received made me feel much more a part of the community at my school, and the community of people in general, than I had felt before I received the prize.

Let me offer one more example, this from the life of Lucy, my daughter. I came home one evening to find Lucy crying. She was sitting at the kitchen table. In front of her was her seventh-grade science project, a model she had made of the human heart and lungs. The assignment had been to think of some physical analogy for what the heart and lungs do and then build a model of it. You were not supposed to build an actual heart-and-lung model but a model of some other entity that could resemble what the heart and lungs do. Lucy chose to make a model of an airport, where each plane comes in to drop off and pick up passengers as blood cells come into the heart and lungs to drop off and pick up gases.

She did a great job, or so I thought, until I came home to find her crying. Then she announced to me that she had got the whole assignment wrong, that when she reread it, she discovered she was supposed to show all the blood vessels and chambers of the heart, and she couldn't do that with her "stupid airport model."

At that point I wanted to call the teacher and tell her the assignment was way too hard for the seventh grade and that she didn't know anything about children. But thank goodness, I resisted. I also resisted my temptation to take over and try to fix the project for Lucy.

Instead, I just sat down and calmly reassured Lucy that she would find a way to fix it. I also tried to make her laugh, and gradually I succeeded. Once she started to laugh, her spunk and creativity kicked in. Soon she was asking me to go down to the drugstore to get some pipe cleaners and nail polish, which she would turn into the blood vessels, while she borrowed some of her brothers' LEGOs, which she turned into the chambers of the heart. Within a few hours, she had redone the science project. Other than providing moral support and going to the drugstore, I had done nothing at all.

The next morning she took the project to school. She felt good about what she had done. She had suffered some pain and touched a bit of mastery. She had moved from connection through play to discipline to mastery. But what kind of recognition would she receive? And what would the effect of it be?

She handed in the project but had to wait to hear what the teacher thought. Other students had said they liked it, but it was the teacher's assessment on which Lucy focused. A few days later, she found out that she had received an A− on the project. Jack chided her, "Why the minus?" but Lucy felt proud. The recognition provided by the grade solidified her sense that hard work can pay off and that even when all seems lost, there is still hope.

Recognition, then, is like a welder's torch. It can connect you to important feelings within yourself and to the outside world. But, if it is not used with care, it can also cripple what we hope it will strengthen.

The Great Harvard Fallacy

This is an example of how the pursuit of recognition can actually do damage.

What I call the "Great Harvard Fallacy" is the overemphasis on a certain achievement as the means of finding happiness in life. In the case of children in America, getting into Harvard (or some other prestige college) can often become that magical goal.

The fallacy is not about Harvard. It is about what many people turn Harvard into, a magical goal worth any price to attain. It is about what Samuel Johnson called "the secret ambush of a specious prayer." Or put more colloquially, it is about how important it is to be careful of what you pray for because you just might get it.

The magical goal may not be Harvard, it may be Yale or Princeton or Stanford or Duke or the University of Texas or West Point. It may not be a college at all but a profession, like being a doctor or a professional athlete. It may not be a profession but a rank, like admiral or professor or CEO. It may not be a rank but a prize, like an Olympic gold medal or the Nobel Prize. Whatever it is, Harvard or some Harvard equivalent, it comes to symbolize the goal that, once attained, confers a godlike status upon the one who attains it. To reach this goal, many people believe, is to be transformed from ordinary to extraordinary and to find the key to happiness. Unfortunately, rather than opening the door to happiness, the pursuit of this key can lock that door forever.

It is a classic case of the tail wagging the dog, the ends justifying the means, and putting the cart before the horse. We have so many clichés to describe it because it is such a common psychological trap. If you fall into this trap, you can do great damage to a child even while you believe you are helping him.

If you stop and think, you will perceive the fallacy immediately. What determines success and happiness in life, *of course,* is not the quality of the college to which a person goes but the quality of the person who goes to the college. Unfortunately many children, and even some parents, are growing up believing precisely the opposite. They subscribe to the cynical and demonstrably false belief that the name of the college will confer success upon them.

A study done by Alan Krueger of Princeton and Stacy Berg Dale of the Andrew W. Mellon Foundation, published in 1999, showed that the immediate advantage in earning power conferred by elite colleges was slight, about 7 percent, and over time was vastly overshadowed by the qualities the individual brought to the college rather than the name of the institution. For example, Jack Welch, former CEO of General Electric, graduated from the University of Massachusetts, a good but not prestigious school.

In their study Dale and Krueger found that certain specific qualities mattered much more than the name of the college in predicting future earning power. These qualities included imagination, ambition, perseverance, maturity, discipline, and some exceptional ability.

If parents and teachers focused on developing those qualities—as the five-step approach I outline in this book does—then success and college admission will take care of themselves. The horse will precede the cart, and the dog will wag its tail.

If you focus on helping your child develop into a good person who does her best to develop her talents and interests as well as her concern for other people, then "success," however you define it, will follow in proper proportion. In addition, you have some control over the outcome.

In the Great Harvard Lottery, you do not have control. You can jump through every hoop, meet every possible criterion for admission, and still not get in. If you have set your heart and soul on getting into Harvard and do all that you were told to do to make sure you get in, and then you are turned down, that can be traumatic. It is also avoidable. Just don't fall into the trap set by the Great Harvard Fallacy.

I have a close friend whose son just went off to college. My friend, whom I'll call Alex, is an alumnus of Harvard, and his son was a stellar student at his high school, getting straight A's and an 800 and a 790 on his SATs (that's a total of 1,590 out of a possible 1,600). He was also on three varsity sports teams and was captain of the tennis team. In addition he was widely liked and admired by his peers and teachers. You would have thought he'd be a shoo-in for Harvard. But no. He did not get in.

What impressed me was how well he and his parents handled the rejection. They were surprised but far from devastated. They knew there was no guarantee; as I mentioned in Chapter 1, Harvard could fill its freshman class with valedictorians if it chose to. Moreover, they knew and believed that it did not matter all that much. Sure, it would have been wonderful to get into Harvard; it is a great college, and it does have a lot of prestige. But they knew that admission to Harvard was not nearly as significant as the process of trying to get in can make it feel. They knew that what really mattered had already been achieved. This young man was on his way to success and happiness because of who he had become, not because of what college he was going to.

From the colleges he did get into, he chose Bates. He enthusiastically enrolled in the fall of 2001. I can promise you that this young man will contribute a lot to this world and that he will be happy within it.

While he applied to Harvard, neither he nor his parents fell into the Great Harvard Fallacy.

But many children are tarnishing the best moments of their lives—their childhoods—in frantic pursuit of a certain goal, like getting into Harvard, in the belief that this is the only sure way to a good life. Unfortunately it is not "the only way," nor is it "sure."

All of these goals—going to a great college, winning Olympic gold—are in themselves wonderful. Harvard is a great college, being a doctor is a fine profession, CEOs keep businesses humming, and our Nobel Prize winners advance knowledge to the benefit of us all.

But when the goals become too important, they become dangerous. They can tyrannize your adult life or, worse, your childhood. If you create within your child the feeling that she is only as good as her latest achievement, that feeling will turn into a lifelong curse. Instead of equipping her for happiness, that feeling makes happiness impossible. She will feel that no matter what she has done, she has never done enough.

The two paramount dangers are these: First, if you fail to reach your goal, you may think you are worthless. Second, what you do in order to reach the goal may prevent you from developing into your true, best self.

It takes great restraint for a parent not to slip into the Great Harvard Fallacy. It stands there inviting us parents to fall in like a psychological Grand Canyon. Most victims even run full speed ahead and jump. After all, who doesn't want the best for their children? And isn't Harvard the best?

The key fact to hold on to in order to keep from falling into this dangerous trap is that there is no best college for all students. There are best matches between college and student, but no one best college all students should aspire to attend; just as there is no "best" profession, just best matches between individual and profession; and no "best" spouses, just best matches. Just as the concept of "smart" damages many children, so the concept of a "best" college leaves many first-rate students feeling second-rate.

Wanting "the best" for your child creates major problems if you do not take into account what "the best" means for the specific child you have. If you ever talk to college placement officers in high schools or admissions officers in elite private elementary schools (and even nursery schools!), you will hear horror stories of the Great Harvard Fallacy in action. They will tell you that some parents are prepping their children from the moment they are born to join the ranks of what author David Brooks called in a cover story in the *Atlantic Monthly* (April 2001) the Organization Kids, a group of young people he believes will become "the next ruling class." These are the super-achieving, extrahardworking, polite, and well-washed individuals who gain admission to the Harvards around the country. Unlike their parents, who were rebellious and wanted to "change the system," these kids compete fiercely to join the system and rise to the top of it.

A high school student told me that she and a friend had talked about committing suicide if they got rejected by Harvard. She told me such talk was not uncommon at her school, a public school in an affluent suburb of Boston. Students and parents can lose their better judgment as they pursue the worthwhile goal of gaining admission to a good college.

The process can become a bit crazy, when parents are angling for their toddlers to get into the right nursery school because that increases their chances of getting into the right elementary school because that increases their chances of getting into the right secondary school because that increases their chances of getting into the right college because that increases their chances of getting into the right medical school (or law school or graduate school) because that increases their chances of getting the best residency (or clerkship or firm or company) because that increases their chances of making professor or earning a billion dollars or winning the Nobel Prize because that increases their chances of, on a distant day, maybe, feeling good about the life they are leading.

Some young children perceive the folly of all this. I have a friend who has a lively eight-year-old son named Bobby. He goes to a public school near Boston that is, like most public schools around the country, frantically concerned about the test scores and achievement records of its students, often at the expense of common sense. In the August before Bobby was to start third grade, he received a form letter from the school that began, "Welcome to Third Grade!" and then went on with three pages of detailed academic expectations for the coming year.

When Bobby's mom showed him the letter, he started to read it, then threw it on the floor. "That is pathetic!" he exclaimed in disgust. "I'm still on vacation. I'll hear all that soon enough." I asked his mother if she really used the word *pathetic*. She assured me he did.

Boy, do I wish Bobby served on school committees around the country. Maybe he could remind the adults that something much more important is going on during the summer of an eight-year-old's life than hearing about the curriculum of the third grade—something that should be protected.

Scene: At a parents' night at a local school, I have been asked to discuss the question of college admissions. In my talk I make the point that not all children will, or should, go to Harvard. During the Q&A I am questioned by a father, along these lines:

"Dr. Hallowell, you noted that not all of our children will go to Harvard. Could you please advise us what we can do to increase the chances that they will?"

"Well," I reply, "Harvard uses the same admissions criteria as other colleges—grades, SAT scores, extracurricular activities, teacher recommendations, whether or not other family members attended Harvard, and the personal interview. So the better your child does on all of those, the more likely he or she will get in. But tell me, do you think it matters a huge amount if your child goes to Harvard?"

"Of course it does!" shoots back the reply. "Harvard opens doors."

"How much of a sacrifice," I ask, "do you think it is worth making to go to Harvard?"

"Almost any sacrifice," comes the reply. "I would give my right arm for my son and daughter to go there."

"Why?" I ask.

"Isn't it obvious? So they can have more opportunities in life!"

"But what if they are not meant to go to Harvard? Would you want them to go there anyway?"

"What do you mean, 'not meant to go'? If they get in, they're meant to go!"

"That's not true. Even the Harvard admissions committee will tell you that it makes mistakes. But what I'm more concerned about is your assumption that getting into Harvard is worth any sacrifice, as if Harvard were the ticket to a happy life. I can tell you, as a matter of fact, that there are happy adults in this world who did not go to Harvard, and there are miserable adults in this world who did. What if all the pressure you put on your children to get into Harvard sours their outlook on life? Is it worth souring children on life to get them into Harvard?"

"Damn right it is," the dad replies.

I doubt that that father, and the millions of others like him, knows what a chance he is taking. Many parents—good, well-meaning parents—infect their children's childhood, and especially their high school years, with a high-pressure message that the goal of life is to get into Harvard or some other school or to make some team or to break some record or to get chosen for some honor—without ever really examining what is being sacrificed to reach that goal.

This is especially dangerous if the child does not reach the goal. For example, Harvard rejects about 85 percent of those who apply, and the vast majority of applicants have the credentials to get in. If the goal of getting in has come to mean too much, then the child is left to feel that he has failed in a major way and that his life is significantly flawed. I have a patient who at age fifty still feels second-rate, even though he has achieved spectacular success, because he "only" went to Lehigh University.

Just for the skeptics, here is a list of individuals who not only did not graduate from Harvard, they did not graduate from any college at all: Edward Albee, Woody Allen, Andrew Carnegie, Walter Cronkite, William Faulkner, Shelby Foote, Bill Gates, Barry Goldwater, Alex Haley, Nat Hentoff, Tom Hanks, Peter Jennings, Fran Lebowitz, Doris

Lessing, Abraham Lincoln, Bill Murray, Jack Nicholson, Anaïs Nin, S. I. Newhouse, Neil Simon, Eleanor Roosevelt, Robert Redford, Margaret Sanger, William Howard Taft, Harry Truman, Ted Turner, Frank Lloyd Wright, and John Wayne, to name but a few. Presidents, tycoons, stars of all kinds.

The fact is that while 75 percent of American high school graduates enroll in college, only about 25 percent ever graduate. And in the achievement of college degrees, the United States is number two in the world, behind only Canada. In Germany, for example, 13 percent of the population has a college degree, and in Japan it's 23 percent. One of the myths under which parents labor is that success in life depends on a college degree, especially a degree from a prestige college.

I am a parent whose children are still in grade school. I have not yet gone through what I have seen can be the agonizing process of college admissions with my kids. For now I am trying to follow my own advice with my children and focus on protecting their first fifteen years so they can connect and play and practice and achieve mastery and enjoy recognition. If they do that, if they have a childhood, they will be much better equipped to contend with the pressures and preoccupations of adulthood when they get there than if they were introduced to them at the age of five.

This issue of goals is a difficult one for all parents. I know it is for Sue and me. We want our children to try their best, and we hope their best translates into high grades and maybe even admission to Harvard or some other prestige college. But if it does not, we will (I hope) not be disappointed. We will recognize our children for having done their best. We will recognize them for who they are, not what we might wish them to be. And that is the kind of recognition children need most.

Feeling Recognized and Valued for Who You Are

As I mentioned in Chapter 5, recognition helps most when you're not wearing a disguise.

Many children strive to act or be a certain way, not because that is who they naturally are but because that is the way they believe they have to act in order to gain approval and love.

A boy whose father desperately wants him to play baseball may feign an interest in baseball, not because he likes the game but because he wants to please his father. A girl whose mother always regretted not having played the violin may play the violin, not because she likes it but, once again, to please her mother.

Boys and girls who feel attracted to members of the same sex may pretend not to feel that way in order to please not only their parents but the rest of the world. Many, if not most, homosexual adults can relate heart-wrenching stories of secrecy, shame, and a desperate fear of being exposed throughout their childhoods.

On the other hand, when you feel understood and valued for who you truly feel yourself to be, that is a golden moment. You begin to feel that there is a place for you in the world. You begin to feel that you belong. This leads you to want to do more and strengthens your connection to the wider world.

It is important for parents and teachers to always look for the real child, not the pretend child or the idealized child. It is the real child who needs our love. It is the real child who needs our help. And it is the real child who will be with us for years to come.

Moments of recognition can happen in a flash.

One morning not long ago, Lucy was arguing about some trivial issue with her mother as they were getting ready to walk out the door to go to school. Suddenly Lucy stopped and looked down at Sue's shoes. Sue instantly knew Lucy was questioning her choice of shoes, and she explained, "Oh, I'm wearing these because it is muddy outside." Lucy nodded, as if to say that made those shoes acceptable, then they went back to hashing out their little disagreement.

In that very brief moment, Lucy felt both recognized and valued. One of Lucy's talents that she values most is her fashion sense. She has an amazing eye for details and a strong aesthetic sense when it comes to clothes. This receives no recognition on her report card, and sometimes leads to teasing from her brothers, but it is a serious interest for Lucy. In fact, she says she'd like to go to Parsons School of Design in

New York, which a friend has told her is the best school for that sort of thing.

When, in the midst of an argument with her mother, Lucy paused and looked at Sue's shoes, and Sue responded by also ceasing to argue for a moment to justify her wearing less-than-lovely shoes, I am sure that Lucy felt complimented. She felt recognized and valued by her mother for something that mattered a great deal to Lucy. That Sue did it inadvertently made it even better, because there could be no doubt about the sincerity of the gesture.

Neither Sue nor I ever dreamed for Lucy to become a fashion designer as we rocked her in her crib. But believe me, if becoming a fashion designer is where Lucy's passion lies, nothing could make me happier than to see her pursue that career. Sue and I recognize and value Lucy for who she is, even as she surprises us all the time.

12

TEACHING JACK TO FISH: PLANTING THE SEEDS OF JOY

I can't fish worth beans. If I am going to lead my children through the steps I advocate from connection on to mastery and recognition, what am I supposed to do if I am not a master of much myself?

There are many potential sources of lifelong joy to which I want to introduce my children, but I am limited in my skills, fishing being just one of those (very) limited skills. I am also not much of an athlete; I am not much of a carpenter; I know nothing about hunting; I can't fix cars; I'm not savvy in business; I'm not particularly good with my hands; if I ever got mugged, I couldn't put up much of a fight; I can't play a musical instrument; I'm low on street smarts; I am not a cool guy or dude—whatever the right word would be, I wouldn't know it— and I don't have any unusual skills or traits, like being a magician or being double-jointed, that a child might find, well, awesome.

Being a father is humbling. I wish—oh, how I wish—I had been a professional baseball player or something awesome like that, or I wish I were one of those dads who oozes confidence or, if not that, maybe, at least, I could have been blessed with the talent of sawing wood well. But no.

The only equipment I have for being a dad is my desire to be one. Thank goodness, that seems to be enough.

I can learn how to do those other things, like fishing, well enough to guide my kids. I don't have to be an expert. All I have to do is be willing to open the door.

I try to open the door for my children to as many possible skills and pleasures as I can. That means I have to be willing to try things I don't know much about, or even like, from fishing to whistling to shining a shoe. Actually I quite like whistling and am pretty good at it. Usually you find you have a knack for some of the things your kids, and you, want to do.

It is crucial that I keep introducing them to new activities, even if it means that I feel foolish or bored, as I do sometimes when I fish. It is crucial because I am planting seeds. Each activity a child takes up is a seed that might just grow into a lifelong pleasure or even passion.

These seeds beget the childhood roots of adult happiness.

The more activities you have that you like to do simply because you like to do them, the greater your chances of living a happy life (as long as they are reasonably safe and legal). Even though I listed earlier the many things I can't do well, there are activities I enjoy—like playing tennis and squash, writing, listening to music, following professional sports, daydreaming, and cooking—that I learned as a child and that continue to this day to give me great pleasure.

It is important to develop reliable, safe sources of pleasure. Most of the trouble that adults get into comes from not having constructive ways of deriving pleasure from everyday life. This leads to the pursuit of pleasure in dangerous or wasteful ways. Eating too much, drinking too much, making love with the wrong person, craving money so much that principles are forgotten—all these and more reflect an inability to find sufficient pleasure in useful ways.

We ought to take seriously the effort to introduce our children to pleasure. We should be at least as diligent about it as we are about getting them to brush their teeth. We should help them find sources of joy to which they can turn their whole lives long, sources of joy that are not damaging or dangerous. If children don't learn how to find pleasure in adaptive ways, then they will probably find maladaptive ways or simply become resigned to quiet desperation.

I think on every report card there should be a category that covers joy. After a child's grades in English and math and other subjects, there should be an entry labeled "Potential Sources of Lifelong Joy in Which This Student Has Shown an Interest," and then those sources should be named. This subject, let's call it lifelong joy, deserves a lot more attention in school—and everywhere else—than it gets. The five-step process I recommend in this book is a good, systematic way of encouraging the development of reliable sources of lifelong joy.

Many unhappy adults never developed constructive sources of pleasure when they were young. Some relied too heavily on the destructive sources, like drugs or alcohol, or vegging out, and so they never learned how to find lasting pleasure from any constructive activity. Others stayed away from the destructive pleasures, but they didn't find enjoyment in anything. They merely achieved. They did all that was expected of them, and some even did more, but they never did much that they actually *liked*. So when they got old enough to do what they wanted, they didn't know what they wanted, or they turned to desperate or dangerous pleasures, never having learned how to find extraordinary joy in ordinary life.

I'll bet you know adults like that. "Successful" people who have no joy in their lives. I'll bet you also know adults who have none of the conventional trappings of success but who are extremely happy in their lives.

It is easy to overlook how important it is to help kids learn how to find pleasure in positive ways. Each school night my main concern is that Lucy get her homework done, not find sources of lifelong joy; and that Jack do his homework and chores and brush his teeth; and that Tucker take a bath if he needs one and get into his p.j.'s on time. So much has to get done, it is easy to forget the larger purposes we have in mind.

That's why it is good to step back and make sure that all your busy activity each day and night with and for your children is in fact leading them to develop constructive sources of joy that can last a lifetime.

So while we focus on helping them get their work done, we shouldn't fall into the trap of overemphasizing achievement at the expense of joy. Ideally the two go hand in hand, but that takes some time. Just ask Lucy, while she practices her violin. It is my hope that she will enjoy playing the violin for the rest of her life, but it has not been easy to learn the skill well enough to enjoy the activity.

As her teacher says, "No matter how much talent you have, you still have to work your butt off."

How does lifelong joy fit into that? This is where teachers, parents, coaches, and friends become crucial. They keep up your spirits as you do the work of finding fun in what at first might feel painful, like practicing the violin or running a long distance or trying to carve a bird out of a piece of wood or trying to speak French.

But learning these more difficult routes to joy is what leads to life-long happiness.

The road to happiness runs from connection through play to practice and discipline on to mastery and recognition. High achievement and material success are often the by-products of this route, but they are not the primary goals.

It can start with fishing.

I have a friend who loves to fish. No matter where he goes, he takes his fishing rod and tackle box with him if at all possible, just in case he finds a body of water that might have a fish in it. When he goes fishing, he is utterly at ease. He is both relaxed and full of excitement at the same time. Relaxed excitement. That's a good state to be in.

I have fished with him in many settings. I have fished with him for bluefish off Cape Cod in his small boat (he is not wealthy, but he is able to afford a small boat for fishing); I have fished with him in streams in Maine; I have fished with him on a lake in Connecticut; and I have fished with him standing on a beach casting into the Atlantic Ocean. For a person like me who is not much of a fisherman, my friend makes fishing enough fun that with him I actually like to do it.

Sometimes I watch him fishing when he doesn't know I am watching. He looks a lot like my son Tucker looks when he is playing by himself in his room. He is totally engaged with what he is doing and seems delighted to be doing it, whether the fish are biting or not. This friend of mine will always have one hand on happiness as long as he can fish.

He started fishing when he was a boy. His uncle taught him how. They would go out early in the morning or at the end of the day, and they would catch bluefish or bass or whatever was biting. At first, when he was a kid, it was catching the fish that made him love fishing.

But then, he told me, the pleasure of the activity expanded beyond just catching fish to encompass the whole enterprise, including thinking about fishing when he wasn't fishing, reading reports of tides and weather to plan future trips, talking to other fishermen about what was biting and what wasn't, what bait was working and what was not, what they'd caught, what he'd caught, and on and on. Not being a fisherman myself, I didn't instantly understand what he meant, but I could certainly hear the many years of enthusiasm in his voice.

When his uncle took him fishing for the first time, I wonder if either of them knew that this boy was embarking on one of the most important days of his life, a day that led to a journey that would last all his days, a journey of finding and catching fish, which amounted to finding and catching happiness.

Childhood is the time to plant these pleasures. If only one of the seeds grows and lasts, that's just fine. Many people have none. If, as an adult, you can have one activity you love that is safe, legal, and affordable, you are blessed. You will always have something to look forward to; you will always have the means of a happy moment in your grasp.

Maybe it is fishing. Maybe it is reading. Maybe it is playing music. Maybe it is more interpersonal, like creating groups or planning parties or bringing friends together in a convivial way. Whatever it is, if you have such a passion, you are lucky. Most of the time, these passions get their start in childhood.

Now, as I write this book, I am away with Sue and my kids at a cottage on Lake Doolittle, where we have been renting for fifteen years. All summer Lucy has been organizing her birthday party. She was born on July 16, but Lucy has postponed her party to August, when we would be at the cottage, some three hours' drive from Boston. She has invited five of her friends to come out to visit us for three days in celebration of her birthday. The logistics of setting this up have been as convoluted as a snarled fishing line. But Lucy has been working them out, with the help of her mom and her friends' moms.

There will be nothing special about this party, except that it will occur at a lake in an old cottage. Lucy has been looking forward to it for weeks, and she has been working hard to set it up. This morning I heard her talking on the telephone with one of the friends who is coming. She was laughing and whispering and laughing again. I didn't hear the words, but I heard the tone, which was bubbling over with life-at-its-best. It seems to me that my most important job as a dad is to protect the time and space for Lucy to do this sort of thing. She is developing a skill, a life skill, as she sets up this party, and she is having fun at the same time.

You can see in Lucy's planning the five steps I have outlined. First, she is connecting with her friends. Then, as she plans, she is playing with ideas of how to make the party and what to do. Setting it up requires her to practice and apply discipline: she has to juggle schedules, figure out who will sleep where and how much food we'll need, and so on. As she sets up what is turning out to be a complicated event, she is mastering a difficult task, namely, organizing friends and planning a party. And when the five girls arrive and they have their three days together, Lucy will feel the pleasure not only of having her birthday recognized but of having her ability to do something complicated recognized as well.

Sue and I (mostly Sue) have been caught up in the headaches of setting up this party—the phone being tied up, the difficulty of reaching parents, the troubles in dealing with changes of schedule, and the challenges of finding enough places for everyone to sleep—so we haven't always kept in mind what a good experience this is for Lucy. She is learning how to deal with adversity and create and sustain joy; she is planting seeds of adult happiness.

What you can see in Lucy's party planning, you can also see in my friend's fishing: the five steps I have mentioned. In my friend's case, it began with the connection to his uncle; then led to playing, the act of catching fish; then led to practice, which continues to this day; then led to mastery, which still grows even now; and led on to recognition, first by his uncle, then by the ever-widening world of his fishing friends; which, in turn, reinforced his connection with the act of fishing itself and with his feeling for his now-deceased uncle.

I don't suppose his uncle knew what a seed he was planting, but it turned out to be one of the most important seeds that was ever planted in this man's life.

I am going to try to follow up on the interest my sons developed in fishing when my friend took them recently. Lucy has stated she has *no* interest in fish; she is busy with her party.

As I said, I am a lousy fisherman, but I want to try to do for my sons (and for Lucy, if she ever changes her mind) what my friend's uncle did for him. Even though I do not know how to fish very well, I can rig up a line and take a hook out of a fish's mouth. I can do the basics. And that's really all it takes to plant the seed.

I don't know if this summer's attempt at fishing will lead to lifelong pleasure for my children, but it is worth a try. I imagine it will provide some funny stories, maybe of dad getting a hook in the seat of his pants, maybe of Tucker catching an old boot, or who knows what.

It will also probably produce some disappointment. Like catching no fish. Or getting bitten by bugs. Or getting bitten by bugs while catching no fish.

In fact, it already has produced some disappointment. I told the kids the day before we went that we were going to a local bait-and-tackle store, and the boys said they were excited to go. Lucy said she was excited *not* to go, as she finds fishing distasteful.

As the hour approached for us to leave, a friend next door called and asked the kids if they wanted to go down to the local Dairy Queen and get a cone. The kids came running up to my office, where I was working on this book, and asked if they could go to Dairy Queen.

I got annoyed and said, "Don't you remember we were going to go to the fishing store? I thought you were excited about that. I guess you don't care." I sounded like a petulant child.

"No, Dad, we want to do that, too!" they protested. I was clearly disappointed that my efforts to plant this "lifelong pleasure" excited them so little that Dairy Queen could make them forget about it.

This is one of the frustrations of planting this kind of seed. Many of the seeds just blow away. Your kids will not always want to do what *you* want them to want to do. And you may be far more interested in their becoming interested than they are. (The notorious example of that is music lessons.)

Jack, however, picked up on my disappointment and said, "Dad, we really want to go to the fishing store. We just didn't know when you would be ready to go." Here's an example of one of my children ministering to me rather than vice versa. I am sure it happens much more often than I am aware of, which points out the intended double meaning of the title of this book. Not only do we plant the roots of adult happiness in childhood, but our children—and their childhoods—become one of the greatest sources of happiness for adults.

Well, the kids got their Dairy Queen, and after they came back, the boys and I went to the fishing store, or what I guess is more appropriately called the bait-and-tackle store. When we got there, a cheerful young man named Brody greeted us. Brody had a buzz cut and wore army fatigues, but beyond that he didn't fit the stereotype of an outdoorsman at all. He immediately understood when I told him I knew very little and needed his help in purchasing a basic rod, reel, and lures for my kids. Brody quickly had us fitted out with inexpensive spinning rods, a plastic tackle box ("Buy the one with two shelves," Brody advised. "It only costs a dollar more, and it holds a lot more"), a net for the fish we hoped we would catch, and a lesson on how to tie a fisherman's cinch knot.

We needed to learn this in order to tie the lures onto the fishing line. I asked if a square knot would suffice, as that was the only knot I knew how to tie, other than a bow. (As I told you, I don't know how to do much!) Brody didn't mock me; he simply shook his head. "You'll lose a lot of lures that way," he said. "Let me show you how to tie this."

Then he set down a length of line and demonstrated tying the knot. I had to run out to the car to get my reading glasses, which made me feel like an old fogy, but no one else seemed to care. My boys and I, along with Jack's friend Noah, stood at the counter practicing our fisherman's cinch knots for about fifteen minutes.

When we got home, it was dark. We took lures and tied them onto the lines of the three rods we had bought, then set aside the rods for the next day. Tucker passed on tying the knots, but Noah and Jack were good at it.

That night the boys slept outside in a tent. The next morning I woke up early, as I often do at that lake, and when I looked out the window, I saw a sight I will never forget.

Standing on the dock, only about one hundred feet away, were the three boys, Jack, Tucker, and Noah, fishing rods in hand. They must have awakened very early and tiptoed back up to the cottage to retrieve their new equipment. Now they were standing on the dock, whispering to one another—I had told them not to make noise when fishing so as not to scare away the fish—trying their hands at casting. Tucker was having a little bit of trouble, but the other two boys were able to cast their lures out pretty far.

I stepped quietly outside and stood and watched. Mists were gathering and rising up off the lake as the sun rose up over the trees. There were three boys—my two sons and a friend—learning how to fish. I could see Jack pause as he tried to get the sequence right: finger on line, flip the brake, tilt the rod back, then flip, let go of the finger, watch the lure arch up, then gently plop down into the water. Reel slowly in. Jack looked excited and relaxed.

This was what I had come all my life to see. This was what I had gone to school, become a doctor, got married, had children, earned a living, paid my taxes, and put up with hard times to find: children having a good childhood, embarking on a happy life.

Oh, no, I don't know that they'll be happy forever. And sure, I know they'll encounter hard times. I don't even know if they'll ever catch another fish.

But as I stood and watched them that morning as they fished off the dock, I felt more moved than if I had been looking at one of the eight wonders of the world. This was the wonder of my world. Nothing could have been better. I am sure it was just the first of many wonders for those kids.

13

WHAT GOES INTO A CONNECTED CHILDHOOD? A CLOSER LOOK

I have emphasized that in the five-step cycle, the most important step is the first one. Creating a connected childhood is the most important task in child rearing. It requires the help of many people, not just parents.

Sometimes people look at me at little vaguely when I talk about "a connected childhood." *Sounds good,* their eyes are telling me, *but what exactly do you mean? What am I supposed to do to create a connected childhood for my kids? I hope you're not going to tell me to quit my job or join a bunch of clubs or get married again, this time to a nice person. Do you have any suggestions that are practical? You know, things I can actually do?*

OK, practical suggestions. This chapter is devoted to practical suggestions for creating a connected childhood. I offer tips on each of the twelve kinds of connectedness that go into a connected childhood. Don't feel that you need to address every area; some will be impossible or simply of no interest to you. But if you can address more than one or two, you will be on your way to a connected life, for your child and for yourself. And connectedness is the most important ingredient of a happy life.

You will not find all of the suggestions helpful, of course. But as you read, you will probably find a few that you can use, and you will also make up many on your own.

Unconditional Love and Family Togetherness

This first element is the most crucial of all.

But take heart; you do not have to have a syrupy-sweet, perfect family in order to create a feeling of connectedness for your children. You do not have to be married; you do not have to subscribe to any particular belief system; you do not have to have had a great childhood yourself. All you have to do is put your love for your children into action.

There is conflict in connected families. In fact, the presence of conflict is a good indicator that there is a connection. So if you argue and get angry and yell and do all those things that families do, that's good! You are connecting.

Of course, how you work out your differences matters. A good, simple rule is, Always try to treat one another other with respect. And never resort to violence. That means don't hit, don't spank, don't use physical violence of any kind. I tell my kids, "I will never hit you, and I expect you never to hit me or one another." They do not always obey that rule, but at least that is the expectation.

These days one of the great obstacles to family connectedness is the pace of life. We are all so busy! To combat this, you need to make time for one another. Here are some suggestions for how to create a more connected family life:

• State the concept of connectedness explicitly, so you can refer to it when you are explaining why you are going to do something or not do something else. Say to your kids, "It really matters to us as a family that we create a feeling of togetherness or connectedness." Then let your kids talk about what that means and why they think it is important—or not important. It can make for some very interesting conversations!

• Make time for family dinner. No, you don't have to do it every night or even every other night, just do it as often as you can. Simply by making it a priority, it will happen more often than if it is a dispensable event. If you can't have family dinner, try having family breakfast. If you can't do that, maybe get together later in the evening after everyone has come home and have a bedtime snack. Making this time is essential. It is hard to develop a feeling of connectedness if you are never together.

• Try not to rule by intimidation. When you are setting limits on your children, do so respectfully, in the name of a principle—like fair play, sharing, or respecting the feelings of others—instead of just demanding a certain behavior because you are bigger and stronger. The same rule goes for dealing with your spouse. Children who bully other children usually learn this behavior at home, either by being bullied by their parents or by seeing one parent bully the other parent.

• Set up family celebrations, rituals, and traditional outings. The most obvious one is the birthday party. (By the way, you don't have to make your child's birthday party resemble the president's inaugural ball. Far from an event that promotes connectedness, an excessively lavish birthday party does precisely the opposite: it promotes envy, competition, and resentment.) In addition to birthday parties, set up holiday celebrations, like a Fourth of July cookout or a Memorial Day softball game, perhaps preceded by a visit to a cemetery to honor and remember family members who have died. Create traditions of your own, like going out for ice cream and a movie on a certain night or reserving Friday evenings for a family board-game night. Discuss with one another what traditions you'd like to set up, then do them, year after year after year. Also, it is great for family connectedness if you have certain daily rituals, like grace before a meal or a TV show you all watch together (yes, TV can be a force of connectedness!) or a game you all play in the car, like finding license plates from different states.

• Read aloud to your children for as long as they will let you. Reading aloud is one of the best activities you can do with children because not only does it promote connectedness, it also promotes literacy and growth of the imagination. A recent study showed that two of the activities that were most closely correlated with high SAT scores were eating family dinner together and being read aloud to as a child.

• Touch. Hug. Snuggle. Kiss. Pat. Wrestle. Roll. As much as I urge you not to hit or spank, I urge you to use physical touch as much as you can. Physical closeness in a family is one of life's greatest pleasures. With touch you can convey love in a much more primal, believable way than you can with words. When you say "I love you" to your children, after a while it almost becomes automatic and easy to ignore. But you can't ignore a hug. After a while, as your kids get older, they will start to resist your hugs and kisses. My advice? Hug and kiss them anyway. Of course, don't force them to do something they do not want to do, but you usually can find a way of hugging that is acceptable to even the most standoffish child, and a way of kissing as well. If you can't, then find some other way to offer physical touch if at all possible.

• Philosophize. I love listening to parents' advice. Even now, at my age, I find it reassuring. Even if your kids pretend to find it boring, offer your motherly or fatherly advice. This is a dying art. Kids need it. I am not referring to the angry diatribes we all find ourselves giving now and then but to the time-honored practice of sharing homespun philosophy. While your kids may roll their eyes and look very bored, chances are these words sink in much deeper than you think. Do you remember such musings from your parents? I sure do from mine. From my dad: You'll always be OK in life as long as you have one close friend. He said that all the time. And from my mom: Always look on the bright side. Simple sayings, nothing profound. The content doesn't really matter.

• Talk. Studies show that the number of words exchanged in families has declined as time spent watching TV and interacting online has risen. Find forums in which to talk—like riding in the car or sitting in the kitchen. Stick up for what you think is right as a parent. As your kids get older, it takes time and effort and a willingness to stay up into the middle of the night arguing about some issue if you are going to stick up for what you think is right. In disconnected families no one argues, because no one cares that much. People are too busy doing what they want to do to spend hours on end trying to supervise the behavior of others. Parents need to be parents. And one of the main jobs of being a parent is saying no and then enforcing what you have said.

• "Take pleasure in every day. Children grow up so fast." How many times have you heard this advice? But it is still the best and truest advice on how to be a parent. Above all else, enjoy your children. If you do, the rest usually takes care of itself. Don't spend all your time regulating them, fretting over them, controlling them, feeding and clothing them, doing what has to be done. Most important of all is that you enjoy them. It is important to enjoy them because when you are enjoying them, invisible good is happening. Depend on it. When you are enjoying your children, formative forces of positive energy—undiscovered electromagnetic microcircuits in the brain— start to radiate from you and from your children and envelop you all. A resonating circuit develops around you, your child, and whatever it is that you are doing, which acts like the magic water that kept the characters in the movie *Cocoon* from growing old.

Don't wait for this to be a proven, scientific fact before you believe it and act on it. I know it is true. *You* know it is true. That's enough. But lots of other people also know it is true. Science hasn't proved it yet, but we do know that when people connect, their physiology changes and their health improves. So science is right on the brink of proving the invisible, magical force of which I am talking.

Nowhere is that magical force more intense than around children. And when you are enjoying them, you are tapping into it. You are adding to their magic with your positive energy, and you are gaining the benefits of their special force. When you are enjoying them, you forget where you are, you forget how old you are or what your troubles are, your hip pain subsides, your financial woes fade from your mind, the boss you can't abide disappears in a poof, and you become as pure a charge of positive energy as you ever can be.

Grab it while you can. Just as our own childhoods disappeared before we knew what we were missing, our children's childhoods can do the same if we get too wrapped up in the process of doing what needs to get done—laundry, homework, dinner—and don't somehow find ways, every day, to relish this, our second chance to enjoy childhood, by participating in it with our children.

Friends, Neighborhood, Community

We all know that friends matter. How much, and in what ways, are the subjects of considerable debate, but for the purposes of most parents and teachers, it is enough to know that friends matter, and they matter a lot. Harvard sociologist Robert Putnam speaks of your friends as being a life asset, social capital, as important as money in the bank. As Putnam documents in his scholarly book *Bowling Alone*, numerous studies show that your friends constitute not only an emotional support but a health asset as well; if you are rich in friends, your chances for a healthy and happy life dramatically rise.

One of the traps into which American children can easily fall is materialism. Kids can absorb the message that "rich equals happy" without even realizing how deeply they are incorporating it into their souls. There are several best-sellers on the market today about how to help children become financially savvy and get rich. The ironic point is that if you teach your children how to make and keep friends, the money will usually take care of itself. Not to downplay the significance of money, but as with grades in school, it has been overemphasized to this generation of children as an end in itself. Both grades and money ought to be natural by-products of a well-lived life, not the goals of that life.

I gave a talk to a group of seniors at a public high school in a New York suburb last year. I told them about the importance of living a connected life and the value of having close friends. One student raised his hand. When I called on him, he stood up and said, "My goal is to have thirty million dollars by the time I'm thirty years old. Then I'll have all the friends I want." The other kids laughed.

"Do you really mean that?" I asked.

The boy who had spoken looked like a big teddy bear: he had a wide smile, was a little overweight, wore a colorful shirt, and looked like someone who had a lot of friends. I learned later that he did have a lot of friends and was a leader in the class. He was simply stating what many of his friends—and many in his generation—have been led to believe: that the path to happiness is paved with money, plain and simple. "Yes, I mean that," he replied to my question.

"Well," I asked, "what will you do when you have your thirty million?"

"Veg out," he said, and sat down to uproarious laughter.

The goal of getting rich so that you can then veg out is a goal most of us have entertained somewhere along the line, in high school or in college, or the first day we worked at a job we hated. But when a person takes that goal to heart, or when too many people start seriously espousing money as their "dream," then we have a problem. Getting rich so you can veg out, while sure to bring a laugh from a crowd, is the goal of a disconnected person. Lifelong happiness does not consist of vegging out.

It is important that parents try to introduce children to pleasures other than vegging out, to goals other than getting top grades or making big money, to dreams other than doing nothing. The alternative I suggest is leading a connected life. It can start by emphasizing social capital right from the very beginning—rather than financial capital or grades, which can become the childhood equivalent of money.

As children get older and go off to school, their social capital—their peers, especially—may be a more pivotal influence than anything else. Judith Rich Harris, in her book *The Nurture Assumption*, showed just how powerful the people kids meet outside the home truly are, especially their peers.

Let your children teach you about the importance of friendship. It is important that we adults let our friends get close to us. Many adults let their adult friends disappear once they become parents. Don't make this mistake yourself. Keep up with your adult friends. You need them as much as your children need their friends.

There are many ways to help your children connect with friends, neighborhood, and community. Here are some suggestions:

• Talk about the importance of friendship with your children and show them in your own life that you mean what you say by keeping up with your friends. While parents typically give many lectures about the importance of achievement, it is just as important to talk up—and model through your own behavior—the importance of friendship.

• Talk about principles of friendship—just as you might talk about math facts or anything else that is important to learn. Here are five that I think matter a lot. You might add your own.

1. Be loyal to your friends. Never try to get out of a date you have accepted because something better comes along.
2. Never bully or brag or embarrass someone else.
3. Try to include kids who are being excluded.
4. Treat others the way you would want to be treated.
5. Remember that uncomfortable feelings like jealousy, anger, and resentment come up in any close friendship. Try to talk it out, forgive, and move on.

Imagine if children were taught these lessons as assiduously as they are taught math facts. Life in schools would improve.

• Tell your children stories about your own adult friends. Ask to hear stories about your children's friends. Try to know something more about them than just their names.

• Make sure you know the parents of your children's friends. They can give you inside information when your children won't or don't.

• Try to know at least one of your neighbors well enough that you could borrow a cup of sugar or ask him or her to pick up your mail when you are away for a few days. While most neighborhoods are not as tight as they used to be, they don't have to fall apart completely. If you make an effort, you can make friends with at least one person who lives near you or down the hall.

• Develop strategies for living in what I call "the new neighborhood." The old neighborhood—with folks looking out their windows or over their fences, keeping an eye on all the kids—has disappeared in many areas around this country. It is hard to bring it back. But what you can replace it with is a new kind of neighborhood. This is comprised of parents and children you know from school or from a play group or from day care or from a team sport or from work. The new neighborhood may include people from many different towns, but you keep in touch by telephone, E-mail, instant messaging, cell phone—all the instruments that have made the new neighborhood possible—along with the chief instrument of all: the automobile. Until your children can drive, you have to arrange for their transportation around the new neighborhood. This is a hassle, but it is better than the alternative of their having little social contact and watching TV all afternoon. Instead of wishing the old neighborhood would come back, learn instead how most efficiently to develop and enjoy life in the new neighborhood.

Here are some tips on living in the new neighborhood:

- Don't say yes to everyone. Everywhere is too far to drive.
- Find other parents and children you *really* trust and treat them as if they were part of your extended family.
- Consider new kinds of groups. In a Boston suburb one mom started a book group—for children in the seventh grade. The kids sit in one room with snacks and a book, while the moms (and even a couple of dads) sit in another room talking with one another. After a while the two groups usually merge.
- Schools can help. One teacher I know gives his twelfth-grade writing students much greater access to him and to one another through the use of E-mail.
- In another school a teacher started a "lunch pal" program where kids could just meet to talk. The teacher started this program because she thought her students were so overscheduled that they never had time to hang out and chat. When she first offered to use her classroom for this lunch pal group, she had no idea how many students would want to participate. Immediately they had to move to a larger room. The success of the program is just another indicator of how much children want to connect—as friends—without an assignment or a goal.
- Take full advantage of the new kinds of communication we now have to promote friendships. Technology should be an ally in the new neighborhood, not a nemesis. For

example, a listserv provides a girls' group of friends daily updates on plans, news, and chitchat.

- But also set a limit on how much "electronic time" your kids can have each day (such as TV, video, Nintendo, computer, E-mail, instant messaging, telephone). In our family the limit is an hour a day on weekdays and two hours a day on weekends, not including telephone. The electronic communications we have today can help develop and promote friendships and the new neighborhood, but if you overuse them, they can lead to a weird, sedentary, virtual way of living. We need the face-to-face contact of human moments on a regular basis to stay healthy.

- Help your child to distinguish between friendship and popularity. Try to help your child learn an ethic of loyalty with friends and not play the popularity game.

- Don't overprotect your child socially. But then again, don't take a completely hands-off approach, either. For example, if your child is getting teased a lot in the third grade, it makes sense for you to go in and brainstorm with the teacher about what might be done.

- If your child has a social problem, get help. There are some excellent books on friendship in childhood—and the problems that can arise, such as cliques, bullying, and amazingly nasty behavior. One of my favorites is a recent book coauthored by Michael Thompson, *Best Friends, Worst Enemies.* If your child is having difficulty in the domain of friendship, this book is an extremely good resource.

- In addition to books, you can get help in other ways. Your child's teacher will have many pertinent observations and suggestions. Also, your pediatrician is a good person to ask for guidance. There are many treatable problems with emotion, learning, and behavior that go undiagnosed—and therefore untreated—in children. Most of these lead to both academic problems and to social problems. Some of the more common problems that can now be treated quite well include:

  - *Depression:* Yes, depression does occur in children. In fact, about 20 percent of children will have an episode of major depression during the course of their growing up. Treatment will shorten the length of the depression and prevent much of the damage depression can do.

- *Learning Disabilities (LDs) and attention deficit disorder (ADD):* I have both of these myself. Contrary to popular belief, these conditions do not equate with being stupid. In fact, most people with learning disabilities and/or ADD have major talents. The job is to find the talents and promote them. Many of these kids have social problems.
- *Anxiety Disorders:* Conditions such as obsessive-compulsive disorder, social anxiety disorder, and generalized anxiety disorder can keep a child socially isolated and unhappy. The treatment for these conditions usually involves both psychotherapy and medication, and it usually is highly effective.
- *Severe shyness:* This is a kind of anxiety disorder, and it is often inherited. Shy kids need guidance and help, not to become unshy but to learn to live well and happily being who they are.
- *Oppositional defiant disorder and conduct disorder:* These conditions, as their names imply, manifest in disruptive behavior and a refusal to obey rules. Although treatment is difficult, it works far better than punishment, which is usually all these children get.

Chores, Work, Responsibility to Contribute

OK, I can't wait, I can almost hear you thinking. *How are you going to help me "connect" my kids with chores? Chores, work, and responsibility to contribute just don't make their top-ten list, I'm afraid.*

Let me quickly add, they don't for my kids either. And, to tell you the truth, they don't for me. I don't connect with taking out the trash or doing the dishes or picking up the dry cleaning or remembering to get my shoes repaired or getting my car inspected before I get a ticket.

Let me also immediately reassure you that I am not about to recommend that you make up a chart and post it on the wall listing everybody's chores, with little boxes to check off when each chore is done. Nor am I going to suggest that you bring in a motivational speaker to charge up your kids into a fury of social responsibility. Nor am I going to recommend a "chores therapist," although I often wish I could find one for my kids and me.

No, I am simply going to state the fact that doing chores and assuming other responsibilities are an important part of growing up that we parents should not let slide. Studies show (ah, the omnipresent "study," but it is true, studies do show what I am about to state, among the most famous being the longitudinal studies done by George Vaillant) that children who do chores around the house and then, when they are old enough, get a paid job outside the home for a few hours a week tend to develop the can-do, want-to-do feeling that Erik Erikson called "industry." If you do not develop that feeling, whether you call it industry or use my term, a *can-do, want-to-do feeling*, then you tend to hold back, not because you are lazy (which is simply a useless, behavioral description) but because you feel inferior.

Believe it or not, one of the most concrete, practical ways a parent can help a child to feel industrious rather than inferior is to insist that the child do chores.

There is something magic about work. When you do it, you feel good. Even if you hate the work itself, as I hate doing dishes, once the work is done, you feel slightly better about yourself than before you started.

You might just think that I am a hopeless Calvinist. That is not true. If anything, my friends will tell you I tend toward being a hedonist. But I do know the formative value of work. It is one of the best tonics for the soul that we have.

With a child you need to define the work clearly, make sure the child is capable of doing it, then hold the child to task to get it done. If you do not do this, the child is at risk of developing one of the worst afflictions a parent can create: a sense of entitlement. Entitled children turn into obnoxious adults.

But you can prevent this from happening! Tell your children, "Do chores! Work! Shoulder your responsibility to contribute!"

If you agree with me, then you might ask, "Just exactly how, dear doctor, do I achieve this noble goal?"

Well, you could have visited my kitchen table the other evening when we were having family dinner. I felt that my three children were not doing their chores faithfully enough, nor were they shouldering their responsibility to contribute. I got all worked up and pounded the table (not too hard, as the table is rickety) and went on a tirade about how hard Mom and I work; and we need a little cooperation from the kids; and it isn't fair for them to think we are their servants; and it isn't right for us not to demand of them what the world will sooner or later start to demand; and they had better learn pretty fast how to get these chores done if they expect to get an allowance ever again; and what's more, they should do their chores irrespective (I don't know if I used that word) of getting an allowance, because part of being a member of the family is contributing something, not just taking; and I don't like to get angry and worked up about this, but it is my job as your dad to lay down the law, that's what dads do, and so you better get with the program or there's gonna be big trouble.

I give that speech about once every four months. It actually does help. The last time I gave the speech, Lucy cried a little bit, which made me wince, but I knew Sue would kill me if I relented and said, "Oh, it's OK, don't worry, Mom and I will just continue to be your slaves," which Lucy's tears almost made me do. Tucker's mouth curved downward so much it practically hit the floor, which also made me want to take it all back and say, "Forget what I said. Being your servant is fine. Just smile, please." But I didn't.

And Jack? Jack kept his sense of humor. And he actually listened to the words. At the end of the speech, I said, "And I expect you to get out of bed in the morning without our having to call you six times and beg. How would you like it if I just stayed in bed all day and never went to work?" At that point Jack saw his opening, and he pounced.

"I'd be glad you were at home more," Jack said, with a little twinkle in his eye.

At that, of course, I had to smile. I ended my lecture. But I didn't take anything back. And sure enough, the chores started to get done more consistently. Not perfectly, but better.

Short of charts and management consultants, I think this is the best method for parents: make a commitment to seeing to it that your children have chores to do and that they do them, at least most of the time. Doing chores, and later getting a paid job outside the home, can be as valuable as eating a proper diet or learning math.

Don't overdo the work ethic, however. In addition to showing how good it is for adolescents to have paying jobs outside the home, studies also show that if they work at a paid job twenty hours per week or more, then the effect is negative. That much work puts them at risk, socially, academically, and emotionally.

One of the most difficult and important tasks a parent faces is helping children develop the habit of doing chores and accepting other responsibilities. Here are some suggestions that might help:

• Explain to your kids the reason that everyone should do work around the house, namely, that it is important for everyone to contribute to the family, because maintaining a family requires a lot of work. You might use some negative examples from stories or movies to illustrate for your kids how obnoxious children can be who are spoiled, entitled, and never have to work. The example we use in our family is a character named Veruca Salt, from the video *Willy Wonka and the Chocolate Factory* (based on Roald Dahl's novel *Charlie and the Chocolate Factory*). Veruca is an insufferable, demanding little girl whose wealthy father gives her everything she wants. All my kids have seen the video, and they all detest the spoiled, annoying Veruca. So when one of the kids acts selfishly, Sue or I can ask, "Do you really want to behave like Veruca Salt?" That usually (but not always; nothing *always* works) shames the kid out of his or her snit.

• Try to involve the kids in a discussion of who ought to do which chore. It is always easier to enforce an agreement, as opposed to an edict. Pick chores that are reasonable and tailored to what the child can do. For example, Tucker, our youngest, can't quite handle setting the table all by himself, so Lucy does that chore, but he can clear his own plate, so he does that, and he can feed the dogs, so he does that, too.

• If you do decide to give an allowance (and I think this is a good idea; it allows children to have some discretionary funds, and it also allows parents to say that a given purchase must come out of the child's allowance, which, in turn, teaches "the value of a dollar," that old message our parents were always trying to drum into our heads), don't consider the allowance as a reward for doing the chores. The chores ought to be done whether the kids get an allowance or not. Parents should expect their children to make a contribution to the work of the family.

• Use work as a realistic chance to develop skills and build self-esteem. When I visited Big Oak Ranch, a home in Alabama for abandoned kids that does an amazing job of saving lives, the man who started and runs the place, John Croyle, drove me around. He told me the whole story of this truly miraculous institution. "In days gone by, we would have been called an orphanage. We take in just about anybody, little children who have been beaten or sexually abused or just left on the side of the road. We give them a loving home, and we raise them until they are ready to go to college. That's what we do here. And we do it well." John is about six foot seven and was an all-American football player at Alabama under Bear Bryant. Instead of becoming a professional football player, he started Big Oak Ranch. Central to his philosophy is helping children learn to take responsibility and gain self-esteem through doing useful work. As we drove past a boy on a tractor who was so young he could barely see over the steering wheel, John said, "See that boy? That's a forty-thousand-dollar tractor he's driving. That boy had to work hard to get cleared to drive that thing. But driving that tractor is going be the best therapy he could ever get." Work is therapeutic. At any age.

• When a child is old enough (and you can decide how old that is), paid jobs outside the home are a great idea. You can prepare for this by offering paid jobs inside the home.

• Try to model an approach to work in your own life that you hope your kids will pick up on.

• Don't sugarcoat the fact that some chores and some kinds of work are indeed odious and onerous. But they still need to be done.

We humans are beasts of burden at times. This is a good lesson for us all to learn and learn early.

• If your child gets a job and has a difficult supervisor, look at this as a chance to learn something. Like having a bad teacher, having a bad boss is an experience everyone has to endure. You can take this as a time to commiserate and to brainstorm how to handle it. Above all, don't encourage your child to quit. It sets a bad precedent.

• Take your child to the bank and usher her through what she will find to be the mysterious and exciting process of opening her own account. Then help her make sense of the monthly statements.

• You may think it is hokey to use words like *responsibility* and *contribution*, but they are important words for children to hear, especially in the context of doing chores and work. They may roll their eyes at you when you say those words, but they will remember them, and their work will feel more meaningful if they can connect it to words like *responsibility* and *contribution*. So take a chance. Be hokey.

Activities, Sports

This section is a lot easier than the last one!

Most children naturally want to get involved with sports and various other activities or some kind of hobby. Unfortunately, as they add time to standard academics, many schools are cutting back in these domains. Parents need to try to help make up the difference.

Let me make some suggestions concerning the connection with sports and other activities:

• Remember, the goal for your child is to connect with the sport or the activity, not necessarily excel at it. I was never much good at any sport when I was a kid, but now I derive a huge amount of pleasure in my life from playing squash. I play once or twice a week, and I have done so for decades, even though I am not now, nor have I ever been, a very good squash player. The people I play are at my level, so we tend to stay at about the same level. But I am devoted to squash. It gives me great exercise, and it also gives me a wonderful way of keeping up with certain friends. I am grateful that I was introduced to squash—when I was in high school—not as a test or an activity at which I was expected to excel but as a game. It has remained a game for me now for thirty-five years, a game I love, a game that improves my health, buoys my spirits, solidifies certain friendships, strengthens my body, and relaxes my mind—even though I am not a highly skilled player.

• Sometimes it *is* good to push your child a bit to play a sport or take up some new activity. Often kids don't want to try a new sport or other activity because they are afraid they will look stupid and mess up, which they probably will at first. This is where kids need their parents to take them by the hand and help them get involved in order to overcome their fears. I know many, many adults who deeply regret that their parents did not try harder to get them to take up tennis or the piano or some other sport or activity that is learned more easily when you are young.

• Let your kids follow their own dreams, instead of your dreams or your idea of what sport or activity you want them to do. For example, my wife, Sue, always wanted Lucy to do ballet but acquiesced when Lucy stated she'd rather try gymnastics. Lucy ended up doing gymnastics for several years and loving it. She stopped doing it when it demanded more of her time than she wanted to give to it, a very wise decision that she made on her own.

• Don't become a crazed, fanatical, hypercompetitive parent. You wouldn't be reading this book if you were such a person, but I have to at least mention the damage such parents can do. I am sure you have read some of the horror stories of gymnasts and figure skaters who get pushed so hard that they attempt suicide or ballet dancers who become so preoccupied with their weight that they develop a lasting eating disorder. (For a well-researched, quite disturbing look at this, read *Little Girls in Pretty Boxes: The Making and Breaking of Elite Gymnasts and Figure Skaters,* by Joan Ryan, a columnist for the *San Francisco*

Chronicle.) Just as excessive academic pressure is ruining the adolescence of many American children, so too is excessive pressure to excel in a particular sport. Many children are pushing themselves way beyond what is reasonable or good for them because they want to star in a sport, believing this will give them a "hook" that will help them get into an elite school or college.

• Children have different bodies, just as they have different minds. As you introduce your child to the world of sports, try to help her learn how to use the body she has rather than force her to try to get a body she doesn't have. The key is for her to learn to enjoy sports and games.

• Beware of what a self-esteem killer a bad experience in sports can be, especially for boys. As much as sports can be a source of confidence and positive self-regard, sports can also make a child feel like a total loser. Being humiliated on the playing fields can do as much lasting damage as being humiliated in the classroom. Indeed, many children who excel in the classroom lose all the confidence they gained there when they have to go outside in the afternoon. The key message—for both the playing field and the classroom—is to foster the connection first; skills will then follow, as far as the child's ability allows. But if you create a negative frame of mind—in sports or in academics—the child will feel bad about who he is, not try as hard as he would if he felt confident, and so he will underachieve. I have no idea why so many coaches and teachers have missed this obvious point for so many years, but they have. Learning—of all kinds—happens best without fear.

• Provide the opportunity to try as many sports and other activities as you can. The more you can expose a child to, the more chances that the child will find a lifelong interest. Even if you are bored by, say, opera, take your child to an opera if you ever get the chance. I confess, I have not yet taken *any* of my children to an opera. But I want to take them someday, and I hope they will not reach adulthood, or even graduate from high school, without my having done that.

• Invite your kids to try your own hobbies, but don't insist on it. My dad introduced me to woodworking, which he enjoyed and I did as well. Don't feel bad if you can't do a certain activity. Just share with your kids the enthusiasms you do have.

• Whatever the activity is, show your children you do not have to be an expert to enjoy it. I am a lousy gardener, but I love my lousy garden. For the past few years, my kids have helped me dig it up and plant it, then watched with curiosity as various flowers and vegetables somehow emerged through the weeds and imperfectly tilled soil.

• Consider music lessons for all your children. If you can possibly afford it, do it. Often the school will provide some lessons and also can recommend a teacher who is good and whose fees are affordable. Playing music is good for children in many ways, from providing good training for the brain to instilling the habit of practice to opening the door to a special kind of mastery and a lifelong pleasure. Children do not have to be prodigies to reap these benefits, and they certainly should not be pressured to become stars. Simply learning the basics of playing music is enough to do them a lot of good and maybe give them a lifelong source of joy.

A Sense of the Past

By helping your child develop a connection to the past, you help her understand where she came from and where she might be going.

For example, my father's father was a schoolteacher. My father suffered from manic-depressive illness, and when lithium became available, my father was able to leave the mental hospital where he had been confined for years and spent the rest of his life teaching public elementary school in New Hampshire, specializing in children with learning problems. My father is no longer alive, but I became a psychiatrist who specializes in treating children, with a subspecialty in children who have learning problems. Because both education and mental illness have been a significant part of my family's past, I have a deepened sense of mission in my current work.

My father died before my children were born. I have told them stories about him, especially about what a great teacher he was, what a great sailor he was (he won many trophies racing when he was a kid on Cape Cod), and what a great ice hockey player he was (he was all-American at Harvard in the 1930s). As my kids get older, I will also tell them about my dad's struggle with mental illness as well as more details about his career as a schoolteacher.

I do not know exactly how this connection to the past and to a man they never met will influence my children. When I was growing up, I certainly was not consciously aware of the amazing parallel that would develop between my choice of career and my father's life. I did not consciously become a psychiatrist in order to help families escape the trouble my father's illness created in my life, nor did I deliberately specialize in helping children with learning problems to pick up where my father's career had left off, but if you look at what I have done, you do see this amazing parallel.

My connection to the past—specifically my connection to my father—has given much greater meaning to my work than it would otherwise have. You might say I am on a mission, a mission to help people like my father and to help children and families like those my father helped. As you plant in your children the seeds of a connection to the past, you never know what those seeds will grow into. But you can be sure that you are extending the range of influences that will shape your child's life, you are deepening the kinds of meaning your child might discover, and you are reducing the likelihood that your child will feel isolated and alone as an adult.

Bruce Stewart, a teacher I have mentioned in this book, likes to quote an old saying that goes, "We are warmed by fires we did not light." A connection with the past teaches your children about the people who actually lit the fires.

Here are a few suggestions on how to promote a connection with the past in your children:

• Tell true stories. This is by far the best way. Tell stories about your own childhood, stories from the parts of your life that your kids know nothing about. Tell them about life before the Internet and life before cell phones and CDs. If you still have some long-playing phonograph records, for example, you might show them some of those relics. Your own life provides hundreds of stories from which your children can develop an active feeling for the past.

• Tell more stories. Make sure grandma and grandpa get in on the process. The oral history of the family is the most gripping history most children ever learn. Funny stories, shocking stories, stories of heroism, derring-do, or scoundrelship.

• Tell even more stories. While you are driving in the car, going past old ballparks or towns you used to visit, driving through parts of the city that used to look different, tell your kids about that. I remember my dad telling me about Scollay Square in Boston. Although that part of town is now entirely changed, I feel the connection to the old Scollay Square through the stories Dad told me.

• Talk to old people. One of the best ways kids can learn about the past is simply by listening when old people talk. Don't let them feel bored when they are around older people; instead, suggest to your children that they can hear some pretty interesting stories if they just ask simple questions like, "What was it like when you were a kid my age?"

• Read aloud. (You will see this suggestion several times in this book, in differing contexts.) There are many wonderful children's books that tell stories from American history and world history. These books are interesting for grown-ups, too, so they make for good reading aloud. I was hooked on history when I was a child by the old classic *Johnny Tremain*, by Esther Forbes. For young teens a good choice is *Constance: A Story of Early Plymouth*, by Patricia Clapp, an actual descendant of Constance and a very good teller of tales; or books by two brothers, James Lincoln Collier and Christopher Collier, especially the classic Revolutionary War novel *My Brother Sam Is Dead*. For somewhat younger readers, Jean Fritz's books are wonderful, like *What's the Big Idea, Ben Franklin?* or *Can't You Make Them Behave, King George?*

• Preserve family traditions. Explain the meaning of them on the days they are observed. An obvious example is Thanksgiving. Why do we all get together and eat on that particular Thursday? Why do we have to go to all the trouble? What is it about? Why bother giving thanks? Isn't it insincere to give thanks on one certain day and forget about it the rest of the year? What if you don't feel thankful, then what are you supposed to do on Thanksgiving? Why has this tradition lasted while others fizzle out? These kinds of questions can turn the discussion in interesting directions.

• Have photographs around of family members or family friends who have died and the places where they lived. Make sure your children know who these people are, how they are related, and what you know about their lives. Point out little details in the photographs, like old-fashioned cars or the style of dress at the time.

• Keep a scrapbook or "special box" for each of your children. Someday looking back at their artwork from kindergarten or their composition about summer from fifth grade or their toothless photo that they demanded you destroy will bring hoots of laughter and tears as well, both to you and to your children. Keep more than just photographs in these boxes and books.

• Visit graveyards. You may think this is macabre, but in fact many graveyards are quite beautiful places to take a walk, eat an ice cream, or have a game of catch. It is one way to lead into the topic of death, what happens after death, and where all the dead people are now. Each person has his or her own views on this, of course, but it is worthwhile to expose children to the subject of death in a comforting way.

• Model for them an active interest in the past. Approach new problems by offering the phrase "Let's see how other people have dealt with this before." The problem could be how to do a science project or how to call up a girl or a boy for the first time. Let them know that you value an awareness of history. Let them know that as curious as they are about the future, the past holds many secrets as well, and these secrets can actually be discovered. As they get old enough to understand, teach them George Santayana's famous dictum, "Those who cannot remember the past are condemned to repeat it." Show them that this applies not only to world politics but to their own lives as well, from their academics to their friendships to their love lives to just about everything.

The Arts

By the arts I am referring to music, painting, drawing, sculpture, film, literature, dance, theater, and the like.

The connection with the world of the arts is one that parents might not immediately think of when considering the ingredients of a connected childhood. But as you give it some thought, I think you will agree that children are natural connoisseurs of beauty—even though they may not like certain museums.

This domain is also one in which parents (and teachers) make a huge difference. What you expose your children to, and how you expose them to it, can determine whether they develop a lifelong interest—or not.

Here are some practical tips on helping children develop a positive connection to the world of the arts:

• Follow your child's lead. Virtually every child wants to paint or listen to stories or sing or get involved with making something or other. This is the beginning of a relationship with beauty.

• Read aloud. (I know. I have suggested this before!) The best way to encourage children to develop a love of stories and words is to read aloud to them when they are young.

• Keep books around. Have them in your children's rooms. Show them how to use a dictionary. Talk about words, what they mean, how their meanings can change. Clue your kids in that English is one of the most beautiful, strange, and expressive languages ever invented. Help them become proud of the English language; it is one of our greatest treasures. Tell them it has more than six hundred thousand words, more than twice the number of the nearest competitor. Richard Lederer's books, like *Adventures of a Verbivore*, are great at pointing out some of the more amusing and playful aspects of English. For example, Lederer asks, Why do we drive on the parkway but park in the driveway? And why do we call the third hand on the clock the second hand? And why are our capitonyms so odd, words like *job* and *polish* that change pronunciation and meaning when capitalized?

• Keep music playing at home. When your kids reach a certain age, you will have no choice in this matter. But before then, try to fill their ears with music of all kinds. It may be their last chance to hear Mozart for years.

• Keep a musical instrument in your house. You can rent a piano for not too much money if your child wants to take piano lessons, and you can rent a violin for even less. Even if you do not do that, you can have a toy guitar around or a small, battery-powered keyboard or some percussion toys, like a tambourine, castanets, cymbals, or bells.

• Go to concerts. If you live near a city that has an orchestra, take everybody and go once a year. Listen to local bands and look for band concerts in the summer. In my hometown of Chatham, on Cape Cod, there is still a band concert in the center of town every Friday night, as there has been since I was a kid back in the 1950s. I used to dance around on the grass in front of the bandstand when I was four years old; other four-year-olds do today.

• Dance. I know, you can't exactly dance around the kitchen every night, but you can dance in the living room now and then, can't you? Let yourself go. This is what dance is all about. It is great "physical education."

• Draw. Paint. Sketch. Kids love to do this, from finger painting to drawing in the fog on a windowpane. You can even introduce them to sculpture through Play-Doh or by making a cake and decorating it in as playful and crazy a fashion as your imaginations concoct.

• Let your children take photographs. Usually there is someone in the family who takes most of the family pictures. Ask a child if he or she wants to help. You can introduce kids to the beauty of photography by making them photographers at a young age. In this digital age, photography is quite a multifaceted skill. Soon your kids will be teaching you.

• Talk to children about art the way you might talk about baseball or cooking. Take the intimidation or fear factor out of it. Many people grow up feeling that art is only for fancy people, while it is in fact for us all. When you see a painting, ask your child what she sees in it. Teach her to look. You can play a game, asking how many colors can you find or how many shapes or how many different faces. The *Where's Waldo?* books and the *I Spy* books make for good introductions to the "game" of looking. From those books you can move on to looking at masterpieces in museums or sculpture gardens. Just don't use the word *masterpiece*, or the child might lose her natural honesty. You want your child to be able to say the *Mona Lisa* is ugly if she thinks it is.

Nature

Most children naturally connect with nature if given the chance. In fact, childhood is when people are often more connected with nature than at any other time in their lives.

Children should be outdoors a lot. The great competition the outdoors faces in vying for children's time these days is electronics: TV, the Net, Nintendo, and so forth.

Here are some tips on how to deal with the competition and promote your child's connection with nature:

• "Go outside and play." Those four words used to ring through most houses. Now, as neighborhoods have weakened or disappeared, it is more difficult for kids to run outside and find a group to go off and play with. But still, you should be able to find some outdoor space where your kids can play. Maybe a public park or a common or someone else's backyard. You might have to go with them or find another parent who can, as the neighborhood doesn't supervise itself as it once did.

• Learn to swim. All kids should learn to swim. Not only might this skill save their lives, but it provides one of the most loved instant connections to nature. If you do not have access to the ocean or a lake, your local Y, school, or other children's organization should be able to help.

• Ride bikes. Even cities have bike paths. Riding a bicycle is still one of the best ways for children to connect with nature and also explore their world and keep up with their friends. Family bike rides can be a lot of fun, too.

• Hike. Personally I hate to hike. I hate the heat, I hate the bugs, I hate the brambles and poison ivy, I hate the sunburn, I hate getting tired and sweaty, I hate the whole experience. But it would be unfair for me only to include in this book what I like to do. I concede that my dislike of hiking is my problem, not hiking's problem. I wish I liked to hike. I am sorry I don't. I hope you like to hike. It is a great way for you and your kids to connect with nature. You can even bring a picnic. (Oh, don't get me started on the perils of that! Bugs, dirt, warm mayonnaise oozing through sandwiches . . .)

• Talk about nature. Kids absorb what you talk about, at least when they are young. If you talk about nature, they will tend to get interested. Also, get picture books about nature. And have maps and atlases around. Maybe subscribe to *National Geographic*. Remember those magazines when you were growing up? Everybody used to subscribe. A whole generation saw their first unclothed adults in *National Geographic*. But that magazine really does have incredible photos of nature.

• Plant a garden. If you live in a place where that is impossible, plant a window box or just have some plants around the house. As the kids get old enough, you can let them choose what to plant in the garden or which indoor plants to raise. And the kids can also start to take responsibility for caring for the garden or plants. The only reason I like gardening now, even though I hate hiking, is that my grandmother and my aunt introduced me to it when I was a little boy. Gardening truly is one of the childhood roots of my adult happiness (no pun intended).

• Look at clouds. If it is a sunny day, lie down on the ground with your kids and look up at the clouds. Talk about what shapes you see. Clouds look like so many different things, from animals to people to mountains. The act of lying flat on the ground connects you to nature quite literally. Then looking up at the clouds, from that unique vantage point, gives you a special take on the world.

• Look at stars. Lie down as you did for clouds. Only this time pick a starry night. Talk about what you see. Some kids will see shapes, some will see gems, some will see constellations, some will see heaven, others will see questions or dreams.

• When you fly, look out the window. This view is passé to most of us adults. But do you remember the first time you looked out the window of an airplane? I do. It was dizzying. Aside from the thrill of it, you get a whole new sense of the dimensions of nature when you look down from an airplane. You can also see the contours of the land and the coast and get a sense of the bigger picture.

• Honor the environment. As your children start to love nature, you can remind them that it will only be there for us as long as we take care of it. I don't think you should scare young children with the harsher realities of environmental crises, but just as you teach them to brush their teeth, it is good to teach them to take care of the land and the sea.

Pets and Other Animals

This is another easy section. For most parents the decision comes down to this: to have a pet or not to have a pet, that is the question.

You don't want me to bore you with all the research that shows how wonderful pets are in almost every conceivable way, do you? And pets are not only good for children, they are good for grown-ups and senior citizens as well.

How are pets good for children (and other people)? Let me count some of the ways:

1. Pets love you. No questions asked.
2. Pets won't disagree.
3. Pets are very good listeners.
4. Pets smile at just the right times.

5. Pets care about you.

6. But pets *don't* care about what you look like, how much money your parents have, what grades you got, what trouble you are in, or whether you have brushed your teeth.

7. Pets teach responsibility, and in the best way. Having a pet is excellent practice for caring for any living being.

8. Pets pick up the mood of most households. For all that they bark and eat and fart (often mercilessly!) and poop, they also wag and shake and lick and kiss. They make friendly noises and pump up the positive energy in homes.

9. Pets teach us how to relax. Pets show us how to chill out. Have you ever seen a human as relaxed as a dog stretched out on the living room floor or a cat lounging in its favorite chair? I have a little Plexiglas box that sticks out of my third-floor, home-office window like an air conditioner. It is a window box for Louie, our cat. He can go out into the box and survey the neighborhood from there, but mostly what he likes to do there is, you guessed it, sleep. When I am at my desk writing, and I look over and see Louie snoozing in his window box, I smile inside and feel a little less stressed by the imperfections of my prose.

10. Pets teach about love and loss. The death of a pet can be one of the most poignant moments in a person's life. It is a good way for a child to learn about death and loss. Some people don't want their children to have pets because they remember how sad it was when their dog died when they were young. But you can't and shouldn't protect children from what is an inevitable and unavoidable part of life. With every love comes loss. It is better to embrace this fact than to avoid it. When I say "embrace" it, I mean more than just "deal with it" or "accept it." I mean embrace it, the way you might sing loudly at a funeral. If you can actually embrace death, then you will be much freer to love deeply and fully, with no tentative holding back.

Of course, if you or your children are allergic, you can't have pets. Or if the zoning laws in your area forbid pets, you are also out of luck.

In these cases, however, you still can nurture your child's relationship with pets through stories and stuffed animals. Stuffed animals can take on a life every bit as real as live animals—and they don't poop! Stuffed animals are one of the great, enduring particulars of childhood. *Every* child should have a stuffed animal, preferably many.

So, here are my tips:

- GET A PET!
- GET A PET!
- GET A PET!
- GET A PET!
- GET A PET!
- GET A PET!
- GET A PET!
- GET A PET!
- GET A PET!
- IF YOU CAN'T GET A PET, GET A STUFFED ANIMAL!

Ideas and Information

Instead of just focusing on grades and SAT scores, it is important that parents and teachers help children learn about the mind each child has. In the past decades we have learned a great deal about how minds differ from one to another. In fact, no two minds—or brains—are alike. The practical implications of this fact are profound.

It means that we need to focus on identifying strengths and talents as soon as possible, as well as targeting areas of weakness. It means that we should do away with misleading distinctions like "smart" versus "stupid" or "normal" versus "learning-disabled" and instead help every child find both those areas in which she is strong and those areas in which she is weak.

As we do that, we should also pay close attention to the emotions a child brings to whatever he is learning how to do, from reading to math to taking apart a clock to skating to speaking up in class to fishing. The more positive the emotions are that surround the act of learning, the more likely it is that your child will become someone who will take pleasure in learning forever. He will become a lifelong learner, and that confers many advantages in life.

So, from as early on as possible, parents and teachers should start to notice the specific qualities of each child's mind, from personality to temperament to learning style to preferred activities to relative weaknesses. As you are noticing what kind of mind a child has, you also want to try to help that child succeed and have fun in at least one area of learning, and hopefully many areas. This leads to a positive connection to the act of learning. A positive connection to the act of learning leads to comfort and joy in the world of information and ideas, which leads not only to enduring pleasure but to high achievement as well.

It is a grave error to focus on grades and ignore the emotions involved in learning. If your child feels comfortable in the act of learning and is able to ask for help without feeling ashamed or stupid, she will learn much more than if she feels tentative or afraid. As Priscilla Vail, one of the world's great experts on education, says, "Emotion is the on/off switch for learning."

Let me give you an example from my own life. When I was in first grade, I couldn't learn how to read. It turns out, I have dyslexia. But back then, in 1955, if you couldn't learn to read, your diagnosis was likely to be that you were stupid. But I was lucky. I had a teacher, Mrs. Eldredge, who intuitively knew there was more going on with children who couldn't read than their being stupid. She didn't know the more sophisticated methods we have today of treating dyslexia—for example, the multisensory approach of the Orton-Gillingham method. But she did know that it was important that I not feel ashamed.

So she did what she could do. She couldn't give me a new, non-dyslexic brain. But she could make sure I felt OK about having the brain I had. So during reading period, when the students took turns reading aloud from the "See Spot run" books, Mrs. Eldredge would sit down next to me, put her arm around me, and hug me in close to her. When it came to be my turn to read aloud, I could only stammer and stutter; but as I stammered and stuttered, none of the other kids laughed at me, because I had the mafia sitting next to me!

What a gift her arm was. What a magnificent IEP (individualized education plan). That arm has stayed around me ever since. I am to this day a painfully slow reader; I still have dyslexia, after all. But I ended up majoring in English at Harvard and graduating *magna cum laude*; without Mrs. Eldredge's arm, that never would have happened.

Studies show that if a child can become comfortably connected to the act of learning and the world of information and ideas, then her chances of pleasure and success in life rise dramatically. On the other hand, children who detect a message early on that they lack brain-power run the risk of believing that message, giving up on learning, and never developing the talents they have.

Nowhere do children sell themselves short more than in assessing their own brainpower. Teachers, peers, and even parents have joined in this sabotage for centuries. It is time for it to stop.

Parents and teachers should make special efforts not only to help children learn but, even more important, to help children get comfortable with their minds. Many children grow up feeling ashamed of their minds because they are not good at what is rewarded in school. Don't let that happen to your child. Help her find out what her brain likes to do and does well; not just spend years being drilled in what her brain can't grasp.

To help in this effort, I have written a children's book entitled *A Walk in the Rain with a Brain*, in which the main character, who is named Manfred, or just Fred for short, is a brain. In the story a little girl (named Lucy; I originally wrote the book for my children) asks Fred to please make her smart. Fred replies, "You're already smart. You just need to find out at what." As the little girl ponders this notion, Fred adds, "No brain is the same, no brain is the best, each brain has its own special way."

Each child needs to get to know his or her own special way. Children need to find the talents—as well as the limitations—of their minds. Although Fred's words are part of a children's story, they are scientifically accurate. No two brains are the same, and no one brain is the best.

So I advise parents to adopt Fred's approach. We're all smart. We just need to find out *at what.*

Tell your children that part of the adventure of growing up is discovering how their minds work, what they do well, what they have trouble with, and what they can do with the good and the bad. Tell them that each brain has its own special way and that, as they grow up, they will learn more and more about the special ways their brains have.

In addition to identifying strengths and interests, it is also important to identify weaknesses and attend to them right away. If you see a problem, talk to your pediatrician, school psychologist, or some other expert right away. Don't wait. It is estimated that *70 percent* of the children who are identified as poor readers in school and end up receiving special help *would never have developed a problem* had they received earlier intervention.

Early intervention means around kindergarten or first grade. The older you are, the more difficult it is to change. A great deal of recent brain research has shown that brain wiring changes in these early years depending on the child's interaction with the environment. If you read aloud to your children and play rhyming games and alphabet games with them at home, and if the teacher in kindergarten and first grade is adept at developing a child's ability to associate sounds with letters, you will go a long way toward preventing a reading problem.

The current model of assessment in most schools waits for the child to fail. G. Reid Lyon, one of the world's experts on learning disabilities, wrote, "Children who get off to a poor start in reading rarely catch up. We wait—they fail. But it does not have to be this way."

If, compared to her peers, your kindergartener or first grader has trouble naming letters, making the sounds the letters stand for, blending those sounds into words when given oral cues, making rhymes, or differentiating between similar-sounding words or syllables, I urge you to take her to a specialist. If, as she gets older, she has trouble—again, compared with her peers—with oral expression (speech), written expression, reading, or mathematics, I urge you to take her to a specialist. If your child complains that she doesn't like to read or that she reads slowly or that she can't remember what she reads, I urge you to take her to a specialist.

Finally, if, at any age, your child complains that she feels frustrated in school, that she knows she is smarter than her grades reflect, that the teacher goes too fast for her to keep up, that she sometimes "gets it" and sometimes doesn't, that she struggles mightily in one particular subject, that she thinks she is stupid or thinks she is bad, I urge you to take her to a specialist.

The specialist can help you develop a plan for your child based on an assessment of many variables. You might be surprised how many different mental functions a good assessment will address. Here is a sampling:

- Cognitive ability
- Problem-solving strategies
- Receptive language
- Expressive language
- Memory (verbal and visual)
- Automatic memory
- Word retrieval
- Perception
- Visual-spatial organization
- Attention
- Phonological awareness
- Reading decoding
- Reading fluency
- Reading comprehension
- Writing fluency
- Writing mechanics
- Written language
- Spelling recognition
- Spelling retrieval
- Math automaticity
- Math computation
- Math concepts
- Math problem solving

This kind of testing is complex and is beyond the scope of most school specialists. You can't always rely on the school specialist for several reasons: a conflict of interest (that is, the school system hires the specialist with the implied mandate of not recommending special services for too many children, since the special services cost the school system a lot of money), inadequate training, or work overload.

It won't cost you as much as orthodontics to see a highly trained specialist, and it is a lot more important.

Finding such a specialist may take some looking. You can begin by asking your pediatrician. However, not all pediatricians understand what is needed for a full assessment. So you may want to ask specifically for a referral to a neuropsychologist. These are the people with the most advanced training in the area of assessment. A neuropsychologist is more than a psychologist. The *neuro* part of the title refers to additional training in neurology, brain science, and advanced assessments of cognitive functioning. I do not mean to make it sound arcane; however, I have seen many times the damage done by a superficial, inadequate assessment.

I have also seen many times the great benefit a child receives from a thorough assessment followed up by proper interventions, from individual tutoring geared specifically to the child's areas of need to consultation with the school to a change in classroom strategies to medication.

What follows are some suggestions to help you help your child develop this extremely pivotal connection to the world of information and ideas:

• Be aware that all minds are different and that no one kind of mind is best. Also, be aware that the "smart" versus "stupid" dichotomy with which we adults grew up is inaccurate and destructive. Try to get to know your child's mind as well as you can and, as you do so, offer her guidance on using that mind. This is a very complicated issue, one that you could spend a lifetime mulling over. Obviously you do not have time for that. But you can clear your mind of misleading labels (of which "smart" and "stupid" are the most common) and try to understand your child's mind, so that you can help her manage that mind most effectively. If you want guidance in understanding your child's mind, I urge you to read Dr. Mel Levine's superb book, *A Mind at a Time.*

• Do everything you possibly can to stamp out the most common, and most dangerous, learning disability: fear. Fear, and its cousin shame, hold more children back than any formal learning disability. Fear of making mistakes is what keeps people from reaching their potential. Make sure your child does not go to a school where fear reigns in the classroom. Make sure you do not slip into using ridicule as a way of "motivating" your child. Once a child feels that making a mistake only leads to being made fun of, then that child will put all his efforts into never making mistakes. Without mistakes, learning stops.

• Praise learning in your home. Make sure learning is honored as much in your family as athletic skill or being polite or cooperating with others. Learning is not the same as getting good grades. You can honor learning by praising your child when she learns to tie her shoes or when he puts together a puzzle or when she correctly concludes that Grandma didn't really mean it when she said she felt "fine." This last example, picking up on a social nuance, is a form of learning that deserves more notice and encouragement than it usually gets, as it is an extremely valuable life skill.

• Have a dictionary in some prominent place in your house. Refer to it. Look words up. When you are having family dinner at home and a word comes up that someone doesn't know, go to the dictionary and look it up. This can become a game if you all try guessing what the word means before the definition is read.

• Play games with numbers. Notice patterns. Everyday life offers hundreds of opportunities to practice math skills, from making change to dividing portions of food to making estimates of large quantities (blades of grass, hairs in someone's head, grains of sand, stars in the sky) to calculating interest to setting odds on various outcomes and so forth.

• Read aloud to your children. I offer this piece of advice over and over, because it's so important in many different areas. Reading aloud builds family togetherness. It also helps build a comfortable connection to information and ideas.

• Introduce children to the world of computers when they are as young as you like. Let computers become a part of their world, especially in providing access to information and ideas. But with computers (and television, video, cell phones, and all electronics), make sure that they promote the connection to information, ideas, and other people—and that they do not become a substitute for any of these or an addiction.

• Expose your children to the world of information and ideas as a playground, not a torture chamber.

• Encourage your children always to ask "Why?" Of course, I don't mean this as a response to being asked to go brush their teeth but as a response to any issue they genuinely do not understand. As with, perhaps, the *first* time you ever ask them to brush their teeth.

• Teach your children always to regard something they do not know as an opportunity to learn rather than feel shame. No one knows everything or anywhere remotely close to everything. Instead of feeling ashamed of what you do not know, you should feel comfortable in saying you don't know and glad to have the chance to learn. For example, when I was a senior in college, I had not yet read *War and Peace*. As an English major, I was expected to have read what many people consider to be the greatest novel ever written. I will never forget what my adviser, Professor William Alfred, said to me when I sheepishly told him I hadn't read this major book. "Oh, aren't you lucky!" he exclaimed, as if I had just told him I won the lottery. "What an enormous pleasure you have in store for you someday!"

• If you can pass the wisdom of William Alfred's attitude on to your children (and maybe their teachers?), you make it more likely they will approach what they do not know with enthusiasm rather than secrecy and guilt.

Institutions and Organizations

In considering a connected childhood, you may not immediately think about institutions and organizations, as they may sound too grown-up. But, in fact, childhood is full of major institutions and organizations—most notably school, but also clubs, leagues, teams, associations—so it is important that children learn how to get along in the sometimes amorphous groups of people we call institutions and organizations.

Learning how to thrive and grow within these institutions and organizations is a life skill of major value, ranking right up there with learning to read and write. We tend not to teach it much; it is one of those skills we let our children learn on their own. I believe that some early practice and some wise guidance can provide children with better tools for living and working in groups than merely throwing them in and seeing if they learn to swim.

It is important not only for the happiness and well-being of our children but also for the health of our institutions and organizations that our children learn how to negotiate life in large groups. As Harvard sociologist Robert Putnam points out in his book *Bowling Alone*, the past decades have seen a massive decline in the strength of all kinds of American institutions and organizations, many of them directly related to children, like the PTA, Scouting, Boys & Girls Clubs, and religious institutions.

As with all other forms of connectedness, connectedness to institutions and organizations will last longer and grow stronger if it begins when you are young.

Here are some suggestions for how to get this special kind of connection off to a good start:

• Explain to your children, in a way that is fitting for their age, some of the basics of life in large groups. A good time to start doing this is when your child goes off to school. You may already have done it with day care or nursery school or just going to a friend's birthday party. You explain the basics of politeness, of waiting your turn, of listening to others, of sharing, and so forth.

• Then, as your child gets older, you can explain some of the practical realities of groups. This way, he is less likely to be surprised and hurt when he encounters cruelty in groups. For example, sometimes a child gets scapegoated in a class at school. If this happens in your child's classroom, instead of wringing your hands at home or charging into the principal's office in a rage, coach your child on how to respond constructively. If your child is the victim, coach him on ways of deflecting the negative attention as well as ways of getting help. Balance the negative messages he may be receiving at school with support at home. If he is old enough to understand, explain to him how the dark side of human nature emerges in groups and how groups typically feel threatened by anything that is in any way different from the mainstream. Then let him know that virtually every advance that has been made in human history came from someone who was brave and talented enough to be different, to think outside the box, to act against the mob, to have a mind of his or her own.

If your child is part of the group that is doing the scapegoating, coach your child on how not to join a mob. This skill is vital at any age. If your child can learn to resist the will of the group when she knows the group is being cruel or doing wrong, she will be on her way to a life of honor. You can help her simply by telling stories in which someone is tempted by a group or by telling true stories from your life or by anticipating situations and coaching her on how to respond. For example, you might ask her, "What would you do if someone on the playground said, 'Let's go beat up Tommy because he looks so weird,' and many other kids said, 'Yeah, let's get him'?" If your child didn't know what to say or do, you could coach her through some responses, like, "I don't want us to beat up Tommy. So what if he looks funny." Or, "I don't believe in beating people up unless they are attacking me." Or whatever response seems fitting with your value system. The key is to try early on to instill the conviction in your child that mob justice is wrong and cruel, that no one is immune to it, and that it is good (although often difficult) to oppose it. If a child can learn to be an independent thinker and not be ruled by the mob, the peer group, the clique, or whatever subculture she finds in whatever organization or institution she is part of, she will become a person of character and honor.

• You can then extend this kind of discussion to talking about courage and honor in general. When faced with real-life decisions at school, children discover how hard it is to be brave or to do what is right. For example, why not cheat if no one is looking? Or why not look the other way instead of breaking up a fight?

• Make friends with your children's school(s). I say *make friends* rather than using a more functional term like *participate in* because I want to underscore the fundamental force that will keep you involved and your children involved with institutions and organizations of any kind. That is the force of human warmth. Once the warmth leaves, then disconnection is not far behind.

But how do you make friends with an institution or an organization? You make friends with the people there. Take school as an example. Make friends with your child's teacher. And the maintenance man. And the principal. And the principal's administrative assistant. And the parents of other kids. Make friends with whoever seems like someone with whom you'd like to be friends.

If you have a friendship with the school (that is, the people there), it is likely you will participate in such groups as the PTA or the curriculum committee or the committee to improve the playground or whatever. It is also likely that, when a crisis occurs, you will not shy away from it, you will tackle it, and the people at the school will help you enthusiastically.

In addition, you will help your child's education if you make friends with the school, because teachers and administrators will be more likely to treat your child well. You will also model for your child how to deal with institutions in general. The relationship you make with the school sets an important example for your child of how to function within an institution.

• Use school as an example to teach your children about what an institution or organization is. Here is a concrete example of the value of people's working together, of cooperation, of social responsibility; without a concrete point of reference, these concepts seem hopelessly vague to your children.

• Explore what clubs and other organizations exist in your area that you or your children might like to join. If you get in the habit of joining—rather than staying at home—that will last a lifetime.

• Talk about politics. Explain to your children how the government works. "Ugh!" you might say. I am merely suggesting that you explain the basics of what once was called civics (and taught in school). Many children growing up today haven't a clue as to what goes on in their democracy.

• Along the lines of the preceding point, recognize that apathy is a major obstacle to the development of political connectedness. Try to think of simple ways to involve your children in their government. Take a trip to Washington, D.C. Meet your congressman or congresswoman. Take your child with you when you vote. Discuss the candidates at dinner. Try to help them become thoughtful future voters in a democracy.

• Point out the dangers inherent in institutions and organizations, like exclusivity, bureaucracy, and political infighting. Help children think of more constructive ways of dealing with these inevitable problems than merely disengaging. Most adults have very immature techniques for dealing with conflict at work, for example. They often resort to gossiping, backstabbing, scapegoating, whining, even lying, or simply quitting rather than trying to solve the problem. Many adults treat their bosses, and the organizations they represent, as if they were their mother or father, and a mean mother or father at that. So they sulk and stamp their feet and throw a tantrum instead of taking a more mature approach. Childhood is an excellent place to learn that more mature approach. If you can help your child differentiate between his teacher and his parents or between his coach and his parents or, when he gets a job, between his boss and his parents, you will have given him a very valuable lesson for later life, both in being a successful employee and in being a successful manager of employees.

• Show your children that you are loyal to certain institutions and organizations, such as your old school or maybe a charity you have helped for many years. You may not talk about this in public, because you don't want to sound boastful or pious, but you should talk about it with your kids. They should know if you are giving money to organizations you value and why you are doing it.

God and/or a Spiritual Life

Children are naturally curious about what makes things happen in this world. They naturally stumble into the hotly contested areas "covered" by systems of religious belief. They wonder what happens to people after they die. They wonder what lies beyond the farthest star. They wonder why some people do evil. They wonder whether there is any force that will protect them against all the bad things that can happen in life. They wonder why siblings have to be born and why they can't have all the attention to themselves. They wonder who will look out for them if mom and dad should die. They wonder who listens if someone says a prayer. They wonder, as my daughter, Lucy, put it, "if anyone is there with me when I am alone."

Developing a means of addressing, if not answering, these questions is what a spiritual life is all about.

I urge parents to explore these questions with your children. It is good for both of you. When you have a child, it gives you a chance to rethink—and refeel—your own spirituality, as you offer guidance to your child.

Membership in some religion used to be a given in a child's life. My generation, the baby boomers, changed that. Now, in many families, not belonging to a religion is a given for a child. In order to avoid the hypocrisy and mistreatment that organized religion can sometimes foster, my generation headed away from it.

This has created a void, but it has also created a great opportunity. No longer do we automatically raise children to believe some inherited doctrine. We may choose to do so—for example, Sue and I have chosen to baptize and raise our children as Episcopalians—but we do not feel the intense social pressure to join a religion that people used to feel. We have the great gift of religious freedom in this country; it is indeed a precious gift, one for which millions of people have died throughout history.

I urge us parents to use this freedom to its fullest rather than ignore it or take it for granted.

Your spiritual life is an intensely personal matter, one that our laws protect, and so is how you encourage such a life in your children, if at all. The belief that there is no one right way is a cornerstone of our democracy and one of our nation's greatest freedoms.

I would urge simply that you do not ignore the issue. Religion can be such a private and discombobulating topic that you may want to dodge it altogether. But you shouldn't do this with your children. They need your help in discussing matters of the spirit just as they need help in dealing with friends or handling money or sorting out their sexual feelings.

You can plant the seeds of a spiritual connection simply by talking about the puzzle of life. If you talk about life's big questions with your children and help them grapple with them, a spiritual life will naturally take root. As you wrestle with the question "Why is there evil in this world?" or the question "What happens to us after we die?" you begin to build a set of intuitions, if not beliefs or faith, and a set of feelings that coalesce into what we call spirituality. This is a part of you that can grow and develop for the rest of your life if you keep tending to it, a part of you that will be there when you need it, and you will need it often when you least expect to.

As you bear with the tension of asking these unanswerable questions, a feeling develops within you for that which is beyond knowledge. Like a person in a dark room, you grope around, gradually gaining a feel for the room, a sense of what is where and how you can be safe. All you have to do is keep the questions open, always seeking but never quite knowing what you've found.

No matter what you call yourself—an atheist; a Roman Catholic; a Buddhist; a rational empiricist; or, like me, an Episcopalian—you still remain human, and being human, you still yearn to know what you don't know.

Children are particularly human in this regard. They want to know *everything*. When they ask the questions that are usually covered by religious belief, you should be prepared to offer guidance. But don't feel you have to have *answers*. There is a prayer I like that goes, "Lord, help me always to search for the truth, but spare me the company of those who have found it."

To help your child develop a spiritual connection, regardless of what you believe, all you have to do is be there while your child searches. Join her in the search. Offer your opinion, whatever it might be, from saying there is no God to saying that God is everywhere. But honor the questions and the search and join your child in it. You never know what you might find.

Here are some suggestions for ways to help your children develop a spiritual connection:

• Search your soul. "OK," you say, "I'll do that right after lunch." I know that you can't just snap your fingers and make this happen, but you can ask yourself two questions: What form of belief am I inclined toward? What form of belief would I like to introduce my children to? Ask your spouse the same questions. "No belief" is certainly a legitimate response. But it is good to address the issue rather than ignore it.

• Make a plan. Based on whatever your spiritual leanings might be, make a plan for how you want to introduce spirituality to your children, whether through organized religion or, if that is not for you, then in other ways. The "other ways" may simply be through spontaneous conversations you have with your children over the years. Or perhaps you might do something more deliberate, like reading certain books with or to your child or attending retreats or festivals together or making a project out of attending different kinds of religious services in your area or learning meditative or prayerful practices.

• Be prepared for the questions children ask. Kids will not tiptoe around these issues. They ask, "Where will Grandma go when she dies?" Or, "Where will you go when you die?" Or, "Who will buy me birthday presents if you and Dad get killed in an airplane crash?"

• Don't feel you have to answer the questions with anything more decisive than "I don't know." All that matters is that you honor the questions and don't get annoyed at your child for asking them. Questions that we can't answer do tend to annoy us, so be prepared to feel stupid or inadequate as you discuss these topics with your children. Encourage the asking of these questions. The questions are like the spade that digs down into the hard earth in search of hidden treasures.

• Remember that children do like answers. So if you say, "I don't know," they are not likely to stop there. They are likely to probe and suggest answers of their own. When this happens, be glad. You may disagree with their answers, but *what* they conclude is so much less important than *that* they conclude, that they delve into the unknown with creativity and energy.

• Be glad, also, because your children can teach you a lot about the invisible world. Be glad, because when your children ask questions, they are reaching. They care. The driving force behind the growth of a spiritual life is curiosity or what some call yearning.

• If you do join an organized religion, be sure to bring it into your everyday life, not just save it for religious services and holy days. Say prayers at bedtime, for example, or grace before meals. Encourage your children to talk to God—that is, to pray—whenever they feel puzzled, unhappy, alone, or on the other hand, thankful and joyful.

• Try to help your kids associate spirituality with joy, not just solemn services or sad moments. Often religion or spirituality is presented to children as frightening, guilt-ridden, formal, stiff, and boring. No wonder so many children flee as soon as they are old enough! This is wrong. Spirituality should be a ball. It should be celebratory and full of joy as well as steeped in pain and sadness. For example, when we arrive at the cottage we rent each August on Lake Doolittle in northwest Connecticut, the lake our children have learned to swim in and have visited every summer of their lives, I unpack the car, then change into my bathing suit and immediately jump into the lake. I am usually the first one in the water, as the kids want to check out what's changed at the cottage or use the bathroom or get a snack. But I make a beeline for the lake. I dive in. The water licks me like an old and faithful dog who's thrilled I have returned. I splash around, swimming nowhere, just exulting in the water and the setting sun (we usually arrive late in the afternoon), the memories of the great times we've had at this lake, and the great time we hope to have this year. I look up at the sky and holler out, "Thank you, God!" Usually by now my children have come down to the dock in their bathing suits, and so they see and hear me thanking God for this wonderful blessing, and they smile. They don't go dancing around thanking God, as that is not their style, nor does their mother, as that is not her style either, but even as they might feel a bit amused or befuddled at Dad's splashing and yelling out thanks to God, I know they feel happy and glad. I try to bring up God when good things are happening so my children will think of God in a context of joy.

• Encourage an appreciation for the diversity of possible religious beliefs. Intolerance is the great enemy of spirituality. Make sure your children know that no one has all the answers.

• Try to translate your spirituality into action. In other words, don't just talk and pray but act in the world. You don't have to go feed starving people in Africa; you can just share a toy with your brother. You don't have to give away everything you have, but you should give away something. You don't have to believe in God, but you should think about the questions.

The Connection You Make with Yourself

This final kind of connection, the one you make with yourself, is, like the connection to the world of the spirit, private and personal. Like the spiritual connection, it also evolves and changes over the course of a lifetime.

The way it develops in childhood often determines whether it is basically a pleasant or an unpleasant connection. This connection can be the ruination of a life; some adults so dislike themselves, usually for no good reason, that they never know lasting pleasure. Most of the time their dislike began in childhood, at a time when it could have been changed—if only someone had intervened and offered a loving hand, a different perspective.

The special connection you make with yourself grows simultaneously with your ability to observe yourself. By the connection you make with yourself, I mean, simply, how you feel about who you are. Since you are yourself, it may seem logically impossible to connect with yourself; it would be like a hand shaking hands with itself. But I use the idea of a connection with yourself as a metaphor, a way of describing how the part of you that observes you feels about you.

Naturally this changes from day to day, even from moment to moment. If you win a tennis game, you might feel good about yourself for the moment. If you break up with your boyfriend, you might feel bad about yourself for that moment. For most people their feelings about themselves change as often as the weather.

But at the same time, there are underlying themes in your relationship with yourself.

As I see it, a healthy relationship with yourself means that you feel comfortable, most of the time, being who you are. You do not put on airs or pretend you are better than who you are. You can enter groups of people and feel more or less OK.

That is not to say that you are in love with yourself. I think the idea of loving yourself has been overdone. And it has been my experience that most people who love themselves awfully much really aren't that lovable.

My goal for my children—and for myself—is that we be comfortable being who we are most of the time and that, when we aren't, we have someone reliable to talk to about our discomfort, someone like a parent, a friend, or a close relative.

In today's world we all feel pressure to live up to ideals that we often can't reach. I know I feel that pressure. I am somewhat overweight, so I feel pressure to become thinner, and I judge myself harshly for not reaching that goal. I am not wealthy, while many of my college classmates are; and even though I do not rate myself as a human being according to how much money I have, there is a little voice inside me that tells me if I had done a better job with my life, I would have more money. There are people in this world who dislike me; and even though I know, rationally, that there will always be some people who do not like me, any dislike of me still hurts my feelings and makes me feel as if I have done something wrong. I can be emotionally insecure, and I often need reassurance; even though I know this is understandable, given my unstable childhood, I chastise myself for being needier than other people.

But even with all that, I am glad to say I am pretty much at home with who I am. I rarely pretend to be anything I am not, and I enjoy putting others at ease by admitting to my own shortcomings rather than putting up a protective facade. I let myself be vulnerable, but I do so intentionally. I believe this is a strength.

In any case, while there are parts about me I would change if I could, I basically like who I am and accept myself, shortcomings and all.

This is my goal for my children. I want to help them feel secure enough that they can relax and be themselves. This is what I mean by a healthy connection to yourself. It is not self-love as much as it is self-acceptance.

The best way to develop a healthy connection to yourself is by first attending to the eleven other kinds of connection I have already described and making them as strong as you can. Connected children almost invariably feel good about who they are.

Then, as your child continues through the five steps, from connection to recognition, self-esteem naturally grows. A healthy connection to self is a by-product. If your child lives a richly connected life, plays, practices, develops mastery in various ways, and receives recognition from different people or groups, he or she will surely feel confident, and confident enough to admit when self-doubt creeps in.

Self-doubt will creep into even the happiest of lives now and then. For children—particularly adolescents, but all children occasionally— the connection to self can hurt. Most of us don't like who we are once in a while. Except for a few serene souls, most of us have wished ourselves thinner or richer or smarter or more popular or prettier or somethinger.

It is crucial that you not let your child become isolated in those feelings.

The feelings themselves are normal and not dangerous. They are embedded in human existence, just as surely as toothaches and bad dreams. I have read enough biographies of great men and women to know that even the people we think of as superstrong and "above" feeling insecure or unworthy, people like Winston Churchill or Eleanor Roosevelt or Abraham Lincoln, nonetheless battled such feelings within themselves now and then. It is as much a part of human life to not like who you are from time to time or to compare yourself negatively with others once in a while as it is to pass gas inadvertently. Not many of us haven't done that.

Just as we offer our children a plan for dealing with a toothache (go see the dentist) or a bad dream (tell Mom or Dad about it and get reassurance that it is all just a dream), we need to make sure our children know that bad feelings about themselves are normal, OK, and deal-with-able.

While the feelings themselves are not dangerous if they are attended to promptly, they can become dangerous if they fester. If we do not attend to a child's negative feelings about himself or herself, the consequences can be as dire as neglecting medical or dental care. If you are lucky, it won't matter. But you have to be very, very lucky.

Try to make sure your children talk to you about such feelings. The great damage is done not by the feelings themselves—as I've noted, they are no more unusual or dangerous than a random fart— but by the feelings' being kept secret. Then they fester. Then they spread. Instead of tooth decay, they turn into decay of the heart and soul. If your heart and soul decay when you are a child, you may never experience hope again.

If, as a parent, you do not know what to say to your child about how she feels about herself—or how he feels about himself—or if what you do say doesn't help, then it is a good idea to consult with a professional. Don't wait for a crisis. In mental health, as in all other fields, early intervention is more effective than crisis management. Your pediatrician or school can refer you to a good child psychiatrist or child psychologist or social worker. These mental health professionals, who only a generation ago were widely considered off-limits for all but the deeply disturbed, now operate in the mainstream and can offer effective, practical help in a short amount of time.

As a parent, you can monitor your child's connection to himself or herself the same way you monitor everything else—by being there, by being curious, by not taking "Leave me alone" for an answer, and by talking to other people, like your child's teachers and friends and parents of friends. Sometimes a relative, like an aunt or a grandparent, will have a special relationship with your child in which the child will open up with him or her but won't with you. Don't feel jealous of that person; feel glad. Oh, all right, you can feel jealous. Just don't act on that feeling by meddling. And above all, feel glad. That relationship may be what the child needs to survive in a tough time.

Remember, the great danger does not lie in feeling bad about yourself; it lies in not having a good person to talk to about those feelings.

Here are some tips on helping your child develop a strong connection with herself or himself:

• Try to strengthen connectedness in the other eleven domains. A healthy connection within yourself is usually the result of healthy connections outside yourself. It is not by looking inward that children grow emotionally as much as it is by reaching outward. The inward growth—the development of such qualities as self-esteem and confidence—naturally happens as the child reaches and stretches outward.

• Let your children feel unhappy. The hardest lesson I have had to learn as a parent is to allow any of my children to be unhappy. At first, I felt I had to wipe their unhappy feelings away, as if I were a large roll of Bounty paper towels and my children's unhappy feelings were a spill in need of sponging. But Sue set me straight. She told me that if I didn't ever allow our kids to say they felt unhappy, then they would get the message that I never wanted to hear about their unhappy feelings. And I knew that would be a big problem.

• As your children come to know that you can tolerate their feeling unhappy, they will be more likely to tell you how they feel. This is all you really need. Remember, isolation does the damage, not the unhappy feelings.

• Promote the cycle of connection-play-practice-mastery-recognition. The best antidote to dislike of self is the process of those five steps.

• Help your child recognize that being unhappy with his or her efforts and saying things like "I am stupid" or "I am a klutz" are part of the process of reaching mastery. The road to mastery is filled with mistakes and moments of frustration.

• Offer a plan for dealing with feelings of envy, self-contempt, or other kinds of self-dissatisfaction. The best plan I know of is to connect. You may do this by talking to someone you trust. But you may also do it by playing with your dog or by talking to God or by shooting a few baskets or going for a run (in the last cases you are connecting with the physical part of you, your body, which, in turn, can soothe your mind).

• Make sure your children know that you love them, no matter what. Make sure they know that there is nothing that you can't take care of as a team.

• Be sure you see your child for who she is, not who you want her to be. One of the surest ways for a child to come to dislike herself is to realize that her parents do not accept her for who she is, only for who they want her to be.

• Do not set standards that are too high or too low. If you expect nothing—if your standards are too low—then your child will get the message that you do not think he can do much, and he may likely agree. On the other hand, if you set standards that are way beyond what your child is capable of, then he may spend his entire life trying to live up to what you expect, never getting there, and will always feel dissatisfied with his efforts. This is one of the most common reasons for unhappiness among high achievers.

• Self-acceptance is an internal state that derives from external experience. You need to make sure your child has moments during which he is enjoying who he is and other people are enjoying who he is as well. You want to guide him toward positive experiences in which his estimation of who he is and the estimations of others coincide. For example, at the end of a basketball game, you say, "Good game!" and he smiles and says, "Yeah, good game."

14

DOING TOO MUCH: THE GREAT MISTAKE GOOD PARENTS MAKE

Good parents often do too much for their children. This is their one great mistake. And its corollary mistake is that they (I should say, we) don't say "No!" enough.

I realized this on a trip to Disney World. All five of us flew down to Orlando and spent four expensive days at the Magic Kingdom and other venues. It was spectacular, it was fun, it was memorable, and I am pleased that we did it. I will never forget waiting in line with Jack (Sue and Lucy were wise enough to decline the opportunity, while Tucker was too short) for an hour, for the "pleasure" of ten seconds of sheer, my-life-is-ending terror, as I slid down the precipitously steep and excruciatingly high slide called "Summit Plummet" at Blizzard Beach.

But I also realized on that trip how hard we parents can work to provide joy rather than letting our kids learn how to create it.

We went from ride to ride, standing in line or wandering around waiting for our reserved, FASTPASS moment to arrive so that we could be entertained for a few minutes on an elaborately engineered ride that provided a thrill not drastically different from what we could have experienced by jumping off a high ledge that overhangs an old swimming hole and costs not a cent to jump from.

We did this for four days.

We had the same squabbles we have at home—what to eat, when to eat, how to eat, how much to eat, why we eat what we eat, what to watch on TV, how much TV we can watch, how much money we can spend, what we can spend money on, what time to go to bed, why go to bed, and so on. As we would squabble about these matters, I would wonder to myself, *Why did we spend all this money to come here and do this?*

But then we would make up, harmony would be restored, one of the kids would say something adorable, and we would all hug and feel good, as we waited to go on another ride.

To the extent that this trip provided a root of adult happiness for my children, I suggest it was not Disney World that did it but the connectedness we all felt on this special adventure. What made it special was more how much we had looked forward to it than what we actually found. What we found was really fun, but what was extraordinary was the enthusiasm we invested in the trip. That's what made it special. It could have been a special trip to anywhere. Disney is an excellent catalyst of the enthusiasm reaction, but it could have happened in our backyard if we had really used our imaginations.

The trip pointed out to me the great danger that we parents must watch for. If I might adapt the proverb if you give a man a fish, you feed him for a day, but if you teach him how to fish, you feed him for a lifetime, we parents must guard against providing too many of the fish and not enough fishing skills. We have to be careful that we do not feel obliged to spend a lot of money to provide the memorable experiences we deem necessary, the ones that we didn't get ourselves perhaps, or the ones that all the neighbors seem to afford. All those fish—all those purchased pleasures—can't compare to helping a child learn how to create pleasure in constructive ways on her or his own.

I often make the mistake of believing that if I furnish the full array of childhood delights for my children—from Disney World to cool birthday parties to skiing adventures to apple picking and hayrides each fall—I will have provided what they need. Of course, I know better. But still, sometimes I deceive myself and believe that the trip to Disney World, the latest sneakers (can we still call them that?), the Big Birthday Party, and the DVD player or CD burner are what my kids need in order to grow up to be happy.

And as they get older, I can deceive myself into believing that admission to the Right College and high SAT scores are what my children need in order to grow up to be happy. I could fall into what I called earlier in this book the Great Harvard Fallacy. It is so easy, as a parent, to do this. We want so badly for our children to have all the advantages we can possibly provide or encourage them to earn, such as getting into the best college. But if we stop and think about it, we realize that what matters is finding the best *match* between college and student. It is far more important that our children go to a college where they will thrive than that they go to a college with prestige. They may be one and the same college, but they may not.

I have to remind myself that the childhood roots of adult happiness do not lie in trips to Disney World or in an acceptance letter from Harvard. I have to remind myself (Sue doesn't forget this as often as I do) that what my children need most is my time, my interest, my love, my guidance, and my ability to say no.

The risk of providing too much is that children can become what my friend John Croyle, head of Big Oak Ranch for abandoned or abused children, calls "shark-eyed." He describes his experience of lecturing to audiences of affluent adolescents and seeing them stare back at him with no excitement, eyes as predatory and humorless as sharks. "They have seen it all, and they aren't even out of high school," John says. "I tell them my best jokes, I tell them stories that make adults cry, and they just stare back at me with those blank shark eyes."

I have seen those shark eyes in many children. They are bored. They have seen it all. They are, in the words of Samuel Johnson, too refined ever to be pleased.

Mihaly Csikszentmihalyi has data to back up John Croyle's observation. Based on his extensive empirical research, Csikszentmihalyi concludes:

The prerequisite for happiness is the ability to get fully involved in life. If the material conditions are abundant, so much the better, but lack of wealth or health need not prevent one from finding flow in whatever circumstances one finds at hand. In fact, our studies suggest that children from the most affluent families find it more difficult to be in flow—compared with less well-to-do teenagers they tend to be more bored, less involved, less enthusiastic, less excited.[1]

Shark eyes mark the end of childhood. Shark eyes mark the end of bright eyes. Shark eyes mark the start of jaded, joyless, cynical adulthood. We need to prevent shark eyes.

One way to do it is not to give too much, too soon. No BMWs for your high school student, please. No unlimited charge cards at Neiman Marcus. One way to protect the innocence of childhood and preserve children's capacity to feel wonder and excitement is to make sure they have to stretch for their pleasure, use their imaginations, save up their money, or simply wait.

All the fancy stuff is OK, I suppose, provided it isn't laid on too thick, but it is dangerous because it can distract parents as well as children from what matters: learning how to deal with adversity and learning how to create and sustain joy.

When you provide too much, you deny your children both the opportunity to deal with adversity and the opportunity to create and sustain their own joy.

The other day I was upstairs working, and Tucker called to me, "Dad! I'm bored!" in the same tone of voice as if he were announcing a fire in the house. We had a crisis at hand.

"Well, Tucker," I called back down, "I'm sure you'll find something to do."

There was a time I would have gotten up from my desk, leaving my work behind, and ministered to Tucker's boredom as if it were a boo-boo. I would have thought this was my duty, that Tucker needed me in his moment of ennui, and it was my job to help him out of it.

Now I believe that nothing could be further from the truth. Now I believe that it was my duty *not* to go to him in his moment of boredom. I believe it would have been a great mistake if I had rushed to Tucker when he was bored as quickly as I would rush if he were hurt.

Moments of frustration and boredom provide opportunities to learn how to deal with adversity and create joy.

My job is to supervise from a distance to make sure no damage gets done, such as Tucker's playing with matches and burning down the house as an antidote to being bored.

So I stayed upstairs working, now with my ear cocked (can you cock an ear?) for any ominous sounds from below.

A half hour later, I went downstairs to see what Tucker was up to. I found him sitting on the floor in his room next to a magnificent structure made out of playing cards. "This is a card hotel," Tucker proudly proclaimed. He had never made a house of cards before, nor had I ever suggested it to him. He must have read about one or heard about it from his friends. In any case, this, his first bit of card construction, was a beauty.

I reminded Tucker that, only a short while ago, he had bitterly complained that he was bored, and I pointed out that, in response to being bored, he had found something wonderful to do. He grunted, not wanting to establish this as an enduring precedent, but of course, he knew that's what it was.

And that's what it should be.

We help our children most by helping them help themselves. They need us to supervise them, but only from a distance, just to make sure they are safe. They do not need us to provide them with entertainment around the clock.

One weary mom said to me, "Sometimes I feel like I am an attendant at a spa. My kids ask me to find towels for them, bring them drinks, cook them meals, and tell them about the day's selection of activities." This is a problem conscientious parents all face now and then, if not every day.

Psychologist Daniel Kindlon wrote a book about this problem entitled *Too Much of a Good Thing: Raising Children of Character in an Indulgent Age.* In it he says, "It is not just a little ironic that our success and prosperity—the very accomplishments and good fortune that we so desperately desire to share with our children—put them at risk."

Instead, we should hold back, not instantly giving them what they want. That can be tough, creating a lot of tension. Like yelling and screaming and fighting and stamping of feet. A generation ago the response to that might have been a spanking; now it is often to give in and provide whatever is asked for. Neither response is helpful.

Instead, do nothing. Keep your kids safe, set limits on rude behavior, but beyond that let them use their own minds to figure out how to deal with the pain and replace it with some joy.

Those moments can be key to planting the childhood roots of adult happiness. Adults who never got much practice in this when they were kids are often the adults who can think of nothing more interesting to do when they are bored than to turn on the TV, have a drink, or get into some kind of trouble.

As a parent, I have had to work very hard to learn how to do nothing or say no. So has Sue. It doesn't come easily, but once you get in the habit, it isn't all that difficult. And believe it or not, children really do want us to do it. The world, after all, will be saying no to them soon, and the world will not rush in with entertainment and food when they are bored; we do them a favor by getting them ready at home.

If your child wants to stay up until midnight watching TV, it would be much easier to say, "Whatever," and go to bed yourself than to enforce a reasonable bedtime. If your child wants to pierce her lips, it is easier to allow it than to draw the line and refuse permission. If your child just *has* to go to the dance, but you know the dance spells trouble, it may be easier to let her go than to endure the brickbats of the fight that will ensue when you say no.

But it is essential for us parents to say no.

Sometimes I surprise a child I am seeing with his parents by saying no for the parents. For example, I saw a twelve-year-old boy—I'll name him Kevin—in my office not long ago who was determined that it was his right to have any part of his body pierced that he wanted to, since it was his body. Mom and dad had brought Kevin to see me about a variety of issues, but this one came up right off the bat. With the four of us sitting together in my office, Kevin started in. "They have no right to tell me what I can have pierced. They have no clue what kids do. Just look at them!" Mom and dad sort of winced as Kevin spoke.

"What do you want to have pierced?" I asked Kevin.

"What does it matter? It is the principle that counts," he shot back.

"I completely agree," I replied. "It is the principle that counts."

Kevin smiled, believing he had found an ally in me. But then I went on. "The principle here is that your parents are in charge, not you. They do indeed have a right to forbid you to have your body pierced. I would go a step further. I would say they have a duty to stop you from doing it, depending on what part of your body you have in mind."

You could almost feel Mom and Dad sitting up straighter in their chairs, as Kevin sputtered, engaging me in a debate that his parents relished watching.

"How can you say that?" Kevin demanded.

"Because it's obvious. Your parents are trying to protect you from yourself. If you don't know enough not to do something stupid, then they have to tell you not to."

"How do you know what I want to do is stupid?" Kevin growled.

"I don't. I bet it probably is, but I don't know for sure because you haven't told me. I'm just arguing the principle."

Kevin looked at me, as if trying to figure out just how much of a jerk I was going to turn out to be. "I still say it's not fair," he protested. "Why should my parents be able to control my body?"

"Because this is what parents do. It is why they get paid the big bucks, telling kids like you to do what makes sense."

"Very funny," Kevin said, as sarcastically as he could.

"I think you know I'm right. Would you really want your parents to let you do whatever you wanted to do?"

"No, but they're unreasonable," he protested.

"I don't think so."

"How do you know?" he demanded.

"Just a guess," I replied.

These parents, like many others, needed to be given permission to say no. More than permission, they needed to see how it is done. They needed to watch a live human being—in this case, me—take on their extremely intelligent, somewhat entitled young son. Kevin knew this, too. It was not all that hard to blow his cover.

In addition to learning how to say no, many parents would love to have information that would help them justify setting limits. Here are some answers to common questions, based on guidelines developed by such sources as the American Academy of Pediatrics and the

American Academy of Child and Adolescent Psychiatry, as well as my own experience:

Q: How much computer time is too much? (Also, TV time, telephone time, and so forth.)

A: We don't know for sure. The average—seven hours a day—is too high, and most authorities would agree. I advise no more than two hours, unless it is an academically related activity. In addition it is very important that you monitor not just how much time your kids spend watching TV, videos, or being on-line but also what the content is.

Q: Should parents allow young children to attend PG-rated movies?

A: This is up to the parent, of course. My advice is to stay within the guidelines of the movie code and not allow children under the recommended age to attend. This makes for a consistent rule, which, of course, you can selectively break if you so choose. Just don't choose to break it too often, or breaking it will become the norm.

Q: What harm is done by watching violence on TV?

A: Dr. Susan Villani published an article in the April 2001 issue of the *Journal of the American Academy of Child and Adolescent Psychiatry* in which she reviewed all the research done in the past ten years on the impact of media on children. The data showed that media exposure can lead to "increased violent and aggressive behavior, increased high-risk behaviors, including alcohol and tobacco use, and accelerated onset of sexual activity." The scientific data are clear. Parents should be careful what and how much their kids watch.

Q: Are there any *proven* safety measures all parents should implement?

A: Yes. Wear seat belts. Have no firearms at home, or if you must have them, keep them locked up and have the ammunition locked up in a separate place. Don't smoke. Childproof your home if you have toddlers. Keep emergency numbers (ambulance, doctor, fire department, police, poison control, and your area's version of 911) clearly posted near all telephones. Practice at-home fire drills. Practice sun protection. (There are four key steps: avoid too much sun between eleven A.M. and three P.M.; wear hats, long sleeves, pants; go into the shade; and use sunscreen with a high SPF [sun protection factor] and apply it a half hour before going outside.)

Q: What's so bad about smoking marijuana?

A: The problem with marijuana is twofold. First, it is illegal, so using it can get a person into trouble with the law. Second, it can undercut a person's motivation to do other things. Kids who smoke a lot of pot often do very little else.

Sometimes you need data to say no, sometimes you need a reasonable argument to say no, and sometimes you just have to follow your gut. Whatever the case may be, it is very important that you say no when you need to.

The old cliché is true: One day your children will thank you for it.

15

FROM PLEASURE TO
SOMETHING BETTER:
THE ART OF GROWING UP

One day my son Jack was playing on the trampoline we have under the magnolia tree in our backyard. As he was bouncing, Jack noticed a little bird sitting on a branch. Unlike most birds that light on that tree, this bird did not fly away as Jack jumped on the trampoline, so Jack began to talk to the bird. He found a new friend. After a while Jack reached out his hand and the bird jumped onto his outstretched finger.

Jack was amazed. He brought the bird inside, put it in his room, and closed the door. "I found a bird outside," he told me. "I put it in my room. We need to get a cage."

"Oh?" I asked. "What kind of bird?"

"A yellow one with some bluish green on it," he said.

"How big is it?" I asked.

"About this big," he said, making a fist.

"And how did you manage to bring it inside?" I asked.

"I just reached out my hand, and Paris hopped onto my finger."

"Paris?" I asked.

"I've named him Paris," Jack replied.

"Why Paris?" I asked.

"I don't know," Jack replied. "That's just his name."

And so on that day Paris took what we discovered later was *her* place along with our dogs, Pippy and Honey, and our cat, Louie, among the animals in our family. We hung up notices around the neighborhood stating that we had found a stray parakeet, but no one came to claim her. So Paris stayed with us.

We went to the hardware store and bought a little cage, along with some birdseed and two dishes, one for water and one for food, that attached to the bars of the cage.

Jack loved Paris. He thought it was wrong to keep her cooped up in such a little cage, so he usually let her out of the cage to allow her to fly free around his room. This was dangerous, however, with Louie in the house. So Jack decided to make Paris a larger cage. A lot larger.

He talked to his teacher in shop at school, and together they designed a cage the size of a pickup truck. Jack set to work on it with gusto. From time to time I would hear updates from him as to how the cage was coming along. He revised his design a couple of times, and he worked hard to learn how to construct such a large edifice. It took him three months to complete it.

I remember going in to kiss Jack good-night one evening during the time he was working on it and asking him what he was going to think about as he went to sleep.

"My birdcage," he said with a smile.

As I went to sleep that night, I thought about Jack thinking about his birdcage. I thought how wonderful it was that he was looking forward to working on it as he went to sleep at night.

Jack's state of mind that night, the state of mind in which you are looking forward to the next step in some ongoing effort, is a key to lifelong joy.

Maybe you are on a hockey team, and you are looking forward to the game the next day. Maybe you are acting in a play, and you are looking forward to rehearsal. Maybe you are reading a book you love, and you can't wait to get to the next chapter. Whatever the activity, when you are so caught up in it that you look forward to returning to it later, the next day, or whenever, you are engaged in prolonged joy.

Freud is famous for, among many other ideas, his idea that maturity is the ability to delay gratification. He explained that the infant and child operate on what he called the *pleasure principle* and that, as you mature, you must learn how to delay gratifying your infantile demand for immediate pleasure.

But what Jack was doing that night was not delaying gratification; he was extending gratification beyond the immediate pleasure of working on the cage to include the wider realm of thinking about it when he wasn't with the cage in the workshop.

To be happy as you leave infancy and mature, not only must you be able to delay gratification, you must learn to derive satisfaction from something deeper and more complicated than mere pleasure. That is what Jack was doing that night as he went to sleep. He was breaking new ground in his ability to take satisfaction in life. He was planning. He was working and playing in his imagination.

The pleasure he took in looking forward to working on his cage the next day was a much more abstract and complex kind of pleasure than the pleasure he would feel when eating a candy bar or opening a birthday present or even actually working on the cage. As he looked forward to getting back to work on the cage, he was not delaying gratification, as he would, say, by putting off eating the candy bar until after dinner. Rather, he was discovering a richer kind of gratification.

He was not in Csikszentmihalyi's state of flow, as he lay in bed looking forward to getting back to work, but he was only one step removed from flow. He was working and playing with the project in his mind, anticipating how much fun it would be to get back to it in reality the next day.

This state of mind lies at the heart of what makes for lifelong joy. The more you find yourself in this state of mind, the happier you are as a person.

Finding it goes well beyond the mere ability to delay gratification. People can work the whole day at a job they dislike, looking forward all the while to the beer they will drink after work. They are successfully delaying the gratification of drinking the beer until after they leave the work site, but they are not what I would call happy. They are mature, by Freud's definition of that word, because they can delay gratification; but they have not found joy that can last.

Jack, on his way to sleep that night, had found it.

He did this not by denying himself anything, not by exercising restraint or willpower, but by enlarging his capacity for joy to go beyond gratification alone. He felt joy in making his birdcage even though it entailed pain, like when he hit his thumb with his hammer. But he also felt joy in making his birdcage even when he was not working on it directly, as when he lay in bed thinking about it. He created this joy actively, not by passively receiving the sweet taste of a candy bar or the excitement of a present.

Being able to do this draws upon the five steps I have outlined. Jack conceived of the project in connection and play; executed it through play, practice, and discipline; felt mastery as the cage grew and he got better at carpentry; and enjoyed the recognition he received from peers, teachers, and family when the magnificent (to my eyes, anyway) cage was complete.

In the long run, the cage itself is of little importance. I don't know how long it will endure, but I doubt Jack will have that cage when he is an old man. However, he will own the experience of having made it forever. The process is what counts.

Prolonged joy depends on your ability to get creatively involved with something or someone over an extended period of time. Such involvement leads naturally to sacrifice and delay of gratification; but it also provides a different, better kind of gratification than sensate pleasure alone can supply.

Helping children discover this process is far more important than making sure they get high scores on their SATs or gain admission to a prestige college. (Remember the list I presented in Chapter 11 of famous people who never graduated from college at all.)

The process is not unlike falling in love. You become preoccupied, enchanted, willing to make sacrifices, energized, and motivated as never before (or since the last time you felt this way). You walk around with a little smile or even a grimace if you are facing a problem, but you are living strong and full.

As a child, you may feel this way when you are playing on a team that has great chemistry. Or you may feel it in a certain English class where suddenly you see for the first time what matters in life. Or you may feel it when you start to paint a canvas and it looks good and you can't wait to get back to it later.

If your child develops a strong interest in taking apart motors or designing her own clothes or setting up a support network for a friend with a serious illness, don't despair that schoolwork will suffer and grades might go down. Instead, rejoice. Your child is learning about a state of mind that will draw her or him back to it over and over again, a state of mind that lies at the core of prolonged joy. Sure, your job is to make certain that grades do not fall *too* far. But it is also important for you to celebrate the project your child has found and to validate the importance of that in-love-with-it, can't-wait-to-get-back-to-it state of mind. That state isn't reserved only for romance.

Indeed, I would say that the art of growing up is learning how to create that state of mind in as much of what you do as you can. If you can bring a lover's enthusiasm, creativity, playfulness, and devotion to what you do all day, you will be happy.

So whenever you see your child light up with enthusiasm, pay attention.

You may say your children only light up at the prospect of going to Burger King, going shopping, watching TV, or playing Nintendo. While some TV, Nintendo, fast food, and shopping are fine, it is important for children to find some activities that engage them more creatively than those do. The TV-and-Nintendo child can turn into the beer-after-work adult. I have nothing against a beer after work, having had many myself. However, if the beer after work becomes the highlight of your day, your main pleasure and reward, you are not nearly as happy as you should expect to be. Life has more to offer, and so do you.

Help your children find the birdcages and other projects that will introduce them to the "more" they should expect to find in life.

Once they find it, they'll tend to want to find it over and over again. And they usually will.

The "more," the something-better-than-pleasure, need not be a concrete project, like a birdcage. It might be an actual love affair. Or it may be involvement with a club or an organization. It may be a love of literature, or, as illustrated in Chapter 12, fishing. The "more" happens when you actively, creatively engage with what you are doing, even when you are not doing it. You could actually be writing an essay about how empty and bleak life is and still feel the something more, still look forward to writing the next page the next day.

Strong interests tend to provide motivation to do more than is expected. This, in turn, usually leads to achievement at the highest level of which the child is capable. But much more important than that, strong interests beget a habit of finding more strong interests. Csikszentmihalyi's research shows this. And when you have a lifelong habit of finding strong interests, you tend to be happy as much of the time as you can be, given your genetics and other life experiences.

The eighth-grade son of a friend of mine came home from school one day and told his father, "My teacher says we should all develop a passion. Do you have a passion, Dad?"

His father, a brilliant litigator at the largest law firm in Boston, is an ironic, witty, seen-it-all sort of soul, not a man given to extravagant shows of emotion. He told me, "I didn't know what to say. Do I have a passion? I don't know. Is this a problem? Do I need help?"

We laughed, knowing he didn't need any more "help" than the rest of us do. He was as happy as an adult as his earned wisdom, mild cynicism, and physical constitution would allow—which was quite happy, in fact. Indeed, he had developed many passions in his youth, and they had all mellowed into a productive and satisfying adulthood. So he didn't need to run out and find a passion right now. Youth is the best time for that.

But the teacher was right in encouraging the man's son to develop a passion. Each childhood passion is a seed of potential adult happiness. Each childhood passion breaks through the barrier that surrounds ordinary experience and introduces you to something more.

The ability to find that something more comes easily to most children. If given the chance, children will naturally find that state of mind, that process that Jack discovered in working on his birdcage and thinking about it as he fell asleep at night. All we adults need to do is not overschedule them or make them crazy with stories about how much pressure they will have to deal with someday; not allow them too much candy, Nintendo, or TV; and rejoice in the joys when they find them.

POSTLUDE: SUMMER'S END:
SETTING FREE THE FROGS

I finished this book at the end of the summer, on the next-to-last day of our vacation on Lake Doolittle.

As I have dedicated this book to summer and to children, it seems right that I should finish the book as the summer closes and my kids return to school.

You might be interested to know that Jack and I went fishing together at 5:30 A.M. a few days after we bought the fishing rods. By then his friend Noah had left. Tucker was too sleepy to get up at that hour, but Jack and I got up, rubbing the sleepies from our eyes. I had a cup of coffee, and Jack had a bowl of cereal. Sitting there in the kitchen together in the early morning light, we spoke only a few words, but the closeness we felt was as warm as the coffee in my mug. We went nearby to Benedict Pond, where there are rowboats you can take out. A man in the know had told me the fishing was good there, much better than on Doolittle, where he said the fish were too wily to be easily caught.

As I rowed, Jack fished. His first two casts brought nothing. But on the third cast, I heard, "I got one!" Bingo! A bass bit, Jack hooked him, and Jack reeled him in. We kept fishing for a while, and then Jack had another strike and another fish. By the time we rowed back to shore, Jack had caught three bass.

I don't know who was happier, Jack or me. I will never forget the look on his face as he reeled the first bass in or the sound of his voice when he yelled, "I got one!"

And Lucy had four friends—she invited five, but one couldn't make it—stay for three nights. I am not sure we will repeat that party, but it was good to do it once. I hope that that sleepover becomes one of the childhood roots of Lucy's adult happiness.

Three days before we had to leave the lake, Tucker caught two frogs and put them in a jar with some rocks and some water. He showed them around to everyone he could find. The next morning I went out to jump in the lake, as I did every day instead of taking a morning shower. As I swam around, I saw Tucker coming down from the house. He had his jar with the frogs in it.

"Hi, Tuckie," I called from the water. "Whatcha doing?"

"Hi, Dad," Tucker said. "I'm gonna let the froggies go free now. We had fun, but it is time for them to go home." How can I tell Tucker how much I love him? I can't. But I do say, "I love you, Tuckie. I am glad you are letting the froggies go home."

This is the same Tucker who told me he couldn't control his heightness when I asked him not to grow up anymore.

Tucker, Lucy, and Jack. These are the childhood roots of my own adult happiness. One day these little frogs of mine will go free, too. Not today, though. Some distant tomorrow—which will be here before I know what's happened. I hope I will have done right by them, by then.

And I hope you have been persuaded by this book that happiness is best not left to chance. I hope you have been persuaded that while genes matter, they do not tell the whole story. I hope you have been persuaded that certain deliberate actions on the part of adults can greatly increase the chances that our children will grow up to be more or less satisfied within themselves and happy in their lives. These actions are simple and available to anyone who wants to join in the most important work in the world: raising children.

Bless you, parents, teachers, coaches, and all who love and help children. And bless you children, everywhere. Thank you for giving us adults new life—and the deepest, most heartwarming, most lively and unpredictable joy we'll ever know.

NOTES

CHAPTER 3

1. Peter Fonagy, *Attachment Theory and Psychoanalysis* (New York: Other Press, 2001), 27.

CHAPTER 4

1. Quoted in Fonagy, *Attachment Theory and Psychoanalysis,* 7.

CHAPTER 6

1. Mihaly Csikszentmihalyi, *Finding Flow* (New York: Basic Books, 1997), 117.

CHAPTER 7

1. David Myers, *The Pursuit of Happiness* (New York: Avon Books, 1992), 44.

2. Ibid., 108.

3. "The State of Our Nation's Youth," Horatio Alger Association, a nonprofit organization (Alexandria, Va.: November 2001).

CHAPTER 8

1. Pamela Kruger, "Why Johnny Can't Play," *Fast Company,* issue 37 (August 2000), 271.

CHAPTER 10

1. Martin Seligman, *The Optimistic Child* (New York, Harper Perennial, 1995), 98.

CHAPTER 14

1. Mihaly Csikszentmihalyi, "If We Are So Rich, Why Aren't We Happy?" *American Psychologist,* volume 54 (October 1999), 821–827.

EDWARD M. HALLOWELL, M.D., a child and adult psychiatrist, is an instructor at Harvard Medical School and director of the Hallowell Center for Cognitive and Emotional Health in Sudbury, Massachusetts, an outpatient treatment center serving children and adults with a wide range of emotional and learning problems. He is the coauthor of *Driven to Distraction* (with John J. Ratey, M.D.) and the author of *Delivered from Distraction, CrazyBusy, Worry,* and *Connect,* among other titles. He and his wife have three children, and they live in Arlington, Massachusetts. He welcomes hearing from readers and can be reached through his website: www.DrHallowell.com.